GARDEN KALENDAR

1751–1771

GILBERT WHITE

GARDEN KALENDAR

1751-1771

Reproduced in facsimile from
the manuscript in the British Library

Introduction and notes by

JOHN CLEGG, HON. F.L.S.
former Hon. Curator of the
Gilbert White Museum, Selborne

THE SCOLAR PRESS
1975

Published by The Scolar Press Limited,
39 Great Russell Street, London WC1B 3PH
Printed in England by The Scolar Press Limited,
Ilkley, Yorkshire

ISBN 0 85967 215 8

CONTENTS

INTRODUCTION

I THE GARDEN KALENDAR

Gilbert White's *Garden Kalendar* here reproduced by permission of the Board, forms Add. Ms 35139 in the British Library. Kept from 1751 until 1771 as a detailed working record of plans and operations, successes and failures, in his garden at 'Wakes', the *Kalendar* illuminates still little explored areas of Gilbert White's life and the development of his interests. Before becoming the great observational naturalist still so justly celebrated, he was one of the most accomplished and enquiring practical gardeners of his age.

The *Garden Kalendar* has only once previously been published, in a rather inaccurate transcript included as an appendix to Bowdler Sharpe's lavish edition of *The Natural History of Selborne*; this appeared in 1900, and is now scarce. It seemed appropriate therefore to issue this fascinating document in a form which captures the immediacy and spirit of the beautifully clear original.

The manuscript is almost entirely in White's autograph, though in his absence an occasional note was kept by another member of the family. The entries were made on loose quarto sheets of letter paper which vary somewhat in size. These were subsequently roughly stitched together. The *Garden Kalendar* remained in the possession of the White family until 1897 when it was acquired by the British Museum. Sotheby's ambiguously described it as being in twelve 'divisions', but it is unclear now what this meant. The individual folios are now mounted on guards, and have been bound together.

Although in subject matter closely related to them, the *Garden Kalendar* is quite distinct from Gilbert White's other notebooks. This explains an apparent anomaly in the present manuscript. During 1765 entries on wild flowers become more frequent, following his purchase of Hudson's *Flora Anglica*. It is clear that White decided to separate observations on wild flowers from his horticultural records, for in the middle of the *Kalendar* entry for 9 August 1765 appear two stray leaves of what is headed *A Calendar of Flora, and the Garden from August 9th 1765*. Folio 192, however, is headed *Garden Calendar* (sic.) and continues the horticultural record without a break.

From the beginning of 1766 the two journals were kept quite separately; the manuscript of the *Calendar of Flora* for 1766 was facsimiled in 1911 by the Selborne Society. 1767 was the last year in which the *Garden Kalendar* was kept in its original form; entries after that declined to a sporadic record of wine and beer making and quantities of 'dung borrowed' until these too ceased in 1773. The *Naturalist's Journal*, which provided a convenient framework within which White was henceforth to inscribe his notes and observations, and which became the source from which much of *Selborne* was to be drawn, was given him in 1767 by Daines Barrington. From early 1768 this seems to have been used to maintain a more or less daily record of White's interests and horticultural pursuits. Only extracts have ever appeared in print, published in 1931 as *Journals of Gilbert White*.

II THE LIFE OF GILBERT WHITE

Gilbert White was born into a modestly prosperous middle class family in Selborne, a small village in Hampshire, on 18 July 1720. His grandfather was vicar of Selborne, and his parents were John White of the Middle Temple, barrister-at-law and J.P., and Anne, daughter and heiress of Mrs Holt, the widow of the Rev. Thomas Holt. On his marriage, John White gave up an unsuccessful bar practice, and the couple stayed first at Selborne vicarage. Soon after Gilbert, their first child, was born, they moved to Compton, near Guildford, and then to East Harting in Sussex. The family returned to Selborne in 1729 after the death of grandfather White to join his widow Rebekah in a cottage across the road from the vicarage, which had acquired the name 'Wakes' from its previous occupants.

During their absence from Selborne the White family had grown at the rate of about a child a year. In addition to Gilbert and three children who died in infancy, there were now Thomas, Benjamin, John, Francis and Rebecca; Anne and Henry soon followed the move to 'Wakes'.

Little is known for certain about Gilbert's early education, although he may have been a private pupil of Thomas Warton, vicar of Basingstoke and father of two remarkable sons, of whom one became Headmaster of Winchester and the other Poet Laureate. The earliest extant record shows that on 17 December 1739, Gilbert White was entered a commoner of Oriel College, Oxford. This choice was a sad mistake in the light of Gilbert's later life, for the living of Selborne was in the gift of Magdalen. So by entering Oriel White was effectively prevented from ever becoming the vicar of Selborne, and the nearest he approached what would have been his ideal calling in life was on the several occasions when through the illness or absence of the incumbent he acted as curate-in-charge.

At this period of his life there seem to be no signs of the deep interest in natural history that was to be so important later, although living in the country as he had always done, White had acquired many of the typical rural interests of his time. During these years his 'attention to the ornithology of this district' seems to have been mainly in those species that were edible or at least shootable. His friend John Mulso, referring in later life to his sporting activities at college wrote, 'I do not ever remember your shooting a snipe at Oxford in summer, where there used to be plenty in winter: at that time you used to practise with your gun in summer to steady your hand for winter, and inhospitably fetch down our visitants the birds of passage'. Until quite late in life his account books show regular purchases of powder and shot.

Gilbert obtained his B.A. in 1743 and proceeded to M.A. three years later, having been elected Fellow of Oriel in 1744. In 1752–3 he was Dean of his college and Junior Proctor of the university. Later he was unsuccessfully in the running for the Provostship of Oriel.

After ordination in April 1747 White became curate at Swarraton in Hampshire, one of the livings of his uncle Charles. This curacy, the first appointment of an active clerical career, probably entailed no more than Sunday duties since the stipend was a mere £20 a year. He was within easy riding distance of Selborne and seems to have spent the mid-week periods either at home or at Oxford, where he still had a mare at livery. He gave up the Swarraton curacy in March 1749, and subsequently held several others all within easy reach of Selborne. From 1757 until his death he was the incumbent of Moreton Pinkney in Northamptonshire, a living in the gift of Oriel, but was never resident.

Offers of profitable livings were made to him from time to time, but White declined them almost certainly because they would have necessitated leaving Selborne. Although never tied by marriage he was reluctant to leave his village for long, and apart from the occasional extended holiday he did so only when studying and following his academic career.

In 1755 Gilbert's grandmother died and the properties in Selborne in which she had a life interest passed to her son-in-law, the Rev. Charles White. To him Gilbert now paid an annual rent of £5.8*s*.0*d*. for 'Wakes'. Gilbert was now virtually the head of the family at home, for his father who seems at best to have been rather ineffectual was now in failing health and died in 1758. It was not for another five years that Gilbert was to become legal owner of the Selborne property on the death of his uncle Charles.

The other White brothers left Selborne as they grew up. Their names appear from time to time in the *Kalendar* and it is clear that they were keenly interested in the development of the garden, took an occasional hand in it, and exchanged both plants and ideas with their brother at home.

The name of Thomas occurs most frequently. Next in age to Gilbert, he went into trade in London but in 1776 came into full possession of estates in Essex. He then retired, prefixed his own name with Holt, and settled at South Lambeth where he maintained a fine garden from which Gilbert received many specimens. Thomas was an authority on trees, gained election as a Fellow of the Royal Society, and was a regular contributor to the *Gentleman's Magazine* under the initials T.H.W. He had at one time contemplated writing the *Natural History and Antiquities of Hampshire* but nothing came of the venture.

John, seven years younger than Gilbert, graduated at Corpus Christi College, Oxford, in 1749. To him Selborne owes the famous zig-zag path up the Hanger. He organised its construction in 1762–1763 with manual and financial help from Gilbert. John became chaplain to the garrison at Gibraltar; while there he corresponded regularly with Gilbert and was in contact with Linnaeus himself. He accumulated material for a book on the fauna of the Rock, to be called *Fauna Calpensis*, and although a manuscript was prepared it was never published in its entirety. Only the introductory chapter has survived and been printed. After John's death in 1780 his widow became Gilbert's housekeeper, a role she filled for the rest of his life.

Benjamin, next in age to Thomas, was educated at Bishop's Waltham and went into a partnership as a publisher and book seller 'at the sign of the Horace' Head, No. 51, Fleet Street, London'. He became the leading publisher of natural history books, his bookshop a meeting place of those interested in the subject. On Gilbert's visits to London he would call at this stimulating Mecca of naturalists.

Among the friends of brothers Thomas and Benjamin whom Gilbert seems to have met in London was William Curtis (1746–1799) for he is mentioned several times in his correspondence. He had been born in Alton, some four miles from Selborne, but had moved to London at about the age of twenty. Curtis, by training a surgeon-apothecary but by inclination a botanist and entomologist, was the author of *Flora Londonensis*, issued originally as a part-work the first number of which appeared in 1775. He was the originator of the *Botanical Magazine*, which started in 1787 and continues to this day under the aegis of the Royal Horticultural Society.

An advertisement for *Flora Londonensis* in 1783 reads 'A new and original Botanic Work, intended to comprehend all the plants which grow wild in Great Britain, beginning first with those which are found *in the environs of London* . . . Published by the Author *at his Botanic Garden*, and *B. White*, Fleetstreet, where any of the Numbers from 1 to 46 may be had, either plain or coloured'.

The London Botanic Garden had been opened at Lambeth Marsh as a commercial venture by Curtis on 1 January 1779, and in the catalogue of plants issued from the garden there appears the following acknowledgement: 'To the generosity and public spirit of the Honourable Daines Barrington and Thomas White Esq., his principal patrons in this undertaking, the garden in a great degree owes its existence'.

It was doubtlessly at Benjamin's, too, that in 1767 Gilbert met Thomas Pennant (1726–1798) a traveller and writer who was then discussing with Benjamin the republication of his *British Zoology*, which had first appeared in 1761. At this first meeting a discussion on the harvest mouse, an animal of which Pennant was unaware, led to White sending him specimens as recorded in the *Kalendar* on 4 December 1767. From this chance meeting the correspondence between them developed which was eventually to be published as the first section of *The Natural History of Selborne.*

The Hon. Daines Barrington (1727–1800), to whom the letters in the second part of *The Natural History* are addressed, was the Recorder of Bristol, and a dilettante in science and letters. Gilbert first met Barrington in London, in May 1769, but he had already been in correspondence with him for White, in an unpublished part of the letter to Thomas Pennant which became letter XIII in *The Natural History*, 22 January 1768, wrote 'Your friend Mr. Barrington (to whom I am an entire stranger) has been so obliging as to make me a present of one of his Naturalist's

Journals, which I hope to fill in the course of the year'. (*Journals*, ed. Johnson, 1931). The journal itself bears an inscription in White's writing 'The gift of the Honourable Mr. Barrington, the Inventer'.

With the encouragement of both Pennant and Barrington, Gilbert White was persuaded to publish a selection of his letters to them. The text of the original letters, of which copies had been kept, was edited and some deletions and additions made. Some additional 'letters', including numbers I to IX of the Pennant series, which were never actually sent to anyone, were written to give readers an introduction to Selborne or to include items that had not been discussed in the correspondence. The finished manuscript consisted of forty-four letters addressed to Thomas Pennant, sixty-six letters to the Hon. Daines Barrington and twenty-six, not addressed to anyone in particular, on the antiquities of Selborne.

Eventually *The Natural History and Antiquities of Selborne* was published by B. White and Son in early 1789. The book was well received in White's time, but since then it has had a truly remarkable publishing history. Some two hundred editions and reprints have appeared, including American, German, French, Danish and Japanese editions. With some justification it has been claimed as the fourth most published book in the English language, preceded only by the Bible, Shakespeare's plays and Bunyan's *Pilgrim's Progress*. In 1972 the publishers of the present volume issued a facsimile of the handsome first edition of *The Natural History* in which the engraved plates, after drawings first commissioned by Gilbert White of S. H. Grimm, provide the best available record of Selborne in White's day.

The natural history observations are outstanding and much in advance of their time. When most of his naturalist contemporaries were concerning themselves mainly with naming and describing dead specimens, White's book brings a breath of fresh air, with its observations of living plants and animals and the original discoveries arising from them. He made the first distinction between the three species of leaf-warblers, the willow warbler, wood warbler and chiff-chaff, and the first description in Britain of the lesser whitethroat, the harvest mouse and the noctule bat. His investigations into the economy of earthworms and their value in improving soil (carried out on the lawn at 'Wakes' by the light of a candle-lantern) anticipated those of Charles Darwin by over a hundred years. He was the first ecologist, a competent geologist and an able meteorologist; but more than all these things he had the ability to write down his observations in translucent prose that is a delight to read.

After the publication of *The Natural History*, the remaining four and a half years of Gilbert White's life were passed quietly. Since 1784 he had again been curate-in-charge of Selborne, as the incumbent was non-resident, and he continued his clerical duties almost until the end. He died on 26 June 1793, and was carried to his grave in Selborne churchyard, as was his wish, by 'six honest day labouring men, respect being had to such as have bred up large families', to whom he instructed his executors to pay 'the sum of ten shillings each for their trouble'.

III GILBERT WHITE AS A GARDENER

It is usually stated, but on slender evidence, that the keeping of the garden journal was probably suggested by the remarkable cleric and natural philosopher Dr Steven Hales who, as Rector of Faringdon from 1722 until his death, was a friend and near neighbour of the White family in the summer months. Hales, as White was to write in 1791, was a man whose 'whole mind seemed replete with experiment, which of course gave a tincture, and turn to his conversation, often somewhat peculiar, but always interesting'. Certainly visits to Faringdon rectory must have had a profound influence on the young Gilbert. At the very least they stimulated the love of experimentation and interest in meteorology which inform so much of the *Garden Kalendar*.

In calling his journal a 'Kalendar' Gilbert White was using

the word to mean a record rather than in the more usual sense. There were, of course, precedents for the name. John Evelyn had written *Kalendarium Hortense; Or, Gard'ners Almanac; Directing what he is to do Monethly throughout the Year* (reprinted in facsimile by the Scolar Press in J. Evelyn, *Sylva, 1664* [1972]). More recently Richard Bradley had published the *Gentleman's and Gardener's Kalendar* in 1718, while Philip Miller's *Gardener's Kalendar* first appeared in 1732 and went through several editions. These, however, were manuals telling the gardener what to do throughout the year. Gilbert White's *Kalendar* was unusual in being retrospective, describing what operations had actually been carried out. As a result, it provides an enthralling record of horticultural theory and practice, and amply evokes the great age of English gardening.

The early eighteenth century had seen the beginning of a revolt against the formal continental tradition in favour of romantic landscaping, led by pioneers like Charles Bridgeman who first laid out Stowe. When Gilbert White was assuming control of 'Wakes', Stowe, in the hands of William Kent and 'Capability' Brown, had become the most important garden in England. Its influence was spreading to every gentleman's grounds. As Horace Walpole wrote, Kent was the man who 'leapt the fence and saw all Nature was a garden'. At this time, too, the English lawn was to come into its own, as it swept from the windows of the house to merge the garden into the surrounding landscape. So that no fences should interrupt the view, the ha-ha was introduced from France: a deep, wide trench with a hidden wall, constructed along the edge of the garden to prevent cattle encroaching while still allowing them pleasingly to animate the view. Bridgeman had used one at Stowe, and it was eagerly copied on many sizeable estates.

Although the professed intention was one of studied informality, this did not exclude the deliberate cultivation of features for their picturesque qualities. For example, the coming of landscaped gardens awakened interest in the growing of fine specimen trees in contrast to the mutilations of the formal style. Arboriculture became a pursuit for gentlemen, but while the trees were to grow naturally, their siting must be carefully chosen.

Just as the return to nature did not imply that the garden was to become an uncontrolled wilderness, nor did it mean that obvious works of man were to be excluded. Kent set a fashion which ran to Palladian temples, rustic arbours, hermitages, statuary, carefully built ruins, and even fake bridges, artfully placed for their maximum visual and emotional effects.

It is clear from the *Garden Kalendar* that Gilbert White's gardening philosophy was permeated by these new concepts. We know that he had known Alexander Pope, the literary prophet of 'natural' gardening, while at Oxford. His account books show that White visited Stowe in 1752, and was sufficiently impressed to return later the same year. We can reasonably assume that the debate on gardening, which was but part of a wider and more general discussion of man's place in nature, was echoed in Oxford's common rooms. We know for certain that White enjoyed contact with some of the most advanced gardening circles of his day: the *Kalendar* provides a record of the current aesthetic of gardening being applied practically and imaginatively to the improvement of his small, difficult but immensely rewarding estate.

Early in the century, stimulated by the introduction of new plants and varieties from the Americas and the Orient, a group of enthusiasts had formed the Society of Gardeners, a body of which the Royal Horticultural Society is a lineal descendant. The secretary was Philip Miller (1691–1771), 'the best gardener in England', and a man in whom 'the perfect botanist and horticulturalist' were combined. From 1722 until shortly before his death, Miller was Gardener to the Worshipful Company of Apothecaries at their Botanic Garden in Chelsea. In this position, and probably with the help of fellow members of the Society of Gardeners, he prepared his *Gardener's and Florist's Dictionary*, published in 1724. This was followed in 1731 by the first edition of a larger work, *The Gardener's Dictionary*, destined to be the standard textbook on gardening in the eighteenth century. The sixth edition (1752) is the starting point for horticultural nomenclature, and in the eighth edition (1768) Miller adopted the Linnaean binominal system for species.

Linnaeus himself was told by a correspondent that Miller's *Dictionary* 'is the chief book that is read by gentlemen who study the art of gardening'. Gilbert White bought a copy in 1747 and in his account book there is an entry on 21 October 1753, 'Miller's Gardener's Dictionary, new edition halfbound in exchange from Br. Benjamin, £01:14:6'. This must have been the sixth edition.

Several entries in the *Garden Kalendar* testify to the close attention he paid to instructions given in the *Dictionary*. For example, an entry on 15 March 1755, has puzzled and amused many writers on White: "Carry'd Mr. Garnier's Cantaleupe-seed (being but two years old) in my Breeches-pocket 6 or 8 weeks'. Reference to the *Dictionary* explains this curious incident. After remarking that seed is frequently exchanged and carefully preserved two to three years before it is sown so that it will not 'be subject to produce strong, luxuriant vines, but will be more productive of fruit,' Miller continues, 'if you cannot obtain seed of that age, and are oblig'd to sow new ones, then you should either carry it in your Breeches Pocket, where it may be kept warm, or plac'd at a proper distance from a fire two months before it is sown, by which means the wat'ry Parts will be carry'd off, and the Seed prove equally good as if it had been left two or three years, as hath been experienc'd by several curious Persons'. More than this, Gilbert White not only followed instructions in the *Dictionary*, but he also corresponded with Miller and visited him at the Chelsea Physic Garden, as the *Kalendar* records on 23 June 1759.

It is clear from the *Kalendar* that when White with his keen interest in both theoretical and practical horticulture was coming to assume control of 'Wakes', he was infused with many of the new and fashionable ideas and applied them in his own garden. When the White family moved to 'Wakes' in 1728 the land attached to the cottage had probably been used as a smallholding and was mainly fields. Gilbert's father laid out seven acres with walks, but even in 1776 the outer garden immediately behind the house was still a field. The land nearer the house was uneven, and sloped towards the back door with a consequent danger of flooding until 1773. Moreover, the soil was not an easy one to work. In letter 1 of *The Natural History* White describes the geology of the gardens on both sides of Selborne street:

> The cart-way of the village divides, in a remarkable manner, two very incongruous soils. To the south-west is a rank clay, that requires the labour of years to render it mellow; while the gardens to the north-east, and small enclosures behind, consist of a warm, forward, crumbling mould, called black malm, which seems highly saturated with vegetable and animal manure; and these perhaps may have been the original site of the town; while the woods and coverts might extend down to the opposite bank.

'Wakes' was on the wrong side of the street and White was writing with feeling as a practical gardener of the 'rank clay' (chalk marl). It forced the Whites to excavate 'basons' in their garden and to bring over from Dortons down 'the opposite bank' the 'black malm' (chloritic marl) to replace the native earth. Gilbert records in the *Kalendar* from time to time the use of ashes and peat dust to make the garden soil more friable. Modern gardeners will envy him the vast quantities of manure he was able to use, and in addition he improved the ground with blacksmith's cinders, soot from the malthouse, tan waste from the tan-yards of Alton, and the soil from mole-hills.

Everything that Gilbert White grew in this carefully prepared ground had to have the best possible chance of success. Whether slugs or bullfinches, pests were eliminated without remorse. On the small scale he delicately amputated diseased shoots; on the large, he built a fruit wall and constructed a melonry forty-five feet long in the field garden. He carefully controlled the temperature of his elaborate hot-beds, and struggled to combat the effects of sudden frost.

Weather indeed takes a considerable share of the entries, as one would expect from a keen gardener. But beyond the noting of 'cold black weather', 'vast rains', 'vehement hot dry weather' and 'vast rimes' with their consequent effects on his plants, there is a remarkable and precise interest in meteorological phenomena. White records the exact duration of spells of wet or dry weather, he discovers the depth to which prolonged frost penetrates the earth, he watches cloud shapes, and he is interested in the microclimate of Selborne, contrasting it with the countryside around, as well as comparing it with weather patterns over western Europe.

In his choice of crops, White was in the horticultural vanguard. As early as 6 April 1751, the *Kalendar* mentions seakale, a plant not generally cultivated for another half-century although gathered in the wild by country folk. White acquired his seeds on a visit to South Devon, and it is clear from a comment on the entry that the planting was very much of an experiment. Similarly, he was among the early growers of potatoes, as an entry on 28 March 1758, shows. This was a vegetable worthy of comment in *The Natural History*; in letter XXXVII to Barrington (dated 8 January 1778), White writes that 'Potatoes have prevailed in this little district, by means of premiums, within these twenty years only; and are much esteemed here now by the poor, who would scarce have ventured to taste them in the last reign'. Perhaps most adventurously of all, 'Wakes' was one of the very few English gardens in which maize was propagated, as the note to the entry of 22 March, 1751, demonstrates.

In common with many of the keenest gardeners of his day, Gilbert White seems almost to have been obsessed by cucumbers and, above all, melons. Miller notes of the latter in his *Gardeners' Dictionary* that 'as there is not any plant cultivated in the kitchen garden which the gardeners near London have a greater ambition to produce early and in plenty, so there is a great number of Methods now practised in the raising and dressing of the Vines in order to obtain them in greater perfection'. This the *Kalendar* reflects perfectly, with its discussions of varieties, its forecasts of success and records of failure, and its close attention to techniques.

Modern gardeners will be interested, and perhaps surprised, at the early planting dates given in the *Kalendar*. The Gregorian Calendar was not adopted by Britain and her dominions until 3 September 1752 (which became 14 September), and so until then eleven days can be added to those given by White to bring them into line with the rest of the entries, but this hardly affects the issue. Two considerations may be relevant, however. Firstly, the tall hedges that surrounded the fields in the outer garden would be effective windbreaks so that the garden would be very sheltered, and secondly, White was using older and probably hardier strains of plants such as peas than those sown today.

It is not always possible to decide which plants are being described, even allowing for erratic spelling, and it is impossible to identify many of the varieties that White mentions. Even so, the great number of plants and varieties grown at 'Wakes' is startling: a dozen types of bean and melon, six kinds of plum, and seventeen sorts of pear.

The size of White's workforce is uncertain. His main helper during the period covered by the *Kalendar* was Thomas Hoar his servant for some forty years, who combined the offices of gardener and groom with that of footman on special occasions. At times 'Dame Turner and the girls' were hired to weed the brick walks; Robin Tull 'planted out in my absence'; and John Lassam, later to become White's permanent manservant, was employed to 'graft stems'. Later, outside the period covered by the *Kalendar*, we know that a curiously masculine 'weeding woman' appeared in the garden during the summer. Besides these identified helpers, casual labour was obtained from the village in abundance, enabling the larger-scaled projects to be undertaken at a strikingly low cost.

From 1751 the *Kalendar* is a record of remarkable achievements for so small a group of people, not merely in the routine management of flowers and vegetables, but also in developing plans for Gilbert's landscaped garden, with its picturesque amalgam of the natural and artificial. He made a shrubbery (without which no gentleman's garden could be complete); he constructed a ha-ha, one of the first if not *the* first in a small English garden. He planted specimen trees; he scattered beech-mast on the Hanger, land not belonging to the Whites, where his brother built a hermitage and constructed paths to reach it. A terrace and sundial were erected, and gigantic urns and a fake statue carefully positioned. Gates were set up in perspective. Gilbert acquired adjoining land whenever it became available, so that the garden eventually expanded to about nine acres.

By the time that the *Kalendar* was coming to its close, the planning of the garden was almost complete. Looking from the back of the house towards the Hanger there was an extensive lawn. It had flowerbeds, gay in spring with crocuses, 'polyanths', tulips and wallflowers, followed by lilies, peonies, red valerian, china asters and scarlet lychnis. At the far end of the lawn was the terrace, with an alcove or arbour at its left side and a sundial in the middle. The ha-ha separated the old garden from the outer garden of about seven acres extent which White referred to as his outlet. Except immediately behind the house this was broken up into small fields, laid out with grass paths and divided by hedges of 'prodigious' height—the maples about thirty-five feet and the hazels and whitethorns twenty feet—in which he delighted to watch many kinds of birds. A rustic field arbour from which he could watch them in more comfort was erected among the hedges, and a narrow brick path was laid from the arbour to the house through a wicket gate so that he would not get his feet wet in reaching it. Mistletoe grew on the hedges, and there were fine specimen trees in the fields including 'the high wallnut', 'the great spreading oak', and the 'Balm of Gilead fir-tree'. A 'forest-Chaire on the Bastion' was sited to take in the surrounding countryside. In 'basons' in the fields were tall flowers like martagon lilies and double sunflowers. In the outer garden, too, were the urns and fake statue.

To the south-east of the house was the rising ground called Baker's Hill. Part of this was still farmland, as the entry for 13 April 1765, shows. It may also have been on Baker's Hill that White planted the wildflowers he brought back from his excursions, like bear's foot or green hellebore, spurge laurel and bird's nest orchid. The opposite end of the garden, to the north-west, was bounded by the fruit wall some thirty yards in length, while the land now occupied by the long Victorian and Edwardian additions to the house was part of White's cultivated garden, his 'new garden against the street'. This is possibly where many of his vegetables were grown, conveniently close to the kitchen. Other vegetables and fruit, including melons, were cultivated on Baker's Hill.

The very house provided a support for vines. Jasmine was placed beneath the windows, and indeed the scent later became so intense that at times Gilbert was to be driven out of his own chamber, as he recorded in his Journal on 7 July 1783. The improvements had come at such a rate that even his friend and contemporary John Mulso, who knew the garden well, found difficulty in following them. In 1754 White mentioned improvements where the 'six gates one above another in perspective' had been set up in the fields between 'Wakes' and the Hanger. Mulso was puzzled, and wrote '. . . you begin to see the effects of your vases and obelisks amongst the green hedges. Your gates still remain mysterious . . .' Eight years later Mulso was again bewildered: 'You tell me of an alcove at the end of your Terrace. Which is your Terrace? . . . I am lost in the grandeur of your outlets, and the multiplicity of your improvements'.

Many of these 'improvements' are clearly to be seen in the atmospheric sketch by S. H. Grimm which is reproduced here as a frontispiece. Taken from the outer garden, with its specimen trees and hedgerows, it shows the fruit wall, sundial, terrace, and ha-ha. A solitary figure probably intended to represent Gilbert White, is facing the alcove. The especial interest of the *Garden Kalendar* is that it enables us to follow the slow growth into this landscaped maturity through White's own eyes. Moreover, as countless visitors to Selborne can testify, with judicious restoration the garden has survived to this day in large measure essentially as he created it.

ACKNOWLEDGEMENTS

I am indebted to Miss J. M. Backhouse, Assistant Keeper in the Department of Manuscripts, The British Library, for information on the history of the *Garden Kalendar*. My thanks are also due to the Curator of the 'Wakes' Museum, Selborne, Mr Clifford Cross, and Trustees of the Museum for allowing access to reference works in the library there, and to the following friends for help with horticultural, botanical and other queries: Emeritus Professor H. W. Miles; Mr Eric W. Groves, Hon. Archivist to the Selborne Society; Mr John Norwood, Keeper of Folk Life, Hampshire County Museum Service; Mrs H. M. Le Rougetel, and Madame N. E. Nannenga-Bremekamp. Miss C. Bane kindly read through parts of the typescript and made valuable suggestions, and Mrs Gifford-Hull helped most efficiently with the secretarial work of preparing the editorial matter for press. Finally, I should like to acknowledge the help and encouragement given me by the publisher's staff, and especially by Mr Martin Bailey.

SELECT BIBLIOGRAPHY

Published London unless otherwise indicated

AMHERST, ALICIA *A History of Gardening in England*, 1875

BRADLEY, RICHARD *The Gentleman's and Gardener's Kalendar*, 1731

BUNYARD, EDWARD *The Anatomy of Dessert*, 1929

CHITTENDEN, F. J. *The R.H.S. Dictionary of Gardening*, Oxford 1951

CLAY, ROTHAM. *Samuel Hieronymus Grimm*, 1941

CURTIS, W. HUGH *William Curtis 1746–1799*, Winchester 1941

EMDEN, C.S. *Gilbert White in his Village*, Oxford 1956

HALES, STEVEN *Vegetable Statics*, 1727

HITT, THOMAS *A Treatise of Fruit Trees*, 1755

JOHNSON, GEORGE W. *A History of English Gardening*, 1829

JOHNSON, WALTER *Gilbert White, Pioneer, Poet, and Stylist*, 1928

KENNEDY, A. E. CLARK *Steven Hales, D.D., F.R.S.*, Cambridge 1929

LAWRENCE, JOHN *The Fruit Garden Kalendar*, 1781

LE ROUGETEL, HAZEL 'A garden kalendar 1751–1771', in *Journal of the R.H.S.*, Vol. XCVI (1971), part 9, 412–8

MCLINTOCK, DAVID *Companion to Flowers*, 1966

MILLER, PHILIP *The Gardener's and Florist's Dictionary*, 1724
The Gardener's Dictionary, 1731, etc.

MULSO, JOHN *Letters to Gilbert White of Selborne*, ed. R. Holt-White, 1906

RYE, ANTHONY *Gilbert White and his Selborne*, 1970

SCOTT, WALTER S. *White of Selborne*, 1950

WEBBER, RONALD *The Early Horticulturalists*, Newton Abbot 1968

WHITE, RASHLEIGH HOLT *Life and Letters of Gilbert White*, 1901

The following works and editions of Gilbert White have been consulted or referred to:

Journals, ed. W. Johnson, 1931 (reprinted, Newton Abbot 1970)

A Nature Calendar, ed. W. Mark Webb, 1911

The Natural History and Antiquities of Selborne, 1789 (Facsimile by the Scolar Press, 1972), and editions by Thomas Bell, 1877, John Burroughs, 1895, R. Bowdler Sharpe, 1900–1901, (also containing *A Garden Kalendar*), E. M. Nicholson, 1929, and James Fisher, 1947

35,139

35 wood ...

Hen?

Mr Henry

```
o : 9  : o : 9
o : 17 : o : 6
o : 17 : 0 : 6
2 : 11 : 0
o : 4 : 3
```

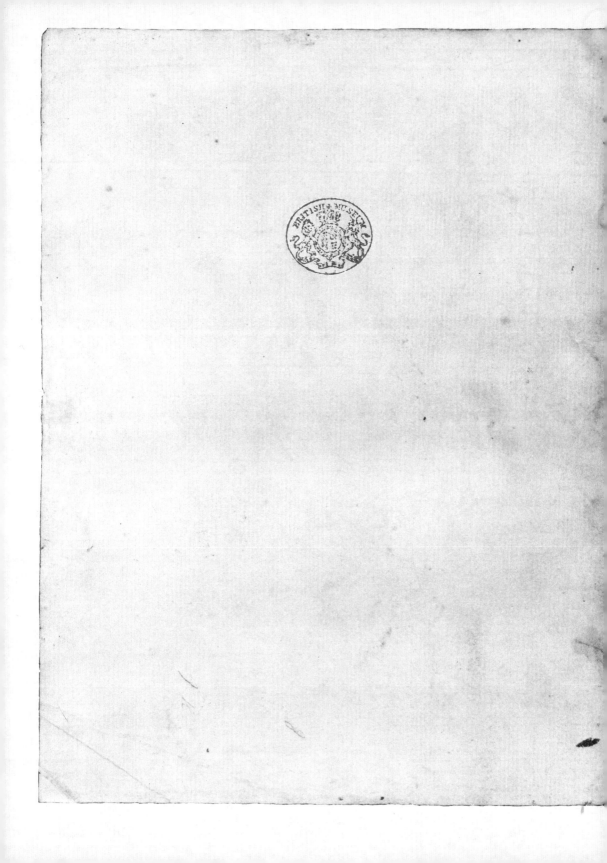

The Garden-Kalendar for the Year 1751.

Jan.ry 7. Two rows of early Spanish-Beans in Turner's plot. The four other rows were set in ye middle of November.

14. Earthed-up ~~the first~~ a row of Celery.

23. Planted 250 loaf-Cabbage plants in Turner's plot.

24. Sowed first Crop of Radishes turnip, & common; lettuce; & onions under the pales in the little Garden.

24. Planted-out five bulbs of the Crown Imperial (which I had from a Seedsman in London) in the middle plot of the little Garden.

14. Planted three slips of the Passion-flower, sent me by Mr Newlin, in the little Garden.

Feb: 23. Planted 14 Cuttings of the large, white, Dutch-Currants (which I brought from Godalming) in the little Garden.

27. New staked the Espaliers.

March 7. Planted five young passion-flower plants, which I had from Oxon. Gave my U: White four.

This bed by means of the great rains lost it's Heat; so that the Cucumbers, Melons, & Squashes never came-up.

March 8. Sowed a Crop of Asparagus seed: & seven rows of pease in the new Garden for the first Crop.

9. Set a Layer of Persian-Jessamin, which came from Mr Budd's.

15. Earthed-up the two last rows of Celery.

Do. Layed-down three twigs of the mulberry-tree.

21. Made first Hot-bed: cleared the strawberry, & raspberry beds.

22. ~~Plant~~ Sowed in the Hot-bed Cucumber, Melon, Squashes, & Mays-seed. Planted-out Holy-oaks, down the field, & in the Garden-border, & before the House: the seed from the Grange. Sowed a Crop of Carrots, Parsneps, Beets, Radishes, Lettuce, Leeks, Onions; a small crop of Salsafy; red Cabbage-seed, Dutch parsley, & Chardoons. There had been a Glut of wet for five weeks, & the Ground was rather too moist; but worked pretty well.

23. In the Hot-bed, two rows of African, & French Marigold seed.

27. Planted four rows of Windsor-beans in the field-Garden in ground just turned in from Grass.

April 1. Sowed in the field-garden four rows of marrow-fat pease.

The Sea cale lay a long while in the Ground before it appeared; six weeks at least.

April 2. 3. Planted four Asparagus-beds with plants of my
own raising in the new Garden: sowed a thin Crop of
Onions upon them. The Ground was well sanded, & trenched
deep with good rotten Dung, but wet when planted.

2. Earthed-up the two last rows of Celeri the last time.

4. Sowed a crop of common, & curled parsley: &
planted 13 Holy-oaks in the orchard, & yard.

6. Sowed a full Crop of Carrots, Salsafy, Skirret,
~~[illegible]~~ Scorzonera, Lettuce, Radishes, Beet. Sowed the
seed of a remarkable large leek. Sowed a large
bed of sea-cale, which I brought from the ~~[illegible]~~
South-hams of Devon. Sliped, & dressed the artichoke-
beds. A small crop of Onions under Kelsey's Hedge
for picklers. The Ground still wet.

3. Made a second Hot-bed: sowed within the frame,
common Cucumbers, Horn D^o Squashes, Melons,
Balsams, French Marygolds, purslain: without the
~~[illegible]~~ frame; Common Celeri, Celeriac, or turnip-
rooted Celeri, Nasturtium, Sun-flowers, & purslain.
Made a cover of oiled paper for the first bed.

18. Sowed nine rows of marrowfat-pease in the plot
just without the field Garden.

The Skirret all run to seed.

23. Planted 300 of Cabbages in the field-garden. Sowed Holy-oak, Oriental-Mallow, & Nasturtium, & Larkspur-seed in the common Ground. Set an old Barrel with the Head beat-out into the Ground to hold water for the Hot-beds, &c.

26. Cut Asparagus for the first time.

27. Made a new Hot bed: transplanted the melon-plants into it: sowed some Cucumber-seed in it: & sowed common Celeri, & Sunflowers without the frame. Transplanted the Mays into the border next Lassams: transplanted the African Marrygolds in the beds, & some of the Cucumbers: sowed 2 rows of Garden Cress, & two of Wh: Mustard on an old bed. Dug-up the last parcel of blanched Celeri.

May 3. Pulled the first Radishes.

7. Sowed a Crop of Parsneps, (the first failed) with radishes, & Lettuce. The first Crop of curled Endive, green, & white. The first Crop of French-Beans, two rows in the new-garden.

9. Second Crop of Skirret; the first failing.

14. Crop of Common Beans in the field-Garden.

No fine weather, but constant wind, wet, & frost till the 18 of May. Then very dry, & hot.

A prodigious Crop of Broccoli by shading, & watering.

May 23. Pricked-out the red Cabbages. Sowed flowering Lupines of several Sorts, & Lady-pease in the basons in the Field, & the border in the Garden.

24. Pricked-out the Chardons: sowed five basons with Cucumber-seed in the natural Ground. Transplanted one Holy-oak into the border in the Field.

25. Planted-out the Melons for the last time, & covered them with oiled papers. Sowed a plot of Roman, & a plot of white Broccoli-seed; & shaded them well with boughs. Sowed some Common, & curled parsley; & some purslane.

27. Planted-out three squashes.

28. Crop of Common Celeri.

June 11. 13. Row & half of Marrowfats; & D^o of French-beans.

20. Gathered first ~~&~~ pease.

21. Planted-out Nasturtiums, Sunflowers, Balsams, & French, & African Marrigolds ~~in~~ in the field, & New Garden.

Latter end of July sowed a large bed of Spinage, & radishes. Came-up very well.

June 24. Pricked-out a large Quantity of white, & Roman Broccoli.

25. Planted-out curled white, & green Endive in rows: pricked out three plots of Celeri: planted-out red Cabbages; & a plot of Leeks from the Giant Leek. Sowed a Crop of Endive (second Crop) both sorts.

26. Planted out the Holy-oaks sown in ye Spring.

27. Gathered first beans, little spanish, set in november.

August 27. Earthed-up the first planted Chardons; planted out more: trenched 6 rows of Celeri. Sowed a small plot of turnip-radishes. Planted out several rows of Broccoli.

Septemr. 9. Earthed-up the first row of Chardons for the last time in pots with the bottoms out.

12. Basketed-up the second row of Chardons: sowed a large bed of Spinage.

Octobr. 5. Planted Stock-gilliflowers from Bradley down the Field. Dug up the two first Chardons.

Octob:r 11. Trenched-out a row of Celery in the field Garden: earthed-up the last Chardons the first time.

Oct:r 14. Sow'd three rows of early Spanish Beans in the field garden

23. Added one row more of small beans from Oxon, never sowed but once in England.

26 Planted seven spruce-firs from North-warnboro' in Baker's-Hill: some flowering shrubs in the lower part next the walk: a Quince-tree in the old orchard. Earthed-up the new asparagus-beds in the new Garden.

Novem:r 2. Finished the Shrubery. A severe frost for planting. Earthed-up the old asparagus-beds.

6. Planted in a border in the old Orchard several cuttings of Gooseberries, Currants, Honey-suckles, & Scorpion Sennas. Earthed-up the Celery in the new Garden.

Decem:r 2: 3. Trenched some Ground against spring. Earthed-up Artichoke-beds for the winter. Earthed-up the last Chardons; & the Celery.

The Year 1751. was one of the wettest Years in the memory of Man. There were constant Storms & Gluts of rain from the 20th: of Feb: to the 20th: of May. Part of May, & all June were very dry, & burning. But all July, & great part of August were as wet as ever: so that nothing in Gardens in a clayey soil grew ~~grew~~ to any size: & nothing came to bear 'till five or six weeks later than usual.

Garden-Kalendar for the Year 1752.

Middle of February: two rows of Beans, & nine of early pease in the field-Garden.

March 4th Hot-bed in the field-Garden: the dung had been cast a fortnight, & mixed with Coal-cynders. 3 hundred of Cabbage-plants in the new, & Turner's Garden.

5. Mulched, & banked-up the Quincunx of firs on Baker's Hill. Dressed the Rasberry-beds, & planted a new one in the new Garden. Sowed a Crop of Celeri on the outside of the Cucumber-frame. Sowed a Crop of Carrots, Parsneps, Leeks, Onions, Skirrets, Beets, Radishes, Lettuce, fine Coss sort. A Large Plot of fine Asparagus-seed from Chalgrave in the new Garden. Sowed in the new Garden Frenchoneysuckles, Columbines, & Everlasting-pease.

6. Weeded Sea-Cale-bed. Sowed Holy-oak seed, & Oriental-Mallow, a good large bed in the new Garden. Sowed two rows of forward pease in the Garden in the field.

appeared all above ground on the 11:th
The bed heats well, without being too fierce.

arch 7. Sowed in the Hot-bed Cucumbers,
rench Marrigolds, African D^o. Indian wheat;
Nasturtiums on the outside. Dressed straw=
rry- beds. Planted a row of Eschallots. Planted
oly-oaks down the field. New-dug the border
t the bench in the Field. Made a screen for
e Hot-bed with pease-haulm.

. Plashed, & banked-up the Quick-set-hedge
etween Turner's, & the Orchard. Planted Holy=
aks in the New-garden. Sowed poppy-seed, &
arkspur-seed in the Borders of the new Gar=
en: Dressed Asparagus-beds: earthed-up the
ate row of Celeri in the field-Garden. Mended
e Sea-Cale with seed, where it was wanting.

. Dunged, & dug-up some Ground in the new
arden. Dug the flower-basons in the field.
owed the ground in the little mead (lately
leared from nettles) with Grass-seeds. Prepared
o basons, one on each side the street-door,
r passion-flowers. Thinned the young bed
l Spinage.

March 11. Sowed seven rows of broad beans in the Quincunx on the top of Baker's Hill. Planted in the new Garden three of the large Dutch-Currant-trees, which I brought in cuttings from Godalming last Year.

Thomas White's writing

April 8. Planted water'd & shaded the Lauresstinus near the Bench in the Field & the Passion flower on each Side the street Door.
Sowed a Row of Laburnum Seed from Ringmer

10 Put sixteen Cowcumber plants under the Hand Glasses.

11. Plant^d. six Cowcumb. plants from W. Wells in the Old Hot Bed.

13. Transplanted the Indian Corn in the Cups in the field by the Brickwalk in Bakers Hill & in the Oats towards Willis's.

Planted each Corner of Bakers Hill within the Rod Hedge with Beans.

15. Sow'd three Rows of French Beans in the field Gard^n. first Row from the Tub in the Barn second from the paper Bag in the Kitchen third from the Chaise

Mem. made a Bed of Sand for the Seed

April 15. Planted some yellow Indian Corn in the new hot-Bed without the glasses to supply those that fail, in the Cups. 12

16. Sowed a Row of purple double Stocks from London & half a Row of Brampton Stocks from Ringmer.

Sowed in the New Garden on the Border by the Brick-Walk, Love lies a Bleeding, Painted Lady Peas, Larkspurs, Yellow Lupines, & Double Poppies.

Mem. Sow'd Radishes with the Stocks as Miller directs.

May 14. Planted some Indian-Corn, & French & African Marrigolds down the basons in the field. Some D^o Marrigolds in the new Garden.

16. Made a new hot-bed in the field-Garden: made a ridge with 10 Cups in the new Garden for Cucumbers in the natural Ground, & sowed them with seed.

?. Sowed a Crop of Broccoli, parsley, & Finochia in the new-Garden.

?9. Removed four plants, with fruit set on them, into the new hot-bed.

May 20. Planted-out Sunflowers, & Nasturtiums down the field: sowed a row of dwarf white french-beans in the field-Garden; mended the early rows of french-beans in Do:

July 23. Planted 200 white, & Roman Broccoli-plants (which I brought from Oxon) in the new, & field Garden. Planted 200 Savoys in the field Garden.

27. Sowed a crop of winter-spinage, with some turnep-radishes, in the new Garden.

29. Sowed a Crop of turneps, ~~for~~ for spring-Greens, in the field-Garden.

A Crop of Do: among the firs on Baker's Hill.

August 3. Trenched six rows of Celeri in the field-Garden. Sowed a Crop of Coss Lettuce, & Endive.

Septem: 15. N: S: Tyed-up several large Endive.

16. Sowed a plot of Rhubarb; & two late Crops of Spinage.

29. Tyed-up the remaining Endive.

Octob.r 19. Six rows of early, African Beans, 14 in the field-Garden.
24. Trenched two rows of Celery in the field-Garden.

Garden Kalendar
for the Year 1753.

January 1.st Planted three rows of small African Beans in the Quincunx-garden.
2. Sowed a crop of Asparagus-seed, of our own saving, in the new Garden.
16. Two rows of broad beans in the fir-quincunx, & two in Turner's Garden.
19. Five rows of forward pease in Turner's Garden.
23. Planted five Bushels of turneps for greens.
24. Thinned-out the raspberry-beds.
26. Sowed a long drill of parsley in New-Gard.n & a Crop of Asparagus seed in D.o

Octob:r 25. 1753. Seven rows of early African-Beans in the field-Garden. Three rows of early pease in Turner's Garden. Laid-down several Branches of the Laurus-tinus in ye little Garden: & some boughs of the Mulberry-tree. Pease destroyed, & most of the beans.

Garden -- Kalendar for 1754.

An uncommon severe winter: most things in the Garden destroyed.

Feb: latter end. A crop of early pease in Turners: & crop of broad beans in the field-Garden.

March 5. ~~March~~ Made a very deep hot-bed: half the dung cast before hand, & half from dunghill at once. The season uncommonly dry, & fine. Sowed a large Crop of spinage in the field-Garden to supply the general destruction made by the severe winter. A wonderful large, useful Crop.

6. Sowed larkspurs, painted ladies, & Columbines in the borders in the new Garden: & a Crop of Parsley.

12. Sowed two pots of melons in the Hot-bed, & one pot of Cockscombs: backed-up the bed to the top of the frame, the frost being very extream.

March 19. Sowed two pots of Mr Missen's melon-seeds; one pot of early Cucumber-seeds; one pot of Gibson's Capsicums. The bed in fine order, but the frost very severe. One pot more of Cockscombs.

The first-sown Cockscombs appear'd about the 21. came-up very thick: the first-sown melons about 23. very strong. Raised the pots as soon as they appeared.

26. Sowed a row of Bosworth's early melons in the hot bed without pots: a row of my own Cucum: seed: & two rows of Bosworth's white-Dutch Cucum: seed, never sowed (never came up) before in England.

29. Cast eleven Cart-loads of Hot-dung in the field-garden for melon-beds, & Cucum^r ridges.

29. Sowed a Crop of Carrots, radishes, white Coss, & green Coss lettuce, Parsneps, Beets, leeks, Holyoaks, & Onions. Planted-out some Laburnums raised in 1752. from seeds in Baker's Hill.

April 4. Made a very large hot-bed for my two-light melon-frame. The Dung very warm.

5. Made four rows of the broken rows of early beans. Laid fine earth 6 inches thick between the Hot-bet; sowed some ~~red~~ radishes, & a crop of Celeri.

April 8. Laid-on the earth on the great Melon-bed. Bed heats finely: wonderful fine weather.

9. Sowed a large Crop of marrow-fats in Turner's.

10. Planted three large, forward Cucumber-plants, given me by Mr Johnson, in my first Hot-bed.

Planted six Laurels ~~on~~ near the pitching in the old orchard; two Larches on the bank near the Ewel-gate; a Scotch, & silver fir in the upper end of the Ewel-close

11. Made a melon-hot-bed with 14 barrows of dung, for my smallest frame cover'd with a paper-light. Made my ridge for three hand-glasses.

12. Transplanted three of my forwardest melon-plants (four leaves each) into each of the lights of my great frame: one to be taken away, from each hill, when they ~~set~~ are settled. Mem: the earth would not turn-out, 'till the pots were broken. The bed in a fine heat The plants had fill'd the pots with their fibres.

Made a slight hot-bed in the new garden with 8 barrows of dung for hardy annuals: put-on my old frame, & old ~~s~~oil'd-paper. Sowed a Crop of Carro & lettuce in the shady quarter of the new garden; spots of Sunflowers, & Nasturtiums in the borders of Do: six rows of broad beans in the field gardens.

Planted-out some cucumber-plants (sadly wire-drawn) under two of the Hand glasses; & sowed six of Mr Burrough's melon-seeds under an other; the ridge in a fine heat. The early melon-plants from Mr Burrough's seed. Those to be put in the paper-frame from Mr Missen's. 16

14. Sowed in the new-garden hot-bed, rows of african Marygolds, & Indian Corn: planted 20 shallot-bulbs, 12 Garlick Do: in new Gard:

17. Planted a pot of Mr Missen's melon's in the small frame ~~uder~~ under the paper light.

15. Brought 4 white cucumber-plants from Waltham; put them under a Hand-glass.

19. Very thick Ice, & the Ground froze hard. Frequent showers of snow, & hail. The Hot-beds maintain their Heat well: the melon-beds too apt to steam; & the air too cold to be admitted in any great degrees.

24. Pinch'd my early melon's for the first time: & added a good depth of fine mould, mixed with sand, so as to fill the frames half way up.

The paper-light torn by a storm, & the melon plants damag'd.

25. Planted-out about 20 of the best Cockscombs on the upper side of the Cucumber, & two-light melon-frames.

April 25. Planted a pot of Missen's melons in the small frame; the other pot being damaged by a storm which tore the paper light. Planted some large french Lupines from Mr. Budd in the new Garden.

May 2. Sowed some Cucumber-seeds under an Hand-glass in the natural Ground, for a natural Crop. Prick'd-out a small bed of early Celeri, just in the first leaf, for early trenches.

8. Earth'd-up the melon-beds a good depth more: took-off a joint with a knife that had been omitted; stopp'd some of the runners: the plants in good vigour, & offering for fruit, & bloom.

The cucumber-plants show fruit; but none yet set.

The Cockscombs wonderful forward, & stocky; & have showed bloom ever since the end of April.

9. 10. Dressed the Artichoke-beds; & sowed three long rows of large, white french-beans in the field Garden

May 21. Made a good strong hot-bed to finish-off the Cockscombs with: plunged 10 large pots in the bed, & half-fill'd them with fine earth.

Lined-out & earth'd very deep the melons-beds for the last time; & rais'd all the frames to the top of the earth. Planted some Capsicums, & pendulous Amaranths from Waltham in smaller pots: & 24 Cauliflowers from Soberton in new Garden.

May 22. Made a wattle-hedge, about 18 inches high,
round the melon-beds, to widen-out the beds. 17
Removed ten of the best Cockscombs into the large
pots in the new beds: the plants were taken-up
with a sheet of tin with a deal of earth, & well
water'd. The plants very fine, & forward, & in
good bloom; & 22 inches high. Two old frames
placed one on the other: & the bed beginning
to heat well.

22. The forwardest bason of Burrough's melons
shewed for fruit. The weather uncommonly dry
& sultry. Planted some forward Celeri from Mr Beaver's.
a large parcel more of my own Celeri in new Garden.

22. Sowed a Crop of turnep-seed in field garden, &
new-Garden after a soaking shower.

25. Planted 300 of backward Cabbage plants.

June 5. The Cockscombs full 28 Inches high;
the combs very broad, & the stems very stocky.

[illegible]. Planted 100 of fine Savoys in the place of the
two Asparagus-beds grubb'd-up in the new Garden.
Sowed a crop of Coss-lettuce, & Endive green, &
white.

6. Planted-out a Crop of Leeks in field-Garden.

June 15. Cut first Cucumber. Cockscombs 3 foot high the ta
1754. widest Comb 3/4 Inches.

28. Lin'd the Cockscomb-bed, which began to grow cool, with 9 barrows of very hot dung:

28. Only five melons set; those very large, & in the two-light frame. Missen's plants still cast their fruit; not one set.

July 2. The best Comb five inches & half wide: the melons swell apace. The Cockscomb-bed very hot with the new lining. Shady, showery weather for these last 3 weeks, & not kind for the melons.

6. Trench'd-out four rows of Celeri in ye field-Garden: planted a large bed of late-sown Coss-lettuces in ye New-Garden.

17. Planted a large Crop of Broccoli-plants from Captain Gwyn's: with Endives between.

23. Cut-away a vast deal of the melon-vines, whi were shot-out beyond all bounds: None of Missen set yet; & no more of Burrough's. Put a brick under some of the Melons. No kind Melon-wea-ther since the beginning of June; but a constan cloudy, windy season, but not much rain. Misse Melons shew plenty of fruit, but it all drops off. The melon's earth too rich; which occasion'd such an

-bundance of vine: besides the seed was but one
-ear old. 18
23. Took the Cockscombs out of their frame:
the best comb full seven Inches wide; the leaves
-ery large, & green; & the largest Stems two
-nches & a quarter round: the Combs well in:
-ented: That Amaranth that was suffer'd to run
- many heads, looks very fine, & makes a pleas:
-ng variety. The wind is very apt to snap-off
-e leaves when the plants are first set-out,
-efore the air has hardened them: heavy rains
-o the same. The tallest plant about three feet
-ur inches. Mem. the constant wet Weather rotted several of the Heads of those that stood abroad
5. Cut first natural Cucumber.

-ugust. 7th. Cut first Melon wt. 4 lb. it was firm & thick fleshed & better tasted than could be expected after such a continuance of Shade & wonderful wet Weather

The best Combs grow mouldy.

-ug: 14. Missen's plants too vigorous to let any fruit
set. Fine weather: cut away the vines from the melons to
- in the full Sun.

Sowed a Crop of Spinage, & Radishes in the field-
-arden.

March 12. 1752. Mem: Left the three new Cucumber-frames, taken to pieces, in the old barn, in the straw-bey, leaning against the boards of the new stable. Put the glass-frames belonging to them (but with no Glass in them) in the lumber-garret: & the oaken-pins in a deal-box in the lumber-Garret.

Mem: Seven very full cart-loads of dung make an exact suitable hot-bed for my great two-light frame: & five D°. for my four han[d]-glasses.

Septem.r 13. 1754. Collected Mushroom-spawn, 19
, laid it up to dry.

20. Laid-down Baker's-Hill with white-clover-
eed; & roll'd it well. A long dry fit of 6 weeks.

8. Made an Horse-radish-bed in the new-Garden:
lanted the buds 10 inches deep.

Transplanted a Row of Mint, one of Balm and
one of Pennyroyal.

30. Parted the Lilly Roots in the Little Garden &
planted the large ones in the Field Basons, & the
Offsets in the Orchard, with the Tulips &c that
if any of them are worth preserving they may
be markt when in bloom & remov'd into the Garden
Transplanted Sweet Williams from Waltham into the
Little Garden from the New Garden with a few Stock

Octob.r 1.st Carryed ten loads of virgin-earth from
Norton into the little mead for the melon-frames.

. A thorough soaking rain, after an uninterrupted
fit of above six weeks dry weather.

Oct. 15. Planted a Bason of Double Per^l. Sunflo
Single D^o. —— N°. 6
—— N°. 7
—— Double Ragged Robin N°. 8
two Roots of Campan. Pysam. in po
two Peach leav'd D^o. —— N°. 9
—— Canterbury Bells —— N°. 11.
two Roots Double Scarlet
Lychnis. one in little Gard^n.
the other in the field —— } —— N°. 12.
two Yellow Lillies
two fiery D^o. } in little Garden ——

20. Planted some Yellow & purple Crocus' for Bord
in the Little Garden

Planted ~~...~~ Slips of Pinks & Cloves in the
Little Garden & in some of the field Basons

22 Planted Fox: Gloves Mulleens, Woodlawrel & Bears foot fro
the Wood & Soap Wort from Gale's Garden Also
Planted three Opulus' from Berrimans

24 Sow'd three New Basons with Larkspur Seed

Sow'd a Row of Laburnum Seed in the No. 1.
Seedling Bed in New Gar[den]

— — — Fraxinella Seed in Do. No. 2

— — — Persicaria No. 3.

Planted Golden Rod & St. Peter's Wort from Dr. Bristow's.

Planted some Xyphiums or Bulbous Iris' in the Little Garden Mem. some Offsets in Seedling Bed. No. 10.

Planted some Tuberous rooted Iris' in the field. Mem. the Xyphiums were sent by Mistake

Planted a Spiraea Frutex from Mr. Budd

Nov. 5. Transplanted a Row of Laurustines into the Gate from the Little Garden

6. Moved the Layers of Laurustinus into the Nursery Bed in the Orchard

9. Planted four Box Trees (which came from behind the old Pales) ~~round the Little House~~ in the vista at the upper end of ye field.

Remov'd four Rose Trees into one Bason in the Field. Very wet Weather, but not very cold

Novr. 20. Planted 9 rows of Mazagon beans in Turner's Garden. ~~Dressed~~ earth'd Asparagus-beds.

21. Made, earth'd, & thatch'd a musroom-bed seven feet long according to Miller.

21. Altered the square-plot behind where the old pales stood, & threw it into a grass plot, with two very wide borders, one towards the street, & one towards Kelsey's Gate.

Planted out 3 doz: of Coss lettuce under two old frames to stand the winter in the new Garden near the melon-beds.

Dec. 17. Put the Spawn into the Mushroom Bed

31. Earth'd up the second Crop of Celeri.

Garden-Kalendar for the Year 1755.

Jan: 6. Sowed a row of Holly-berries behind the Filberts against Kelsey's Yard.

Feb: 7. Made an Hot-bed with the small frame for White-mustard &c: & an other with an hand-glass for Celeri. Sowed it last week in Feb:

Feb: 19. Sowed half a pound of spinage in the field-Garden: 6 rows of forward pease in ~~the~~ Turner's Do. Planted 200 of Cabages in Field Do.

20. Sowed a Gallon & half of broad beans in ye field-Garden. Very severe frost.

21. Made an Hot-bed for early radishes, hoop'd it over, & cover'd it with a large mat.

March 12. Very ~~deep~~ snow, 7 inches on plain ground.

13. Made a very deep & large Hot-bed for my melon-seeds; &c: with seven cart-loads of dung: thatch'd the edges of the bed ~~beyond~~ without the frame.

14. Made slight Hot-bed for the Arbutus-seed.

March 15. Sowed two pots of Mr Garnier's Cantale-
-Melons 1753: two pots of Mr Hunter's of Waverly
Do 1752: two pots of Cockscombs: one pot of
pendulous Amaranths: one pot of sensitive-
-plant-seed: one pot of Arbutus-seed: two pots
of my own large Andalusian-Melons:
Mem: Carry'd Mr Garnier's Cantaleupe-seed
(being but two years old) in my Breeches-pocket
6 or 8 weeks. Sad snowy, wet, cold weather.
17. Scattered the overplus of the Arbutus-seed a-
-mong the new-planted Filberts in the orchard.
Mem: To observe if any grow.
17. Hot-bed heats well.
19. Sowed five rows of Marrow-fat-pease in field G
20. Planted 74 Laurels from Waverley down Bak-
-er's-Hill with two Ilex-acorns between each two:
one portugal-laurel, one weeping-willow, one
parsley, one black mountain-Virginian-Elder,
one flowering-Rasp: two stoneless barberries, 6
roses, down the basons in the field: 2 Dutch Ho-
-ney-suckles against the Trellis in new Garden: &
some Pine, & Chili-Strawberries in new Garden.

21. Sowed 12 seeds of Cedar of Libanus, a Crop of Larches, Weymouth-Pines, & Cluster-pines, in two Boxes standing to the morning sun in the field-garden; & hoop'd & netted ym:

Planted Ivy round the little-house, & a Bed of Rasps at the north end of the House:

Planted a fine Mulberry-tree, of my own raising from a layer, in the new opening in the new-Garden.

27 Sowed more Melons in the Pots that fail'd. John White Senr handwriting

Sowed one pot of Mr Garniers Cantalupe 1753. one pot of Lincolns Green Cantalupe 1751. one pot of Mr Hunters Yell-ow Cantalupe 1752, and one pot of Millers very fine old seed.

April 1. Sowed a Crop of Carrots, Coss-lettuce, & parsneps in the New-Garden.

2. Cast 20 Cart-loads of Dung in the melon ground.

3. Planted 13 Laurels round the necessary, & against the street.

14: 15: Made a large melon-bed with 20 loads of dung for six lights in the field-garden. The weather wet, & unfavourable. The melon-seeds in the pots came-up weak, & poor, the season not favouring.

April 16. Sowed a pot of Romania-Melon-seed 1753: & a pot of Zatta 1751: a pot of three-thorned-Acacia-seed; & a pot of seed mark'd only ~~A~~ Acacia: Evergreen-Oak Acorns: Bird-cherry-seed: cut-leaf'd tulip-tree seed: Boorcole, red & green: savoy seed: Campanula Pyrimidalis: Scarlet Lychniss: Holy-oak-seed [illegible] leeks: Beets, parsley, & Onions.

17. Sowed Basons of Double-China-Aster, Double-Larkspurs, Nasturtiums, Nigella-Romana, Venetian-poppies, Oriental-mallow, Venus-Looking-glass, Candy-tuft, & Chrysanthemums in the new borders in the Garden; & in the Basons in the field.

Sowed some Orange-Gourds, & long-Gourds under the Arbutus mat. Painted-Ladies in the New-Garden.

19. Planted some foxglove-roots from London in the shady Border in the new-garden.

April 19. Turn'd-out two pots of Cantaleupe, & two pots of Andalusian-melons into the two great frames. The plants in thriving condition, but the bed hardly shews any signs of Heat. The weather uncommonly dry, sunny, & sultry.

20. The Romania, & Zatta-melons appeared out of the Ground.

21. Turn'd-out two pots of Cantaleupe-melons into the two single lights, the one Glass, the other paper.

22. Made an Hot-bed for two Hand-glasses, & one paper light, with seven loads of Farmer Parsons's dung: earth'd the basons with Dorton-mould. The Acacia-seeds appeared to day. Sultry weather. Cut a good mess of Asparagus for the first time.

23. Planted large plot of Artichokes from Dr Bristow's in the new-garden; & sowed a Crop of Coss-lettuce between. Made a slight hot-bed with 1 load of dung for sunflowers, African-Marrigolds, double Asters, & Celeri; & hoop'd, & matted it. Made Cucumber-ridge

with two loads of dung for two Hand-glasses.
April 25. Transplanted out of their pots some Zatta-Melon-plants in the paper-light; & some Romania-Melon-plants under the two hand-glasses: the bed heats very finely. Transplanted some Cucumber-plants under the two other Hand glasses. Showry, warm weather.

26. Turn'd-out a pot of Cantaleupe-Melons into the original seed-bed, & earth'd ~~the~~ it up a great depth.

28. Planted-out 6 Acacias in 6 penny-pots: very long tap-~~[illegible]~~-roots.

29. Transplanted some Cockscomb-plants, not very forward, into one of the two-light melon-frames. Transplanted three Orange-gourd-plants under the melon-ground-Hedge. Planted two Storax-trees, from Guernsey, sent me by Will: Galden, in one of the basons of the field.

June 23 Cut the first Cucumber.

July 17. Planted-out plots of Endive-plants Turn'd-out remarkably fine & large.

July 18. Only six brace of melons set.
The Acacias in the pots very fine. A fine
Crop of Cluster-pines: 10 or 12 Weymouth-
pines: 2 Cedars of Libanus: not one Larch,
nor Arbūtus.

An uncommon hot, dry summer to this time.

18. about 500 savoys-plants, & about 6 score
boor-cole plants, all of our own raising, in
Farmer's Garden.

August. 1. Cut the first Melon. Mem. It hung too long, & was mealy. This was intended for a Cantaleupe, but proved a common sort.

26. Gather'd the first Mushrooms from spawn
put into a bed last Decem.^r^ ye 17.th

Only six brace of melons set: hinder'd in their
ripening by a long run of cold, shady weather.

28. Planted-out a great many Holy-oaks in
the new-Garden, ye Yard, & field.

28. Tyed-up 30 Good Endive-plants. More
should be tyd-up about the 18.th of Septem.^r^
with different-colour'd yarn.

Septem:r 1. Planted a plot in New-Garden with Hine-strawberries brought from Waverly. Those planted in the spring dyed.

2. Cut two Cantaleupe-Melons: the biggest weigh'd 3 pds 5 oun: they were perfectly dry, & high-flavour'd, notwithstanding the weather had been shady, & cool for three weeks; & uncommon wet & stormy for the last week.

2. Made a large Musroom-bed, eight feet long; used eleven Barrows of hot-dung with no layers of earth intermix'd.

15 Planted the mushroom spawn brought from Dean on t
new made bed, it was moderately warm. the larger lumps wer
set on the ridge, the smaller earth near the bottom. NB I plant
the SE side & Thomas the NW.

19. Tyed-up more Endive: those tyed-up before not well blanch'd, for want of being ty'd with double yarn, & in two places.

The new Musroom-bed heats gently.

The double China-asters make a fine show.

Mem: The green-Endive, by being so much longer, tyes-up, & blanches much better than the white.

Septem.r 23. Put the Acacias in their winter-quarters in a frame under the Hedge of the melon-ground: planted some lettuce to stand the winter in the same frame, & along the border: placed an old frame for a Quart.r of an Hund: of Cauliflower-plants: put the two boxes of the seedling-pines under the sunny-hedge. Sowed a Crop of persicaria-seed, & green-Coss-lettuce on the same border. Sowed a Crop of Belvedere on the same border.

Octob.r 6. Sent the Cauliflowers from Dene.

30.th Planted two basons in the field with Canter=bury-bells. Planted a nursery of some Scorpion-sena, & Spiræa-suckers in the New-Garden.

Nov.r 2. Planted ten rows of Mazagan-beans (never planted in England) in the field-garden.

Planted four Pyramidal-Campanulas in four large pots, & plunged them in the Border under the melon-screen.

Planted 30 full-grown perennial-sunflower-roots in the border against the street, & Kelsey's Gard; & in the upper part of the basons in ye field.

Nov:r 2. Planted some slips from the perennial-sun-
-flowers in a nursery.

Fine settled weather for 9, or 10 days before: the only good weather since July.

The Campanulas, & sunflowers lay in the ware-house in London, & were somewhat damaged by the closeness of the Box.

6. Sowed two more patches of ye last year's persicaria-seed under the melon-hedge. One plant of the last sowing come-up very strong.

11. Most uncommon frost for one night, & consider-
-ing the season of the Year: Ice near an inch thick, & the dirt hard enough to bear an Horse.

6. Planted 12 cuttings of Tamarisk sent down from London with the Peren:l Sunflowers, &c:

24. Turn'd the Horse-path at the Bottom of Baker's-Hill, & continu'd-out the Quincunx-
-basons, & prepar'd them for shrubs.

25. Staked & tyed the Quincunx of Firs that were much loosen'd by the late violent rains, & winds.

Decem:r 1. Earth'd-up the Artichoke-beds for the winter.

Eleven evergreen-oaks alive down Baker's-Hill.

Decem:r 27. Finished two large three-light Melon-frames, each ten feet & an half long, & five wide in the clear; & containing 97 feet of Glass in ye lights, & an half foot.

A terrible winter for Earthquakes, In:undations, Tempests, & continual Rains. No frost worth mentioning except on the 11th & 12th of Novem:r

Garden-Kalendar:
for ye Year 1756.

Jan: 23. Made an hot-bed on the dung:
:hill in the Yard, with Mr Johnson's frame,
for white-mustard, & cress.

30. Earthed-up the backward Celeri.
31. Planted two Cuttings from the weeping-wil:
:low in the New-Garden.

Feb: 14. Planted 200 of Cabbage-plants in
ye field-Garden.

14. Made a Melonry in the Field-Garden
45 feet long, & lin'd it at ye back very warm, & secure
with some damaged rushes of John Berri:
:man's: lin'd ye two side-screens in the same
manner; & in particular that towards ye
Cucumber-bed, that it's Farina might
not mix with ye melons.

Mem: The winter-Coss-lettuce, which stood
very safe under frames during the severe
dry frosty winter 1754: are this winter
rotted by dampness, tho' there have been no
frosts at all to touch ym.

Feb: 18. Snowed very hard from morning to night: by ye evening the snow lay 14 inches deep on plain Ground; & lodged so heavy on the Hedges that it broke ym. down in several places; & weigh'd all the shrubs flat to the Ground. Went-off with a gentle thaw without any rain.

23. Cast eight of our little Cart-loads of hot dung in the field-garden for ye melon seed-bed.

24. Sowed quartr. of a pound of spinage in the field-garden.

25. Planted six rows of large Winsor-beans in ye field-Garden: six rows of Marrow-fat-pease in Turner's Garden.

27. Planted a row, & an half more of broad-beans.

28. Made the melon-seedling-Hot-bed with the whole eight loads of dung, except a little for the Celeri. Weather very fine, & the Ground in good dry order.

Made a Celeri-Hot-bed for an hand glass, & sowed the Celeri-seed.

Planted some lilac-suckers from Bradley in Turner's; & some Cuttings of the parsley, & Mountain-Elder. Planted a large lilac-sucker in a field-bason.

March 1. Sowed ten pots of Mr Hunter's red-seeded Cantaleupes 1752: & two pots of Mr Hunter's white-seeded Cantaleupes 1754.
Sowed a pot of early prickly Cucumbers.
Fine weather; & bed heats well.
Sprinkled the bed with quick-lime to kill the small snails, & grubs.
2. Raised the fence of the Cucumber-Ground equal with that of the Melon-Ground, & lined it with pease-haulm: so the two fences screen the whole North-end of the field-garden the length of 70 feet.
6. Removed the two Larches from the Ewel-Close, where one had been damaged by ye Horses, into the Basons in Baker's Hill.
Cucumbers began to appear.
Removed one of the Laburnums into a gap in the Orchard-hedge. Planted some layers of Jasmine in Turner's Garden.
7. The Melon-plants began to appear.
8. Sowed 12 basons in the field with double Larkspur-seed. One ounce will sow 8 basons very thick.

March 8. Sprinkled more quick-lime round the young Melon-plants.

9. Sowed a box of Polyanth-seed: cleansed the moss & filth from off the Acacia-pots, & sifted-on a little fine earth. Sifted a little fine Earth over the seedling Cedars of Lib: & pines in the boxes.

10. Sowed a Crop of Carrots in the New-Garden, & mixed with it some radishes, onions, & coss-lettuce both green, & white.

11. Sowed one pot of Mr. Hunter's White-seeded Cantaleupes. 1752.

Forked the Asparagus-beds; & raked ym for ye first time.

Made a rod-hedge round the Quincunx of firs.

Very dry March-like weather: no rain since the great Snow Feb: 18.

13. Hot, sunny days, & fierce frosts at night. Thick Ice.

15. Brought a four-wheel'd post-chaise to ye Door at that early time of Year.

16. Cast 15 good Dung-carts of hot dung for the melon-bed: 9 of our own dung, & 6 of Farmer Parsons's. The Ground as dry as at Midsumr.

March 17. Sowed an ounce of Onion-seed in ye New-Garden. Transplanted the Cucumber-plants from the pot, to the full Ground in the frame. Planted some very large potatoes from Swarraton in Turner's Garden. The Ground was double-trench'd in the winter; & ## some rotten dung, & old thatch were dug-in at planting.

18. Sowed two pots of Arbutus-seed, & one pot of Magnolia-seed, & plunged them in the Hot-bed.

19. Snowed hard almost all day. Several of ye Melon-plants go-off with a mouldiness that spreads on the leaves.

20. Received a large Cargo of Shrubs, & flower-roots from Brothr Thomas in London.

22. Planted in the Basons in the field, a Moss-provence, & some damask, Monday, & red roses; Spiraea frutex; blue, & white lilacs; Syringa; early golden-rod; sumach; Althaea frutex; guelder-rose; coccigrya; female dogwood; double flowering-thorn; & Persian Jasmine.

In the New-Garden forward honey-suckle; Lavender-cotton; golden-sage; double, & single Lychnis; blue, & white Campanulas; catchflies; blue, & peach-bloom Mich: daisies; striped bulbous Iris; ribbon-grass; double, & variegated perriwinkle: & fruit-bearing Passion-flower near the brew-house-door. Snowy, frosty, untoward weather for planting. Four new hand-glasses f.m Alton.

March 23. Back'd-up the seedling-bed, which began to lose almost all it's heat, with seven barrows of hot dung.

Drew a parcel of the cast-dung from the side of the heap, & made an Hot-bed for an Hand-glass: sowed three pots with Yellow, & white-seeded Cantaleupes 1752: & several cucumber-seeds round the pots for the ridge-hand-glasses. The first Melon-plants continue to go-off with mouldiness. Danger of a scarcity of plants for the frames. The Cucum.s plants in the same frame very healthy. Storms of Hail, & rain all day.

24. Hard frost, & thick Ice.

March 27. Frost so fierce that it damage[d]
the flowers, & shrubs very much: Ice nea[r]
an Inch thick: heavy snow all the mornin[g]
29. Dress'd the Rasberry-bed.
31. Planted four limes in the Butcher's Gar[den]
to hide the sight of Blood, & filth from
ye Windows.
April 2. Planted out of their winter-box a be[d]
of Cauliflower-plants. Sowed two pots of Lar[ch]
-seed; two pots of China-Arbor-Vitæ; & a po[t]
of Arbor-Judæ-seed.
3. Made my great ten-light melon-bed with
fifteen dung-carts of hot-dung. Laid an
Hillock of Dorton-earth in the middle of each ligh[t]
& cover'd the whole bed about two inches
thick with earth. The earth wet & cloddy
& not [illegible] in condition for the purpose
Supply'd the Artichoke-bed (which had los[t]
most of it's plants) with very good slips
from Dr. Bristow's.
5. Sowed a large Quantity of Holy-oak-see[d]
with some radishes for the bugs; crop
of parsneps; crop of Leeks; row of parsle[y]
Row of Larch, & Judas-tree-seed in the comm[on]
-ground: four rows of Evergreen-oak-acorns;

plot of Tree mallow, & curled mallow; some Honesty-seed; Date stones: crop of red-beet: & some cress, & white mustard.

April 6. Made a Cucumber-bed for three Hand-glasses with two dung-carts of Parsons's Dung. The trench 16 feet long, & two & an half broad, & one & half deep: the dung did not reach to the level of the Ground by some Inches.

Made a slight Hot-bed for hardy annuals with seven barrows of dung: laid fine earth over it five inches deep.

Sowed the border against Parsons's yard with Sunflowers, Lady-pease, Venetian Mallow, Nasturtium, Larkspurs, Candy-tuft.

10. Sowed in the annual Bed Sunflowers, African Marrigolds, Orange-Gourds, Double-China Aster, Marvel of Peru, Celeriac.

10. Turn'd-out eight pots of Yellow-seeded Cantaleupes, & two of white into my ten great Lights. The white-seeded ~~..~~ under the tiled lights. One pretty good plant under each light. The bed but in indifferent condition by reason of

the continual rains, & black cloudy weather.

~~March~~ April 10. Sowed some Yellow-seeded, & white-seeded Cantaleupes in the old seed-Bed, for fear some plants in the lights should miscarry: some Romania-melon-seeds in Do. for ye Hand-glass-ridge.

Mem: Those melon-plants that were once seized with a mouldiness constantly dy'd away by degrees, 'till they were quite devour'd by it; except ~~such plants~~ those plants on which I tryed the experiment of clipping-off the ~~[illegible]~~ infected part with a pair of sciss[ors] ~~those~~ when they recover'd, & afterwards grew pretty well. The only method I can find of preventing the earth from falling from the melon-plan[ts] in turning them out of their pots, is by plaistering-down a cake of wet Clay over the mouth of the pots. Those pots turn-out best that have two or three plants; because there are ~~[illegible]~~ more roots to hold the earth together.

No snail ever comes a near a place well sprinkled with quick-lime, especially in a frame where the wet is kept-off. And what is very strange, quick lime, tho' plentifully shaken upon them, will not injure the youngest, or tenderest plant. 31

April 12. Sowed plot of Savoy-seed, very good sort; & plot of Borecole red, & green: some Pendulous Amaranth in Annual bed.

Planted quart.r of Hund: of laurels against the street in the new-Garden to thicken y.e screen; & down Baker's-hill, where the turkeys had destroyed them.

13. Planted some Laurestines down Baker's-Hill, where the Laurels were dead. Constant heavy rains day, & night.

Six rows of Marrowfats in Turner's Gard.n

This April, tho' a most surprizing Season for wet, & frost. The 20th was a vast rain: but on the 26th: it rain'd for 22 Hours without ceasing, & brought on such a vast flood as has seldom been seen; the meadows round Oxon being entirely cover'd a great depth.

May 1. Received from Broth.r Thomas an Arbutus, common Cypress, Portugal-Laurel, Cluster-pine, Silver-fir, Swedish-Juniper, Evergreen Cytisus, Passion-flower,

& some small evergreen Creepers. Fine plants, & most of them turn'd-out of pots & sent down with all their earth about ym:

My ten-light Cantaleupe-bed so flood= :ed by those vast rains that all the plants are dead.

Planted ye evergreens in the basons in the field.

May 4. Heavy storms of snow, & thunder.

5. Frost so hard that the dirt carryed.

6. Broke-up my ten-light Cantaleupe-bed, & work'd it up with five dung-carts more of hot-dung. Sensible heat ~~in~~ remaining in the bed, ~~so~~ tho' it had been so flooded. Put earth into the boxes, in good dry order. Soft mild shower.

7: 8: 9. Very wet season.

10. Planted my ten-light melon-bed a second time with Waverley Cantaleupe, & Roma :nia melons. Bed in fine order for Heat. Planted-out the seedling Cedar of Liba: :nus in a penny-pot.

Four lights of Cantaleupes, & six of Romagna-Melons.

May 11. Violent rain, snow, & hail: Ice in the night.

12. Made a ridge for ~~seven~~ five handglasses, with four dung-carts of dung.

Received from Kensington one Holly-leaved Oak, one Olive-leav'd Do: one red Cedar of Virginia, one White Do: one Spanish-Evergreen-Creeper, one Balm of Gilead-Fir, two Weymouth-pines, one Acacia-leaved-Cypress. All nicely pack'd with a deal of earth about their roots; & about a foot & half high.

From Williamson Nursery-man at Kensington.

14. Sowed some common green, & white-Dutch Cucumber-seeds under an Hand-Glass.

Set up my first Oil-Jar Vase at the bottom of the Ewel-Close with a pannel only in front: Mount, pedestal, & Vase nine feet high. Dripping season still.

May. 15. No one Day so much as spring
:like before: now absolute Summer.

Sowed a crop of Green-Coss-lettuce
among the New-planted Artichokes.
Planted three of the Hand-glasses with Cucum
:ber plants, three plants in a Glass.

May 17. Pricked-out the seedling Weymouth,
& Cluster-pines in the New-Garden.
Prick'd-out a plot of Celeri in Turner's.

18. Planted 300 & quart.r of Cabbage-plants
in the field-Garden. Very hot sun-shine
with a cold East-wind.

19. Set-up my second Oil-jar vase at the
top of the broad walk, with a face to the cross
-walk. Mount, pedestal, & Jar some inches
above nine feet high.

19. Pinch'd my melons to make them throw-out
runners: the melons, for want of having been
in pots, a long while in taking to ye Ground.

20. Planted six rows of large white Dutch
Kidney-beans as long as ye Spinage will
permit.

May 24. Earth'd-up the melon-hillocks for ye first time with Dorton-Mould. Mould in fine order.

28. Bright sunshine, & smart frosts for this fortnight past, with a cutting East-Wind most part of the time: now a small shower. Ground strangely bound, & parched.

Cucumbers begin to set.

31. Cut the first Cucumber: 3 more al:most grown on the same plant.

Planted all the Standglasses with cucumber-plants, white, & green. Planted some basons in the field with Sunflowers.

Bright, settled dry weather; the Ground bound as hard as a stone.

June 1. Five of the melon-plants have runners with two Joints.

3. Pinched the forwardest of the melons at the third Joint: & pinch'd-off all the small buds about their stems. Best Cantaleupe knit for bloom.

7. Three weeks & three days drought, except a shower once for a few minutes. Now moderate showers.

June 10. Earth'd Melons second time with Dorton-earth: second runners show second Joint. The Glazier cemented the large lights, which drip wretchedly: mended but not cured. Frequent Showers.

16. Prick'd out five Hund: of Savoys; & 175 of Bore-cole. Lengthened-out rows of French-beans. Melons ~~then~~ throw-out plenty of fruit; & Male-bloom full blown. Hot, dripping weather, which makes the melons grow wonderfully. Prick'd-out more Celeri.

19. Lined-out the melon-bed with 8 dung-carts of Dung; & laid-on the full thickness of earth without, & within the frames. Earth'd the frames twice with Dorton-mould, & the last time with common Garden-mould.

27. Gather'd Mazagan Beans.

Several melons set.

Sowed Crop of Endive.

July 24. Full twenty Brace of Melons, most of them well-grown: the plants in great vigour

July 26. Planted-out Crop of Endive in the field-Garden.

27. Planted-out first plot of Savoys.

29. Planted-out Borecole, & rest of Savoys.

Aug:st 2: Cut first Melon, a Romania: very early, considering the first bed was destroy'd.

3. Cut brace & half more, of Romania: turn'd, & ~~tyles~~ tiled the rest, which was much wanting.

Cut 70 Cucumbers.

Aug: 4. Trenched-out 8 rows of Celeri: plant-
:ed some of the Borders in the New-Garden
with Polyanths of my own raising.
Cut four brace & half of Melons this week.
15. Had cut eleven brace of Romania-Melons
one from the plant that was put a seed
into one of the great frames on May ye 10.
18. Planted six pots ~~of~~ with Cuttings of
Geraniums.
Mushroom-bed bears pretty well at one end.

Aug: 18. Sowed Crop of Turneps in the Quin:cunx, & among the Savoys.

21. Sowed half pound of spinage; & with it ~~turnp~~ turnep-radish seed; & brown dutch, & green-Capuchen-Lettuce to stand the Winter.

22. Cut the first Cantaleupe, a very small one: it was almost cleft in two: was high-flavour'd, & vastly superior to any of the Romanias. This Melon set the first of any; & was full 8 weeks in ripening. The plant on which this grew was one of the first crop, the only one that survived; & was moved in a careless manner back into the seedling-bed; & brought back again when the bed was new-worked-up.

Constant heavy rains for ~~[illegible]~~ a week: the wheat that is down begins to grow.

24. Cut second Cantaleupe, the largest in ye Boxes; weigh'd 3 pds 7 oun: sent it to London to Broth: Tom. Turn'd colour before it began to smell, which is unusual.

Aug: 25. Planted-out Holyoaks in the new-Garden next the street; & among the limes in the Butcher's Yard.

26: 27: 28. Cut a brace & half of Mr. Hunt-ers Cantaleupes: a brace were not much emboss'd on their Rind, & not so high fla-voured as might be expected: the other was very rough, very firm fleshed, & very high flavoured, weighty for it's size. N: B: All the Canta-leupes yet have chang'd colour, & smelt without cracking at the Stalk.

28 ● True fine Harvest-weather. Wheat much grown about the Country; some grew as it stood.

29. Cut one Waverly, & one Miller's Canta-leupe: & sent the Waverly one to Bradley.

Miller's tho' it promised well was very abominable; being about an Inch thick in the Rind, without any flesh or flavour. The rine was finely emboss'd, & the shape Compressed like a Turnep.

Brought the only flowering Pyram: Campan into the parlour: it produced only a single stalk

Septem^r. 2. Tyed up 30 Endives: first tying.
7.. French-beans so backward that not above three boilings have been gather-:ed yet.
11. Cut the other Miller's Cantaleupe: turn'd out as execrable as the former.
16. Brought a large Cantaleupe from Wa-:verly, weight 3 p^ds. 9 oun: turn'd-out very high-flavour'd, & curious: saved the seed.
18. Tyed-up the Endives in the new-Garden.
25. Planted 300 laurel-Cuttings in Turner's.
Octob^r. 3. Cut brace & half of Romania-melons: good for latter Crop.
Octob^r. 9. Set nine Hyacinths, given me by M^r. Trinley, to blow in Glasses in ye parlour.
25. Cut last melon: the 41st.
Novem^r. 9. planted ten rows & half of Maza-:gan-beans in the field-garden.
One Quart of true small mazagan-beans will plant eleven good rows.
9: 10: 11: 12. Extream hard frost, & bearing Ice. From the 18th to ye 25: uncommon fierce frost, & some snow.

Mem: Put the pins belonging to my new melon-frame in the small leathern trunk in the man's room.

Pins in a box in the lumber-garret.

Spring 1755. Borrowed seven of our Cart-loads of Hot-dung of Farmer Parsons.

March 1756. Borrowed six good Dung-carts of hot dung of Farmer Parsons.

April 6. Borrowed two dung-Carts more of Parsons's dung.

May 6. Borrowed seven loads of dung of John Berriman.

June 18. Borrowed of Berriman four loads of Dung.

22 (1.) 37

Garden-Kalendar:
1757. 1758.

Jan: 1:st Planted a row of Tulips, & Ranunculus's, given me by my Broth:r Thomas, in the Border in the New-Garden next the street. Dug out the soil, & filled the trench with earth well-mixed with lime-rubbish.

3. Planted the Fir-Quincunx with five rows of Winsor-beans: dunged the ground, that was very poor, with ten wheel-barrows of very rotten dung. After the beans the ground to be trench:d with Celeri.

Levelled, & widen:d the Area of y:e melon-Ground; having made an underground Drain to prevent it's being flooded any more.

4. A most extraordinary dry season for wheeling-out the dung of the old Hot-beds; & for trenching the ground for Crops.

On the 2nd began a frost, which on ye 3rd & 4th by means of a strong East wind became very severe, so as to freeze-up all the pools & ponds: the ground, which had been ~~[illegible]~~ quite ~~dry~~ drained before by a fortnight's dry weather, look'd white & dusty, & was not the least relaxed or greasy at noon for many days together. On the 10th came a thaw, & a little snow. The Laurustines, & other tender Ever-greens began to suffer a little, especially on the severe windy days. Froze up again, & lasted (tho' there were frequent hasty showers) without the frost ever being out of the Ground till Feb: 6th Great Quantities of snow fell,

which being half melted by the rain made
the Country slippery to a strange degree.
The frost penetrated deep into the ground,
& seems to have been the severest since
that in 1740. Seems to have done no mate:
:rial damage to vegetation; but has made
the Ground very light, & mellow.

Feb: 10. Sowed half a pound of spinage in
the field-Garden, with some Browndutch,
& Capuchin-lettuces; some common, & white-
-turnep Radishes.
11. Several of the Hyacinths are tall, &
just ready to blow.
12. Planted six rows of Hotspur-pease, &
two of Marrowfats in the field-Garden.
Summer-like weather: the ground by means
of the frost perfectly mellow. Sowed a crop
of parsley in the New Gardens.
17. Made an Hot-bed in the Yard with 16
wheel-barrows of dung, only to raise ye

(4.) Cucumber-plants, & a little Cress, & white-mustard. To be taken away, & work'd-up in a future Bed.

Feb: 18. One of the Sunbury Jacinths (ye only one not decay'd) in full bloom. Those from Mr Budd drawn-up very tall, but not blown.

19. Sowed some early Cucumber-seeds unde one of the Handglasses.

21. Planted 100 of Cabbages in Turner's: sowed hand-glasses in the Yard with Cress, & white-mustard.

24. Carryed eight of our little Cart-loads of dung into the field-garden for a seedling melon-bed.

28. Made a very stout hot-bed above three feet thick for the melon-seeds, & to forward the Cucumber-plants, with [illegible] 8 Cart-loads of dung: Saved about two barrows of dung, & made a Celeri-bed for one Handglass.

March 2. Sowed the New Hot-bed with Yellow-seeded Waverley Cantaleupe 1752: & White-seeded Waverly D^o. 1752: & 1754: with Dutch Cantaleupe (never sowed in England) 1754: & with John Bosworth's Zatta-melon from Florence 1754. Sowed also a few early Cucumber-seeds for fear the plants should fail.

Sowed a small Hand-glass Hot-bed with Celeri, & Celeriac. Dress'd Rasp-bed: & hoed beans: but a thin Crop.

4. Sowed 14 basons in the field with double upright larkspur-seed; & bush'd them well.

Sunk a wine-Hogshead in the field-garden for a well.

5. Sowed some Asparagus-seed to mend the beds that are decaying.

Very dry weather, & severe frost.

8. The seedling-melon-bed, tho' made so strong, would not come to any Heat:

6. so I cut away the bed sloping-in on every side, & lined it very thick with four little cart-loads of dung just fresh from the stable.

March 11. Bed begins to heat very well: prick'd the cucumbers from under the Hand-glass into it. Melons not yet come up. Lost about a week in the forwarding the Cucumber-plants by the bed's not heating. Sowed the Hand-glasses in the yard with more Cress, & Mustard. That little bed keeps it's heat well still.

14. Sowed 22 Mazagan-beans, all worm-eaten, to try if the ~~[illegible]~~ rest will be fit to plant next year.

Tyed the melon-bed, that crack'd & was like to bulge-out, with a strong cord, that seems to secure it.

Made a melon paper-House 8 feet long, & 6 feet wide: to be covered with

the best writing paper.
Planted two seedling white-Elders in the little mead.

17. Supplyed the basons where the shrubs were dead, with new ones.

Melon-plants come-up very fast.

18. Planted a weeping-willow, a fine plant, & one Year from a Cutting, in one of the basons in the field: planted a black Virginian-Mountain-Elder in the little mead.

19. Sowed 20 more Yellow Cantaleupe-seeds Selborn 1755: to supply the room of any plants that may fail.

Sowed 9 basons in the border next parsons's Yard with double Larkspurs. Some of the forward Cucumber-plants show a rough leaf.

21. Sowed Crop of Carrots, White & Green Coss-Lettuce, & common radishes

8. in Turner's Garden. Headed-dow
the limes in the Butcher's Yard; & took
several Cuttings from the Weeping-wil
& planted them in the Nursery.

March 22. Sowed the Clover in the wheat;
& mixed with it the white-Dutch-Clover
that had been in the House two or
three years.

Sowed 40 of Murdoch Myddleton's
white-Cucumber-seeds in the seedling
-bed. Bed heats very well.

23. Raked, & weeded the Asparagus-beds.

24. Sowed 20 seeds of prickly Cucumbers
just come from London.

26. Cast six loads (dungcarts) of hot
dung in the field-garden for the cucumber
-bed.

Planted Quart[r] of Hund: of Cauli:
-flowers in a well-dung'd plot in the field
-Garden: from Greedy at Farnham.

March 28. Made a very stout Cucumber-bed five feet wide, two feet & half deep, & thirteen feet long for three lights, with the six loads of Dung: cut very deep holes in the middle of each light, & rais'd a hillock of fine earth to receive the plants: cut also a trench at the back of the frames, & plunged 12 pots to the brims to receive the melon-plants.

Sowed nine more basons of double-upright Larkspurs in the border in the new-Garden against the street.

31. Planted the plants of Cucumbers in the new bed, three in an Hole: they shew each four leaves; but have not grown much for some days past. Bed gives a very strong Heat.

Planted a Quart of marrot-fat-pease in three rows in the field-Garden.

~~10.~~ April 1.

Planted out twelve pots of melons: fi with yellow-seeded Cantaleupe plants, old seed from Waverley, with ~~in~~ one D^o: new seed of my own saving in the same pot. three with new Yellow D^o three with ~~wt~~ White-seeded Cantaleupes, old seed from Waverley: & one pot with Dutch Cant:leupe from Holland, never sowed in Eng:land. Left six Selborn Cantaleupes, & two Zatta-plants in the seedling bed.

Mem: To soak the earth well beforeha with water, or else the fine earth is ver apt to crumble away, & leave the roots naked in moving.

2. Sowed two or three white Cantaleupe-see in each of the ~~wt~~ pots that contain the white Can:taleupe plants.

Sowed a good Quantity of the old green Cucumber seeds; & D^o of Middleton's White D in the one-light Cucumber-frame.

The former sowing of Middleton's white Cucumber-seed, & of the new green D.o from London came-up wretchedly.

Sad wet, cold weather, & constant high winds (some of them very terrible, & mischievous ones) for three weeks past.

New Cucumber-bed heats well; & Cucumber, & melon-plants have struck-root already.

April 5. Sowed a Crop of leeks, beets, pars-neps, turnep-radishes, & onions.

Unusual Hot weather this week: during which, John, who was but a very young Gardener, scorch'd-up, & suffocated all his forward Cucumbers: & drawed his melon-plants in the pots, but has not spoiled them.

21. Snowed very hard for sixteen hours: the greatest snow that has fallen this year; & must have been a foot deep had it not for the greatest part melted as it fell. Went away without any frost, & seems to have done no damage.

April 23.^d Made the melon-bed for the six large lights, & two of the small ones, with 18 dung-carts of dung, just 30 feet long, & about two & half high, & all above ground.

25. Dressed the border against Parsons's & sowed in it, Sunflowers, Candy tuft, Venetian-poppy, & Venus looking glass: sowed large plot of savoy-seed, plot of sweet William-seed, & some rows of sorrel & parsley.

Sowed some Celeri on the melon-bed between the frames; & some white-seeded Cantaleupes for the paper-House in one of the large lights.

On examination it appeared that the earth in the Cucumber-bed was burnt by the fierce heat of the bed: dug it out of the basons, & put in fresh: One bason of the early Cucumbers will recover the other two must be new-planted.

My Polyanths, which I raised from seed
given me by Mrs Snooke, & sowed last
spring, make now a most beautiful appearance; many of them have large, upright stems, producing many flowers, which
are large, beautifully striped, & open flat.
Mark'd the finest blowers with sticks,
intending to save seed from them.

April 26. Turned-out five pots of
Waverley Yellow-seed Cantaleupes, &
one Selborn Do: into my six great
lights: & only one pot of John Bosworth's Dutch Cantaleupe into the
middle of my two light frame.
All the pots were turned-out well
except the Dutch-Cantaleupe, whose
earth stuck to the pot, & pull'd-off many
of it's fibres.
Sowed Crop of Borecole, green & red;
a vast plot of Holy-oak-seed: & a row
of tree-mallow seed.

April 26. Sowed four rows of dwarf white Battersea-kidney-beans in the New Garden. An handful of beans left out of one pint. Ground in good dry order.

Supplyed the two basons of Cucumbers that were burnt, with some white, & green prickly plants. —

May 9. Made an Hot-bed for my melon paper-house with four loads of dung joined on to the former bed.

Made hot-bed for seedling-annuals with three barrows of weeds, & four of dung.

Early Cucumbers shew nothing but male bloom.

Planted two rows of large white Dutch Kidney-beans

10. Sowed Annual-bed with African & French Marrigolds, Marvel of Peru, Gourds, & double China-Asters.

Sowed some rows of Sunflower-seed.
Plants shew some few Cucumbers.
Some of the melon-plants decaying in their seedling-leaves: turned-out some more pots into the basons. Shall save but one Waverly melon-plant; all the rest Selborn seed, except the two White-seeded plants under the paper, that are Waverly.

May 12. Sowed an Hand-glass on ye cold ground with several sorts of white Dutch-Cucumbers; & a few green prickly Cucumrs:

Sowed a late Crop of green, & white Coss-lettuce. Prick'd-out some rows of Capuchin-Lettuce.

13. Earthed-up the melon-hillocks for ye first time with Dorton-earth. The reason that ye first melon-plants that were turned-out did not succeed, seems to be, that the earth in the pots was press'd down too hard,

so that the fibres could not push thro:
Laid-on the hillocks upon the new-made melon-bed; & put-on the paper-house. Earth'd the forward Cucumbers, & water'd them all over.

May 16. Pinch'd, & turned-out two pots of white-seeded Dwarf Cantaleupes under the paper-house: the bed very hot. The plants strangely rooted for their age. One of the plants under the two-light-frame has got a runner with two joints.

18. Mended-out the Artichokes that were decayed with some plants from Johnson's

Very hot, sunny weather: no rain for five weeks; the ground very much burnt.

20. Pinched one of the melon-runners at the third Joint. The weather full fierce for hot-beds under Glass.

May 23. Earth'd melon-hillocks the second
time with garden-mould, which had
been turn'd & prepared on purpose, &
is in excellent order. The melon-plants
in general weak, & puny: pinch'd some
of their runners at the second & some at
the third Joint according to their strength.

Sowed three rows more of large
Dutch-Kidney-beans in the field: garden
the sowing of White dwarf Do: seems
to be rotten in the Ground, notwithstand:
ing the great dryness of the Ground.

24. Sowed an other Hand-glass with
white-Dutch-Cucumbers in the cold
Ground.

26. planted 200 of Cabbage-plants in
the Field-Garden.

27. Earth'd-up the melons under the
paper-house the first time: the
plants thriving.

May 29. Cut first Cucumber. Seve
more set. Fine soaking shower after
six weeks drought.

June 1st Prick'd-out first bed of Celeri
& transplanted from their seedling-bed a
large Crop of leeks. Ground thoro'ly
moisten'd by a long gentle rain.

2. Planted-out the natural Cucumbers
under the hand-glasses. Planted some
variegated Gourds in the Corner near th
Brewhouse-door. Sowed a row more of
large French-beans in the field-Garden

3. Widened-out the early Cucumber-bed
with the dung of the seedling-bed, & laid
on a good depth of stiff earth.

6. Sowed five rows of dwarf white-kid-
-ney-beans in the new-Garden, where the
early crop fail'd. Soak'd the beans ove
night in water, the weather & ground
being extreamly dry.

June 7. Tyed-up a few of the best Coss-Lettuce: a fine Crop.

Several of the melons show bloom, but are very weak in vine.

Earth'd-up melons the third time.

Weeded & thinn'd-out Carrots: a good Crop.

10. Earth'd-up melons the fourth time: the boxes almost full of earth. Extream dry weather. Melons mend by more frequent watering.

11. Staked the Holy-oaks in the Garden, & Butcher's Yard, & tyed them up.

Water'd melons pretty much at a distance from their stems. Great drought.

Melons shew fruit. They, & Cucumbers require constant shading from ye fierce heat.

13. Prick'd-out second Crop of Celeri in Turner's Garden.

Earth'd-out the melon-frames with their

20. full depth of earth; & watered them well. Extream hot weather. Melons improve every day, & shew several fruit; but are still scanty in vine. Those under the paper-house thrive well.

June 17. Gathered first pease.

19. The Coss-lettuce, that were tyed-up, well-grown, & finely blanch'd.

20. Lined-out the melon-bed with 18 Dung-Carts of Dung, & earth'd it the full depth within, & without the boxes. Bed 13 feet wide, & contains 40 loads of Dung. Plants under the boxes still but weak; those under the paper-house very thriving. Gentle rain: the ground before burnt to ashes.

21: 22. Prick'd-out about 650 savoys; & about 280 Bore-cole-plants.

24. Buried the stones, & rubbish from ye Butcher's in the Yard to make it sound. Dry, scorching weather.

June 25. Watered melons well: burning
season, & no signs of rain. Fruit in
plenty; but none set.
27. Earth'd the melon-bed still deeper on
account of the extream Heat; & pull'd the
Lights quite off for the whole day, & covered the frames with mats. Plants
draw very long without any fruit setting.
Cucumbers raised in the cold ground
very forward, & thriving.
28. Planted several Bassons in the
field with Sunflowers.
30. Sowed a plot of Endive, & shaded it
with a mat.
July 5. Pull'd-up the two melon-plants in
the two-light-frame, which had never showed
a fruit so far as to blow; & planted in their
room two Selborn-Cantaleupes, sown about
the 21 of May, just shooting into runners.
Drought continues; & the Garden suffers
greatly.

July 16. Planted-out, after waiting five or six weeks for a shower, the Af: & Fren. Marrigolds, & double China-Asters, in the midst of an unusual drought: the Earth quite dust spit-deep.

17. Gathered first natural Cucumber from a seed put into the cold Ground the 12th of May.

20. Great tempest of thunder & lightening, & vast rains after 13 weeks drought.

Frequent showers 'till the 15 of August; then ~~a whole weeks wet~~ sixteen days wet, & very bad Harvest weather.

August 22. Found on my return from Sunbury six brace of moderate-sized Cantaleupes; & about the same number of small ones, that will ripen, if the season be favourable. No fruit would set 'till the rains came, & the intense heats were abated: & what did set was all on the third wood, the second casting it's fruit, & drawing very weak.

Planted-out in my absence near a thousand savoys, & a large plot of Borecole; was sown a pound of spinage, mixed with turnep-radishes, & lettuce of many sorts: & trench'd-out eight good rows of Celeri.

The Pyram: Campanula in beautiful bloom; but has only two stems.

Aug: 29. Planted-out 43 Holyoak-plants before & behind the melon-screen, & in the border of the New-Garden against the street.

Septem:r 17: Tyed-up about 25 Endives: they run very small this year.

18: Cut first Cantaleupe, a small fig-shap'd one, & not thick-fleshed. The leaves of the plants unusually decayed.

Septemr: 19: 20: 21: 22. Slip'd & new-planted the pinks in the Borders against the House: dug-up the Crocuss, & planted them in double rows before the pinks; they are encreased to near 500 roots: slip'd the best of the Polyanths, & planted them in two rows in the border against the broad walk: planted a border of seedling Sweet-Williams against Parsons's Yard: planted three rows of green-Capuchin, & Brown-Dutch-Lettuce the length of the melon-ground on a border just under the rush-screen to stand the winter: planted several Basons in the field with Sweet-Williams: took-up the yellow-lilys & a fine large Martagon under my Father's window, & planted them in a bason in the field: the two Xiphiums were encreased to a great number; planted some of them in the Basons round of lilies

& some in a row ~~so~~ under my Father's
window: planted my Tulips in the same
place; & a few Ranunculus, & Fritillarias:
planted a row of Crocus-~~roots~~ on each
side as you go out of the new Garden:

Septem.r 27. Put nine Hyacinths to
blow in the Glasses over the Chimney.
They were given me by M.r Trinley, &
brought me by M.rs Mulso.

28. Planted a row of Sweet Williams, & a
row of Polyanths under the back of the melon-
screen: some ~~&~~ Polyanths along the dark walk
in the orchard.

Delicate Autumn-weather, & no rain
for more than a month. Roads perfectly
dry.

Cantaleupes come-in apace: very high-
flavoured, but small; as they were all on
the third wood. The white-seeded sort very
good.

Octob.r 1:2. Cut two very high-fla=voured Cantaleupes, both under two p.ds in weight. They were very weighty for the size; & their coats very black, & em=boss'd. Sent them to Lord Keeper.

11. Tyed-up second tying of Endives with red Yarn. Earth'd-up three rows of Celeri quite to the top.

Cut three Brace of Cantaleupes for Mangoes, that were too backward to ripen. Left two braces & half, that may ripen toler=ably well, if the season favours.

Octob.r 16. Received from my Broth.r Thomas 50 double snow-drop-roots; & six very large double Narcissus-roots.

17. Set three of the largest Narcissus's to blow in sand.

17. Sowed a large quantity of Laurel=berries in all the gaps of the Hedges;

down Baker's Hill; at the top of Turn=
er's Garden; & in the New Garden against
the street. Berries very large & ripe. 50
from Mr Bridger's.

Octobr 24. Planted in the Basons in ye
Field five double rockets, six scarlet Mar=
tagons, six Fraxinellas, 3 tallest purple
Asters, 3 Dwarf Do 2 German Goldy-
locks, 6 double Sunflowers, 3 tall smelling
Sunflowers, 2 Carolina Sunflowers; from
Murdock Middleton. In the broad borders
under my Father's window; 6 Solomon's-
seals, 6 double Narcissus's from Mur:
Middleton: several double rockets from
Mr Budd; striped Epilobium in the field.
Put two Jonquils to blow in the Glass=
es; & changed ~~to~~ some of the Hyacinths that
did not thrive for some of Mr Myddleton's.
26. Finished digging up a new piece of Garden-
Ground 60 feet by 30 in Baker's hill beyond
the Field-Garden.

~~28.~~ Octob.r 27. Sowed a large Quantity of Elder, Buckthorn, & dog-wood-berries in the ditch by the sand-walk.

28. Planted seven rows of small, early Beans in Turner's Garden.

Took away the two three-light frames. The Ground very dry, & in fine order.

29. Planted 50 snow-drops in three Clusters under my Father's window. Turn'd-out double Dunged, & earthed the Asparagus-beds.

30. Cut a melon; tolerable for the season.

31. Turn'd-off the earth from the melon-bed; & cut two brace of unripe fruit.

Novem.r 1. Planted in the Border next ye street 24 tulips from Mr Budd: 12 Hyacinths from Do: 5 Hyacinths from Murdoch Middleton: 12 Jonquils from Do: 8 Narcissus's from Do: 2 Dutch Narcissus's from Bro: Thomas: & two Groups of foxgloves from Mr Budd. Trenched the border well with lime-rubbish; & put the roots into the

Ground in fine dry order.

Planted in a double-trench'd plot of Ground five rows of Horse-radish 10 inches deep.

Planted several slips of Mich: Daisies round the basons of Golden-rod; & in the new-planted basons of double-perennial Sun-flowers. No rain for many weeks, & the ground as dry as in Summer.

Cast the Dorton melon-earth, & mixed some rotten Dung with it.

Nov.r 6: Cut-up a Cantaleupe that had been cut green, & laid in the Buffet to ripen. It had a very good flavour, & was better than many a common melon ripened in the Height of the Season.

26. The early beans come-up very well. mild growing weather as yet.

Decem:r 1. Eat a Cantaleupe that had been a month in the House. It was firm, & well-flavoured.

~~30.~~ Decem[r]: 9: Earth'd-up the Artichok
Stoc'd the beans, that are grown pretty ta
Very mild weather till this time.

26. Cut the last Cantaleupe, a very small o
& not very good.

Very mild weather; hardly any frost y

The spring & summer 1757 we
remarkably hot & dry. The dry weather bega
in passion-week, & continued-on without any
Interruption (except ye 29 of May) till the 20th of July. The air was
rather cold in April & May: but the sun, shin
:ing all day from a cloudless skie for many wee
dryed the ground in a very uncommon manne
& the heats of June, & July quite burnt it to du
I observed that our wet clay withstood the
drought very well for many weeks: but when on
it was thoro'ly parched (as it was more than spi
deep) vegetation suffered more than in the gra
:velly soils. The barley, oats, & pease, having
no rain to bring ym up, did not yield half a cro
but the wheat (which is never known to be inju
by dry weather) turned-out very well. On ye

twentieth of July fell a very heavy, & ex:
tensive thunder-shower: after which there were
moderate rains, that restored a little verdure
to the grass-fields. From the 16 of August set:
in a very wet season for 15 or 16 days, which
made people in some pain for the wheat that be:
gan to grow. About the beginning of Septem:r
began the most delicate Autumn, & lasted quite
into Novem:r with very little or no frost quite to
the Close of the Year. On a large well-
prepared melon-bed I could get no melons to
set 'till the great rains fell; all the watering
& shading not being sufficient to keep the plants from
drawing. By my Brother Barker's
account they had seasonable rains in the spring
& summer; for their lent-crops in Rutland
were very good.

(1.)

Garden-Kalendar:
1758.

Jan: 1: 2. Fierce black frost; went-off with an heavy rain.

9. Wheeled into the Cucumber-ground 17 barrows of very hot dung for seedling-Cucumb:

Earth'd two rows of Celere.

Very mild, spring-like weather.

10. Sowed a box of Polyanth-seed of my own saving, & set it under an Hedge where it could only have the morning-sun.

Hoed the beans, which are very prosper:ous, the second time.

13. Made a deep one-light Cucumber-bed, for my smallest frame.

16. Laid-on the earth three Inches thick: it was cold, & lumpish tho' mix'd-up with a good Quantity of rotten dung, & two spade's full of wood-ashes. Matted down the frame very close.

Jan: 17. Finished an earth-house in
he melon-ground. ~~The sides are~~ It is worked
n a circular shape with rods & coped over
ith the same, & then well thatched: ~~It~~ is
ine feet over & eight feet high; & has room
o hold a good Quantity of mould, & a man
t work without any inconvenience.

8. Sowed about 40 early Cucumber-seeds of
e Year 1752 in the hot-bed. Bed comes to
'ts heat very regularly. Hard frost, & great
ime; & no sun for some days. The bed matted
own a nights with three mats.

. Carryed out three moderate dung-carts
ashes from the ash-house, & sowed on
akers-Hill, which is now laid for natural
rass; & has been Clover for two Years past:
pread also the upper part of it with the
ung out of the melon-bed.

20. Turned all the melon-earth; & mixed it
ith a good proportion of the Dung of
e last melon-bed. Dung hardly rotten
nough.

~~3.~~ Jan: 20. Hot-bed works very well. Ha
frost for two or three days: now ground
covered with snow.

One of the Hyacinths in the glasses seem
to promise to blow soon.

22. On this day, which was very bright,
the sun shone very warm on the Hot-bed
from a quarter before nine, to three quart:
after two. Very hard frost.

24. Set-up about 20 yards into the Hanger
in a line with the six Gates, a figure of
the Hesperian Hercules, painted on board,
eight feet high; on a pedestal of four feet
& an half. It looks like a statue, & show
well all over our out-let.

Cucumber-seeds swelled for sprouting, bu
not up yet: lined the end of the bed next the
screen with two barrows of hot dung. Sor
of thaw.

27. Finding the hot-bed scarce powerful
enough to heat the three inches of earth thro;
which was full wet when laid-on; I took-off the

mould half the depth, & put the seeds in again. 4
Some of the seeds sprouted. Sowed about 20 more. Earth very warm towards the bottom. 54

27. Planted about 40 Ranunculus-roots, given me by Mr Budd, in the Border against Parsons's, to blow after those that were put into the Ground in October.

29. Cucumber-plants come-up apace.

29. On this Day the mercury in the weather-glasses, which had been mounting leisurely for many days, was got one full degree above settled-fair in the parlour, & within half a degree of the same in the study.

My Father, who has been a nice observer of that up stairs for full 37 years, is certain that it never has been at that pitch before within that time. Very still, grey, close weather, with the wind at full east, & quite a thaw: tho' there has been somewhat of a frost for more than a fortnight past. Ground very dry; little rain having fallen for these three weeks past.

~~5~~ Jan: 30. Mercury continues at the same height. Same still, gloomy weather.

Sent for 42 bushels of peat-ashes from the forest-side. Sowed fifteen bushels on the broad-mead, & 15 bushels on the Cowslip. Ashes very dry, & curiously preserved. Laid-up the remainder in ash-house

Brought at the same time an old sand-stone-roller from Mr Bridger's at Oakhanger. It was, it seems, formerly the property of Mr Hmass of Oakhanger, Father to Sarah Hmass; & may probably have been made these 60 or 70 Years; & yet is very little damaged by age or weather

31. The Narcissus's, planted in sand in common blowing-glasses, have crammed the glasses so full, that tho' they budded very strongly at first, they have hardly advanced at all since in height for many weeks: one of ye Glasses, that was crack'd by accident, is quite split to pieces by the large, strong roots.

Took it out of the Glass, & planted it in
a pint-mug fill'd with sand.

Feb: 2. Sowed about 20 more cucumber-seeds;
the third sowing: the first, & second come-
up very well, & begin to get some greeness.

4. Lined one end of the hot-bed with one
Barrow of Dung. Bed declines in heat.

Sowed two samples of white-clover-seed,
from different Seeds-men, in the Hot-bed.

6. Backed the hot-bed with six barrows
of hot-dung.

Took away the suckers from the filberts
against Parsons's; & planted some of them
where they have failed against Turner's.

6: 7: 8. Trimm'd, & tack'd ye vines, (as much
as old neglected trees could be reduced the
first Year) according to Hitt's directions.
Covered many parts of the wall very well
with horizontal wood. Left the disbudding
till the budds are more swell'd. Trimmed ye
figtree, which was full of young wood, & flies
very well to the wall.

7 Feb: 9. Put in about 20 more Cucumber-seeds. Former sowings do not come up well.

11. One of the Hyacinths in the glasses blow-:out in several of it's buds.

Some in the Garden, thro' the mildness of the winter, budded for bloom.

14. Had 20 bushels of tan from Alton for the Cucumber-bed.

23: 24: 25. Made a cucumber-bed full four-:teen feet long, & almost four feet deep at the back for my two two-light frames with ten Dung-:carts of dung, which is very ~~...~~ short this year on account of the scarcity of litter; & was very cold & wet by reason of the vast rains about that time. Covered the dung the space of one of the frames about five inches thick with tan, & filled a deep hole in the centre of each light with the same. Laid a leaden-pipe into the frame that has got the tin-chimney, (accord-:ing to Dr Hales's proposal) up thro' the back of the bed, in order to convey in a succession of fresh air a nights.

Made an hot-bed for a single hand-glass for Celeri.

Planted half hund: large forward cabbage plants.

27. Planted 100 brown-Dutch, & green Capuchin Lettuces from Bradley that had stood ye winter, in the room of our own, which rotted thro' the wetness of the soil.

28. Sowed the Celeri-bed.

March 1. Great flood: wet for a long time.

2. Laid the hillocks of earth in the middle of each light. No earth fit to have been used, had it not been for the earth-house, thro' the vast rains.

4. Plunged nine melon-pots in the tan-frame, & three in the other frame. Contrived some wodden bottoms to the pots to make the earth turn-out more easily. Sowed plenty of Cucumber-seeds in a good depth of earth. Bed comes well to it's heat. Sad wet, stormy weather.

March 6. Sowed one melon-seed, from that curious Melon brought from Waverly in 1756, in each of the twelve pots. Bed heats well. Weather still so stormy, & wet, that there is no removing the Cucumber-plants. It has rained of late from all Quarters of the Skie.

7. Found an opportunity at last to plant-out the Cucumber-plants, three tolerable ones in each Hillock; some of which shew a rough leaf. Bed in fine warm order both in the tan, & dung part.

Sowed two more of the same Cantaleupe-seeds in nine of the pots.

9. Transplanted a large Laburnum into the Butcher's Garden. Planted half Hund more Cabbage-plants.

11. Laid that part of the leaden-pipe, which comes-out behind the Cucumber-bed, called up in a large box made out of ye seed-box; & filled the box with about two barrows & half of Hot dung. The nose of the pipe comes-out about

three inches beyond the box.

March 13. Planted 100 more Cabbage-plants, in all 200; the rows two feet apart, & the plants one foot from each other in the rows: every other plant to be pulled-up early in the summer. 57

14. Melon-plants begin to appear.

16. Planted Gallon of broad-beans in the lower field-garden, almost seven rows. Sowed pound of spinage, with some common radishes, which ought to have been sowed 5 weeks before, but was prevented by the wet, in the upper field garden. Sowed some Celeriac between the Cucumber-boxes. Sowed eight basons in the field with double-upright-Larkspurs; & the two lowest with large-single-branching D^o:

Perfect Summer for these two days.

18. Earthed-up Cucumber-hillocks the first time. Plants thrive, & many of them shew four leaves. Melons up some in every pot; they look healthy, & grow apace.

11. March 18. Turned-out a large Narcis=
=sus, that was intended to blow within, into
one of the borders. planted some bunches
of single snow-drops in bloom under my
Father's window.

Sowed about 30 more green Cucum=
=ber-seeds in the Hot-bed. Filled-up the box
that contains the leaden pipe, with one
more barrow of dung: the dung begins to
heat in the box: the nose of the pipe hot
in the morning, & cold towards the even=
=ing. Very wet afternoon.

19. Vast heavy rains most part of ye day

21. Great snow all the day, & most part
of the night; which went off the next day
in a stinking, wet fog. Very trying wea=
=ther for Hot-beds, more like Jan: than Mar
No sun for many Days.

23. Planted among the Holyoaks next the
street in ye New-Garden 2 Austrian Briars
1 black Belgic rose, 1 York & Lancaster
Do 1 Marbled Do 1 monthly Do: from Mr

Budd: & two large roots of the Aster-
kind in the Border before the roses. A
very late-blowing sort.
25. Planted three more Provence-roses
from Mr. Budd in the same place.
Forked Asparagus-beds: dressed Rasberry
-bed: sowed the lower plot of the new field
Garden with seven rows of marrow-fat
pease, at four feet asunder. Ground
in a cold clammy Condition.
Tryed an experiment late in
ye evening with a Candle on the two
Cucumber-frames after they had been close
covered-up some Hours. On putting the
Candle down a few Inches into that frame
that has leaded lights & no Chimney, the
flame was extinguished at once three sever:
al times by the foul vapour: while the
frame with the tiled lights, & Chimney was
so free from vapour that it had no sensi:
ble effect on the flame. I then applyed
~~then applyed~~ the candle to the top of the

18. Chimney, from whence issued so much
steam as to affect the flame, tho' not put
it out. Hence it is apparent that this In:
:vention must be a benefit to plants in
Hot-beds by preventing them from being stew:
:ed in the night time in the exhalations
that arise from the dung, & it's own leaves.
The melons confirm the matter, being un:
:usually green & vigorous for their age.
I applyed the Candle to the nose of the
leaden pipe; but it had no effect on it:
so that what air comes up thro' it must
be wholesome, & free from vapour.
March 28. Planted 59 potatoes in Turners;
not very large roots. Sowed the wheat with
white Dutch Clover: Baker's-Hill with Rye
Grass, & black-seed: the vase-mount, & hollow
way into the Ewel with D^o^. Fine weather.
Set up the vases: put on two bold Handles
to the lower one; & two side-pannels to
the pedestal. Sowed two rows of pars:
:ley, & transplanted some mint.

24

59

Garden-Kalendar:
April: 1758: 1759.

April 1st Unusual sunny, scorching weather for a week past. The heat drew the forward Cucumbers, notwithstanding they were constantly shaded; & would have spoiled the melons (as ye same kind of heat did this time twelvemonth) had not the pots been raised. Forward Cucumbers weak; & begin to shew for bloom.

3. Sowed 14 of John Bosworth's curious large white Cucumber-seeds in one of the frames, in order to raise some plants for one of the Hand-glasses to save seed from.

4. Sowed almost an ounce of Carrot-seed, mixed with Coss-lettuce green & white, & some common radishes, in Turner's Garden. Sowed in the field-Garden ounce of onion-seed, half ounces of Leek-seed, & a small Quantity of parsnep-seed.

6. Made a one-light hot-bed for Annuals with six full barrows of dung.

April: 9. Very dry weather for this
fortnight past: for the last week fierce frost
10. Several basons of sunflower-seed sowed
among the Holy-oaks in the new-Garden
against the street; & some among the Butc-
er's Vines. Sowed the annual-bed with
French & African-Marrigolds; Double-
China-asters, & single Do: & white Asters;
pendulous-Amaranths; & some Gourds for
Dame Tyrrel.

9: Saw two Swallows: one was seen in ye
village on the 3rd.

11. Sowed in a seedling-bed in the field-Garden
Sunflowers, French-wall-flower, Columbine,
Sweet-Williams, Double-China-pinks under
two hand-glasses, Everlasting-pea, French-
Honey-suckle, Evergreen-Cytisus, & Holyoaks
in the new-Garden in the broad-border, &
against the apple tree, painted-Lady-pease,
Nigella romana; in the Kitchen part half
ounce more of Leek-seed, & small plot of
red beet.

April 12. Sowed third Crop of Marrow-
fat pease, one row in Turner's, two rows in
old field-garden, two rows in new field-garden.
13. Worked-up a nine-light melon-bed with
18 good dung-carts of fresh, hot dung, &
30 bushels of fresh tan. I had made this
bed just a week before, only two days
after the materials were brought in;
but finding it to heat violently I order=
'd it to be pulled to pieces, & cast back
again, that it might spend it's violent
Heat. The bed is 36 feet long, six feet &
an half wide, & about about two feet &
half high. The tan makes a covering
all over of about 8 inches thick. In the
middle of each light I laid a patch of
rotten dung about two inches thick, which
I beat-down hard to keep-off the fierce
heat from the hillocks of earth.

Fierce east-wind; & no rain for near
three weeks: the ground, & roads unusually
dry.

April 15. Raked-over the Aspa:
:ragus-beds the second time: stuck the
first Crop of Marrowfat pease: filled
the box that contains the leaden-pipe
with hot dung the second time.
Cutting winds all day, & thick ice every
night.

16: So fierce a frost with a South-wi[nd]
as to freeze the steam which run out
in water from between the panes of ye
melon-frames into long Icicles on the
Edges of the lights.

17: Prepared & dunged the basons in
the field, which are to be planted with
Annuals hereafter. Fine shower.

18: Put a barrow of fine mellow eart[h]
into each melon-light. Bed seems now
to be very mild. More soft showers.
Earth-house of great Use to keep a
constant supply of fine mould dry &
ready for the frames.

April 20. Found the melon-hillocks so hot that I durst not turn the plants 62 into them: plunged the plants in the pots into the hillocks.

Turned out some Hyacinths that were out of bloom from the blowing-glasses into the flower-border.

Sowed Crop of Boorcole green, & red.

Polyanths in full bloom; but not so fine, as last year. Several Hyacinths in the border very large & handsome.

White & yellow Narcissuss with golden Cups blow very well, both in glasses & abroad.

21. Found the melon-bed so hot still that I did not trust the plants out of the pots. Earthed the bed all over an inch thick to keep down the steam, which in the night had spoiled three of the plants. Bored some holes very deep in the back of the bed to let out the violent Heat. I find a moderate thickness of tan, when

6. laid on a good strong bed of dung, to occasion a very dangerous, & unequal Heat, so that there is scarce any Judging when the earth is free from burning. For in shady weather it will appear very mild; but on a hot morning will rage again as fierce as when it first cam to it's full heat. Tan gives a mild & last:ing heat by itself, but does not seem suit:able with dung.

22. Took out the tan the whole depth as wide as the Hillocks, & mixed up the hil:locks with a little fresh earth. Did not find the earth burnt, but much too hot. Filled the space whence the tan came with barrows of rotten dung trod down very hard, about four Inches thick.

Sowed four rows of dwarf kid:ney beans, the white sort; & a crop of Savoy-seed. Perfect Summer weather.

April 24. Ventured to turn-out ye melons, tho' some of the hillocks were full hot: mixed-up a good deal of fresh earth in each hillock, & set ye plants as high as possible: left the wodden bottoms under some of the plants to see if they will pre:vent the roots from burning. Intend to cover the frames but slightly, while the bed is so hot

Made an hot-bed for the small:est one-light frame, to prick the annuals in, with 5 barrows of dung, & ~~two~~ of Grass. Made two beds for two hand:glasses with two barrows of dung each to forward some of Bosworth's large white Cucumbers to save seed from. Dressed Artichoke bed. Forked up ye seedling Asparagus; only 16 plants to be found. Layed some boughs of Laurustines; & planted a Laurustine by ye pitching.

April 27. Planted-out John Bos:worth's large white Cucumbers, three under each Hand-glass, to make early plants to save some seed of that fine sort from: pricked-out the annuals in ye two one-light frames, & sowed some more Afr: Marrigolds, & more of Bosworth's Cucumber-seeds. Weeded all the basons, & flower borders. Melon-bed steams greatly; but seems to be past it's vehement Heat.

Fine soft showers all the Afternoon, & evening.

Disbudded the vines that were laid on the walls according to Hit.

May 1. Planted about 20 bulbs of Eschal:lots in the New-Garden.

Some melon-plants continue to fail, tho' the bed is very mild, & the mould sweet & unburnt.

12. On my return from London I found several of the melon-plants very large &

thriving; except in two of the basons, where they were puny, & withered: supply'd those two basons with some late-sowed Cantaleup plants from Seed saved at Selborn 1755.

May 15. A most extraordinary dry season ever since the end of March: all our worst roads have been dryed-up many weeks. For this fortnight past the heats have been very great. Grass & lent-corn must suffer unless rain comes soon. Apples-trees finely blown. Bosworth's Cucumbers come-on well under the Hand-glasses.

17. Widened-out the Cucumber-bed four feet with the dung of the seedling-bed; & laid-on a thick covering of earth.

Prick'd-out a good plot of Celeriac.

Vines trained according to Hit full of Bloom.

20. Sowed a Quart, four rows, of large white kidney-beans in the field-Garden: watered them well beforehand. Earthed the melons, & watered

them stoutly: trod the earth round the stem
down very hard to keep out the heat. Plan
four Handglasses in the cold ground with
Mr Bosworth's large white Cucumber-plan
raised in the annual-bed. Very hot, dry weat.
Sowed some Cucumber-seeds under a hand-gla

May 22. Prick'd-out a plot of Celeri: sowed
a Crop of Coss-lettuce green & white.

24. Made a melon-bed for four Hills with
six loads of dung in front of the large bed:
it is five feet wide, & seventeen long.

25. Turned out a pot of Selborn Cantaleupe
into each Hill, & covered them with Hand-
glasses. Intend to cover the plants, when
they spread, with the two two-light frames.
Violent hot weather: no rain for some
weeks. The ground burnt, & cracked to an
unusual degree. Things in both fields, &
Gardens suffer greatly. The fierce heat
has lately damaged both melons, & Cucumbers
notwithstanding constant shading, & unusua
watering.

May 26. Planted 6 basons in the field with Indian-pinks: set the plants pretty near together. Fine soft rains all day: every thing greatly refresh'd after so tedious a drought. Sunny days & east winds for the most part ever since the last week in March.

29. Weeded the Carrots, & Laurels, & hoed the potatoes: weeded the seedling-flowers.

Tacked the young wood of the vines all perpendicular, for the first time, according to Hit.

30: 31. Raised & earthed the melon-frames almost their full quantity. Melon-bed very warm still. Many of the melon-plants very thriving; abound in vine, & shew male bloom, & fruit.

Planted 100 of late Cabbages; & pricked-out some Broccoli plants given me by Mr Budd. Shady moist weather for a week past: now frequent heavy showers that have well ~~~~ soaked the Ground down to the roots of Corn, & Garden-stuff.

~~12.~~ June 2. Sowed four rows of large white-Kidney-beans, & one of dwarfs in ye field-Garden: five rows of dwarf D^o. in the Quincunx.

3. Gathered first beans.

5. Cut a brace of Cucumbers. Shady, moist weather.

6. Earth'd the hand-glass melons the first time: the bed not earth'd all over yet. The plants are strong, & produce plenty of wo[od] but are strangely blistered in their second leaves by being exposed to ye fierce sun while the night-dew was on them:

9. Mulberry-tree shews several Blossoms for the first time. Fine summer-weath[er] with now & then a shower. French-beans that had been watered all night, & were sow[n] on the 2^d. of June, began to appear on the 8th

9. Raised the Cucumber-frames the thickne[ss] of a brick above the mould: turned down ye large white-Cucumbers from under the hand-glass; they are strong plants, & shew fruit.

June 10. Went to raise the melon-frames, 66
but found the melon-roots have extended
hemselves all along against the sides of
he boxes, & require room by lining.
Watered the Mulberry-tree well
to make the fruit set.

12. Gathered first Marrowfats.
Soaking rain for ten Hours.

13:14. Lined the melon-bed three feet on each
ide with eleven loads of dung; & laid on
a good depth of earth: raised the frames
o the top of the earth. Lined the ends of
he bed with one load of Dung: the bed is
ow full 40 feet long, & 12 feet wide. Earth'd
t deep as far as the earth would last:
un a slight hedge round the edges to keep
p the earth.

15. Earth'd the Hills of the melons under ye
and-glasses: stop'd some of the plants at
he third Joint: plants very vigorous.
Sowed Crop of Endive.
Soft showery weather

~~th~~ June 15. Prick'd out 600 Savoys, & 350 Boorcole-plants, green, & purple.
16. Planted-out all the leeks at six inches asunder: about 200.
Pricked-out a little more Celeri.
Planted-out a bed of small Coss-lettuce.
Sowed a row of parsley.
Wet, blowing weather.
17. Planted 100 Cabbage-plants in the room of those planted May 31st: which were dead.
Tyed-up first Coss-lettuce.
Some of John Bosworth's long Cucumbers set.
20. Planted-out the greatest part of my annuals, African & French-Marrigolds, Pendulous Amaranths, & China-Asters: They were pricked into a second bed, & are very forward, & large.
Pricked-out an 120 Roman-Broccoli-plants from Waverley.
Two Labourers have been working for 5 or Days in the Garden, & have hoed & weeded

ll the Crops, & cleaned all the paths, & borders
hat were in a foul Condition.

22. Planted more Annuals, Sunflowers, &
China-Asters, in field, & Garden.

27. Nailed, & trimmed the vines: the second
time, according to Hit. The bunches in full
bloom.

28. Earthed the hand-glass melon-bed the
full depth, took away ye hand-glasses, &
put the two two-light frames over the plants.
Plants strong, but shew little fruit, or bloom.

Planted some of Mumd: Middleton's white-
Cucumber-plants under three hand-glasses.

July 1. Stuck the sticks to the large kidney-
beans. Heavy thunder-showers.
Melons swell apace. The late bed shews fruit.
Dwarf kidney-beans in full bloom.

3d. Lined-out the two-light melon-bed a yard
wide with three loads of dung, & laid on
earth very thick. Prick'd out a good many
Sweet Williams. Planted out more annuals:
sowed a small spot of Endive.

July 4. Pricked-out bed of Holy-oaks to p
them in less room: pricked-out vast Quant
of Sweet Williams.

Blowing, wet weather on to the 14: when
there was quite a storm all night, & such qu
tities of rain as made quite a flood: the tr
& flowers were much damaged by the wind.

15. Found on my return from Dene abou
thirteen brace of Cantaleupes set; some
very large. Plants in vast vigour with
leaves near a foot in Diameter. More fru
setting every day. Those plants in the two
light frames seem to be full late; hardly an
of their fruit blown-out yet. Two plants
new frame have 8 brace of fruit betweem y

18: 19: 20. Showery, black weather. Trenched-ou
seven rows of Celeri. Planted-out second
plot of Endive: first plot about a fortnight before. Planted large plot with
Roman-Broccoli from Waverley.

On examination it appeared that the Ca
taleupe-fibres have run the full extent of

the 12 feet bed: laid-on some more earth behind
to secure their Roots from the Sun. Some
of their branches, on which are large fruit,
are attack'd with mouldiness this wet weather.
Raised the frames behind, the thickness of a
Brick, to shoot-off the rain, that drips thro;
& rots some of the Haulm.

1. Quite heavy showers to day, & strong wind.
Some of the melon-leaves measure 11 inches
& three Quart:rs in diameter.

20. Gathered first French-beans; white dwarfs.

24. Stringed pine strawberries.
Continual showers.

25. Dug-up Hyacinth, & tulip-roots: Hya:
cinths bloated with the wet weather. Planted
in their room African & French-Marrigolds.
Vast rains still.

26. Great rain.

28. Vast rains with Thunder.

29: 30. Dry weather: on 31:st rain for 14 hours.
The melon-vines suffer with the continual
wet, which has continued now more than a month.
Cut-off a full-grown Cantaleupe that was rotten.

August 1. Black, moist weather all day: vast rains at night.

2. Sultry, bright morning: turned the large Melons.

3. Tiled, & turned all the largest melons: full twenty brace set; tho' perhaps they may not all ripen

4. Sowed half pound of spinage, & some white-turnep-radish-seed in the new field-Garden: began planting-out savoys, & Boorcole. Two hot, bright days.

5. Cut-off the small side-shoots from the bearing wood of the vines, leaving one joint on; according to Hitt's directions. Grapes pretty larg The fourth hot, dry day.

7. Drawed-out the boorcole, & savoy-bed to a foot & half apart, & planted the new field-Garden with D^o:

8. Brought in a doors the Pyramidal Campanula: it has seven Stems, & just begins to shew some bloom.

Aug: 11. Trenched two long rows more
of Celeri. Vast rains the two days before.
12. Finished the hay-rick: hay-making
was in hand just seven weeks. A deal
of Hay much damaged.
13. Beautiful harvest-weather.
16. Tyed-up some of the forwardest endives.
Vast rains last night, & this evening.
The wheat is all cut, & must soon be dam=
aged if this weather lasts. It has never
been dry more than four days together, &
that only twice, since the first of July:
in general only two days together; & that
but seldom. The Cantaleupes have had
a very disadvantageous season; nothing
but black, wet weather since they have
been set. Sr Mat: Featherstone's Canta=
leupes, I hear, have very little flavour.
19. Earth'd one row of Celeri half the way up.
Planted a row of Savoys between every two
rows of dwarf-kidney-beans in the Quin=
cunx. Housed the wheat not in very good order.

~~20.~~ Aug: 21. Tyed-up more Endive.

22. Cut the first Cantaleupe, the largest of the Crop: weighed 3 p.ds 5 oun: & half. It proved perfectly delicate, dry, & firm, notwithstanding the unfavourable weather ever since the time of setting. Saved the seed.

23. Cut second Cantaleupe: weighed 2 p.ds 5 o[un:]
Fine, bright weather for five days.

24. Cut a brace more of Cantaleupes; one weighed 2 p.ds 6 oun: one 2 p.ds 4 ounces.
Great rain in the afternoon.

25. Sent a brace of the Cantaleupes to Lord Keeper: eat the third at Home, which turned out perfectly delicate; rather superior to ye first, eaten at the Hermitage. Saved the seed.

26. Cut & set-up in the sun ye six large white seed-Cucumbers: the biggest weighed 2 p.ds 14 oun: & the longest measured 13 inch: in length.

Sowed a small plot of Coss, green-Capuchin & Brown Dutch Lettuce-seed, for plants to stand the winter.

28. Cut small Cantaleupe, weighed but 15 oun:

vast rains all day, & a great flood.

29. Tyed-up about 30 more Endives.

31. Heavy rain for about 30 Hours, which coming upon the back of such vast showers before, occasioned an extraordinary flood, which ran over the foot-bridges, & was greater than any winter-flood for many Years past. It filled James Knight's biggest pond, which had been fished this summer, brim full: & raised the Landsprings in ye fields, so as to damage the paths.

Septem.r 5. Earth'd-up early row of Celeri to the top.

Eat a brace of Cantaleupes at the Hermitage: the black, rough one very high flavoured. Shady, showery weather. Saved the seed.

Pulled-up the Onions, & Eshallots, & laid them to dry. Onions begin to rot with ye wet.

7. Eat a very delicate Cantaleupe: it had a bottle-nose, & grew close to the stem. Sav'd ye seed. Shady, showery weather: now a vast rain.

~~22~~. Septem^r 8. Cut first Endives.
Vast rains still.
9. This day ten weeks the wet season began
10. The Cantaleupes threaten to come all together. Cut two brace, & half to day.
12. Held a Cantaleupe-feast at ye Hermitage: cut-up a brace & an half of fruit among 14 people. Weather very fine ever since the ninth.
13. Planted-out two rows of Polyanths down the border next Dashams. Should have been transplanted many weeks ago, if the wet weather had not prevented.
14. Eat a brace & half of Cantaleupes. Saved the seed of one that grew near the stem, & was very fine.

Tyed-up more Endives.

17. Had been dry for 8 days: now very wet.
18. Cut a Cantaleupe ~~for~~ from one of the later plants: weighed 2 p^ds 5 oun: Esteemed very curious: saved ye seed.

Septem^r: 26. Earthed about half way seven rows of Celeri.

27. Cut two Cantaleupes, & took away two of the frames: only one fruit remaining. Dug up the Carrots, & Potatoes: the potatoes not a great Crop, nor very large. Dry, pleasant weather.

28. Continued ~~down~~ the dug-ground down Baker's Hill for more Garden. Dug a border down the Shrubbery under the rod-hedge.

Octob^r: 2: 3. Chip'd the best of ye Polyanths in ye broad shady walk, & planted two rows again in the same place.

4: 5: 6. Planted three beds of Pine-strawberries, & two of scarlet D^o: in the New Garden. Planted a few large strawberries call'd Collinson's, Nova Scotia, & white Strawberries sent me by Brother Thomas.

6. Cut last Cantaleupe; & housed the frame very dry. Firm, good-flavoured Fruit.

~~24~~. Octob.r 8. Fine still weather in gener
since the 9.th of Septem.r now rain, & a
vast storm of wind, that blew-down some
shrubs, & beat to pieces all the flowers.

17. Transplanted about 100 Green Capuchin, &
Brown dutch Lettuce to Dame Tyrrels garde
to stand ye winter. Dressed the border at
ye back of ye melon-screen, & planted a row
of Sweet Williams: planted a row of D.o in
the border in the New-Garden against ye
Street.

21. Received from Mur: Middleton 12 double
blue Hyacinths, 12 early-blowing tulips, 6
Polyanth-Narcissus, 6 double white-Hyacinth
Quart.r p.d of Anemonies, 50 good Ranuncul
two Moss-Provence-roses.

21. Planted the two Moss-provence roses be:
:hind the border next ye street in the New-Garden
Put to blow in the Glasses 3 double blue, & 3
double white ~~Hy~~ Hyacinths; & one early Tulip

Octob:r 27. Slip'd-out the buds of the Pyramidal Campanula, which blowed this Year, & planted them in several pots, four in a pot.

Nov:r 2. Saw a very unusual sight; a large flock of House-Martens playing about between our fields, & the Hanger. I never saw any of the swallow-kind later than the old 10: of Octob:r The Hanger being quite naked of leaves made the sight the more extraordinary.

Warm wet weather for many days, with blowing nights, & sunny mornings. The leaf fallen more than usual.

Nov:r 8. M: Middleton's large late Aster just blowing: a fine shewey flower of a beautiful purple.

8. Set to blow in Glasses four Polyanth-Narcissus, & two Hyacinths brought me by Brother Thomas.

14: Planted in the Butcher's Yard between ye limes one white, & two purple lilacs.

~~26.~~

Novem^r: 16. Planted in broad border next Parsons's;

No: 1. Double blue Hyacinths.

2. D^o White.

3. Early tulips.

4. Quarter of a pound of Anemonies.

5. 50 Ranunculus.

6. My own Hyacinths.

7. My own Tulips.

8. Bro: Tho: Polyanth-Narcissus, & Jon---quils: some have been in Glasses.

9. Mr Budd's Ranunculus.

10. Mur: Middleton's Narcissus.

11. 16 Coronæ Imperiales.

12. Mr Budd's Narcissus.

The border very dry, & in very fine order

Nov: 20. Planted four Damascene-plum-trees from North-Warnboro'.

Nov: 24. Set up two wickets from ye upper end of my Ewel-close thro' Parsons's field to the pound-field.

Planted 9 long rows, 3 pints of early beans, in the field-garden. Ground in very dry, good order.

25. Trenched & dunged very stoutly a piece of Ground for melon-earth next spring.

Decemr: 14. Earthed-up Artichokes.

The spring, & Summer of 1758 were much in the extreams. From ye last week in March to the first of July was one long dry fit, with very few showers between. At one time, I think, the Ground was more scorch'd than even in ~~xxxxx~~ summer 1757: & the lent-corn began to suffer greatly. But on the first of July the great rains began to set-in, & continued with very little intermission till the 10 of Septemr: The Autumn was moderately dry, & pleasant; & continued very mild, one short frost excepted, to the end of ye Year.

1.

Garden-Kalendar
for the Year
1759.

Jan: 19. Wheeled-in, & cast 18 barrows of hot dung for the seedling-Cucumber-bed.
20. The season has continued uncommonly mild to this time. Many kinds of flowers are got above ground some weeks before their usual time: the snow-drops, & some Crocus's were in bloom before old Decem was out: & Farmer Knight complains that several of his turneps are in blossom.

Covered the tulip, & Hyacinth-buds with a thin coat of tan that is rotten.

Have got some mould in excellent order for the early Cucumbers; it is a mixture of strong loam, ashes, & tan, tumbled about & well incorporated all the winter.
The Glass has been very high for many days with a falling mist, & blustering west-wind.

2.
74

Jan: 22. Turned the earth trench'd for ye Melons, & gave it an other sprinkle of very rotten. dung: turned the Dorton-earth, & mixed with it three barrows of rotten tan.

23. Made the Cucumber ~~Hot~~ seedling-Hot-bed, turning the front to the south west to take all the sun these short days.

Hard frost for two nights, & bearing Ice

24. Laid on the mould on the hot-bed; fill'd & plunged four pots for Cucumber seeds.

Sowed a pot with Cucumber-seeds, & set it by the parlour-fire for experiment-sake. These seeds came-up, but would not advance beyond the two first leaves.

26. Bed come to a kindly heat: sowed above an 100 Cucumber-seeds within & without the pots.

30. Cucumber-plants begin to appear.

Feb: 3. Sowed a small Quantity of curious Polyanth-seed, given me by Mr Hale of Ham=bleton, in a box; & set ye box where it may receive the morning-sun.

Sowed 20 more Cucumber-seeds in the frame.

First plants thrive, & look of a good Co=lour. Unusual sunny, fine weather.

~~8.~~ Feb: 3. Cucumbers in ye pot by the fire:side come-up very well.

5. Set in a nursery-bed a good parcel of Hyacinth, & Tulip-offsets.

7. Finished trimming, & tacking the vines ac:cording to Hit. Took away abundance of ye old wood: The vines in one year more will be quite furnished with new.

Ashed the great mead, Clover-field, & part of the slip with three dung-pots of ashes: quite cleared the House.

Cucumber-plants thrive so fast, that to da[y] the 12 day from sowing the seeds, many of th[e] plants have got a rough leaf.

Fine dry weather, with a good deal of Sun-shine; more like April, than old Janu:ary. Paths quite firm.

8:9:10. Set on three Labourers this fine weath[er] to dig all my Ground ready for Crops: turn'[d] my plot of melon-earth the third time: & wheeled out of the way all the old rotten dung & tan.

10. Sowed Gallon of early pease; & half poun[d]

f spinage: planted Gallon of Winsor
eans, & 200 of Cabbage plants.
eb: 9. Turned-out of their pots, & planted
n deep mould several of the best Cucum:
er plants: plants strong, & thriving.
Notwithstanding the long dry weather
the Ground will but just work decently.
12. Carryed into the Hot-bed Ground
eight loads (dung-carts) of hot dung
for the forward Cucumbers.
Perfect summer: the air full of Gnats:
& the surface of the Ground full of
piders webs, as in a fine day in Au:
ust. The sun lay so hot on the frame
that the Cucumber-plants wanted to be
haded. Some plants have a broad
ough leaf.
13. Made the bank against the new-garden
retty fine, & smooth by the advantage of
his fine weather. Planted it with flowers
n two rows: the upper row was Colum:
ines, French-honeysuckles, & rose Campi:
ns, at a Yard apart: the lower row all

5 sweet-Williams, at a foot apart. Orde
the bank to be well-beat, & the water-tab
to be cut so deep, that no mould can tum
ble on the brick walk. The bank lays ver
handsome, on a hanging level.

Feb: 15. Cucumber-plants thrive strangely
Some have got a fourth leaf quite expan
ed; & their first rough leaf as broad as a
Crown-piece. No rain at all since
this day month. Great fogs for these
two days past, that hang 'till the afternoon: then bright sun-shine.

Planted Holyoaks in the new border under the rod-hedge down Baker's-hill, & mended-out the borders in our own, & the Butcher's Yard.

17. Received from Mr: Philip Miller of Chels
about 80 Mellon-seeds 1754: immediately from
Armenia; which he finds to be better than the
that have been first brought to Cantaleupe
& thence to England.

20. Made my early Cucumber-bed with 8 loads of dung; & cased it round well with a Coat of refuse-hay, well sparred-on.

Feb: 20. Black, rough, March-like weather:
seems to threaten snow. 76

22. Laid-on the hills of earth on the Cucum=
er-bed. Now rain after many weeks
dry weather.

23. Turned-out two pots of Cucumbers
n one of the two-light frames: the Plants
ave got a fifth leaf, & a joint: the two
first rough leaves are as broad as the
alm of my Hand. This day month the seeds
ere put into the frame. Plunged 14
ots for Cantaleupes in the two two-
ight frames.

24. Sowed six of the pots with Canta=
upe-seed from Waverley 1756: & eight
f the pots with Armenian-Cantaleupe
754 from Mr. Miller. Fierce, piercing
ast-wind with a low, sinking Glass.
The Glass has been up at, & above fair
ver since new-year's day, 'till yesterday.

25. Vast rain all night.

26. Transplanted more Cucumbers in the
ther two light-frame. Bed full hot.

7 Feb: 27. One pot of Miller's Cantaleupes begins to appear. Continual heavy rain
28. Sowed one more Armenian seed in eac of the six pots: so there are three seeds in every pot. Plants came almost all up in general last night: raised the po allmost out of the mould.

March 1. Sowed some Cucumber-seeds to give away.

3. The Cantaleupes looking not quite right I plunged the pots up to their brims in the mould.

4. Cucumbers grow away, & put out long wires; have six leaves, & three joints. Sad heavy showers.

Put in a few more Cantaleupe-seeds into the worst-looking pots.

6. Ventured to mat-down the Cucumber-frame untriged for the first time. Continual rain

7. Bright sun-shine all day; scalded some of the Cucumber-leaves.

8. Continual rain all day.

9. Raised the frames the thickness of one bric Cantaleupes look in general very well: plenty

l plants at present. Vast storm in the
vening, & very heavy rain. 77
March 10. Vast tempest all night, & this morn-
ng; which at noon blew down the weather-
ock on the tower.
2. This day 6 weeks the Cucumber-plants
ppeared above ground; & have now five,
six joints apiece, & are full of budds
r bloom, & fruit. Watered them gently
r the first time over the leaves with ye
atering-pot. Promises for dry, & cold.
3:14. Carted 20 loads of hot dung into
he melon-ground for ye Cantaleupes: seven
f my own, & thirteen borrowed.
5. One of the Cucumber-plants has a
nale-bloom fully expanded.
The weather very wet, & stormy.
Sowed ye Celeri Hand-glass.
17. Vast storms still.
Cucumbers thrive, but not the Cantaleupes.
19. Received from Brother Tho: three sorts
f the double-flowering Sweet Briar; & two
oots of the large tap-rooted Lathyrus; & three
oots of the Lathyrus. earth-nut with a tuberose
(root.

~~9~~ March 19. Vast rain most part of the day. Wind abated. The late storms have done considerable damage among our ship[s]

20. Cucumber-plants showed plenty of fru[it] for the first time; all on the second wood. Black weather, & continual showers.

22. Moved the seedling Cucumber-frame nearer to the two-light frames, & sowed it with radishes on very deep mould. Beautiful day.

21. Mowed the grass-plot for the first time a vast plenty of Grass, which lined the Cucumber-bed. Made two beds, with one barro[w] of ~~earth~~ dung each, for two handglasses, for whe[at]-mustard, & cress.

23. Planted 4 of the double-Briars in the new Garden against the street, & one in the front of the House; & the two long Lathyrus-roots against the apple-tree next Parsons's. Grubb'd the orchard-walk, & planted it with Holy-oaks, & Wall-flowers. Potted so[me] sweet-williams. Removed the double jonquils, out of the orchard, ~~into~~ under Hassam's hedg[e]

24. Dressed the Rasps. Removed half the Capuchin, & Brown-Dutch Lettuces from

Dame Tyrrel's Garden back to the New-Garden.
Sowed four Drills of Marrow-fat pease in Baker's hill. Sowed a drill of parsley. Yesterday a beautiful Summer's day. 78

Grafted my three Cantaleupe-frames, & raised
them 9 inches behind, & in proportion before.
Hyacinths in bloom in the open air; & one
Narcissus. Early Tulips have been blown
above this fortnight.

25. First Cucumber-blossom fully expanded.
Still, grey weather, with a very high Barometer.
Some fruit shows on the first runners of some
plants. The lining of grass-mowings gives a great
Heat to the Cucumber bed. Hyacinths abroad full
as early, as those in ye Glasses.

26. Work'd-up the 20 loads of dung (brought
in on the 14th) into a Cantaleupe-bed for the
nine large lights. The bed is tucked to six
feet & half broad, & 36 in length. Laid some
very stiff loam all over about an inch thick;
& put on the boxes, & lights. The bed is about
two feet thick. Housed seven more barrows
of dorton-loam; in all 14.

27. Sawed-down those two espalier-trees in ye
New-Garden, that bore angular apples; & employed John Lassam to graft

the stems with some Cuttings from the Royal russet in the Orchard. Grafted two of the Golden pippins in the Orchard with Cuttings from a tree of the same sort.

March 28. Put the male-bloom to three of the first fruit-Cucumber-blossoms, that were just turning-in, in order to set them.

Sowed three pots more of Miller's, & three pots of Waverley-Cantaleupes, two seeds in a pot; to supply the hills in Case of any failure. Miller's marked as usual with sticks. Plunged the pots in one of the Cantaleupe-boxes.

29. Sowed half a Gallon more, four rows of Marrow-fats, in the lower field-garden: the rows are four feet a-part; the former sowing five.

30. Put a brimful Barrow of Dorton-loam into each light of the Cantaleupe-bed. The Hills will require, now the boxes are raised, a barrow & half each at least. Bed comes slowly to it's heat; & is very mild yet.

31. Planted groups of Sweet Williams in the border under the rod-hedge down the Shrub:bery.

Put half barrow more of loam to each Cantaleupe-Hill. Bed very mild.

Finished a bastion, & Haha, fenced with sharp'ned piles, in the vista from Baker's Hill to the Great mead: & a conical mount, about six feet diameter at top, & five high, at the bottom of the great mead. Mount about eight days work; Haha about sixteen.

Fierce frost, & vast ~~white~~ hoar-frost on the Grass: the ground continued very hard, & icy all day in the shade.

April 2. Sowed ounce of Carrots with green, & white Coss-Lettuce; ounce of Onions; & a few parsneps. Fine weather.

3. The Cantaleupe-bed not coming to a proper degree of Heat, I ordered it to be pulled to pieces, & worked-up with 10 loads of fresh hot dung just brought-in. The Labourers made use of about 16 loads of the first bed again: so the new bed contains 26 loads. Laid some loam all over to keep-down the steam; & some turfs under the Hills. Put one barrow of loam to each Hill.

17. Bed more than seven feet wide; & two feet & half thick behind.

April 4. Widened out the Cucumber-bed in front three feet with about two loads of the dung, which came out of the Cantaleupe bed; & laid on a thick covering of strong loam: lined it behind with Grass, & weeds. Some fruit set, that grows apace.

Planted some everlasting-pease of my sowing last year; & some earth-Nut La:thyruss under the rod-hedge against Par:sons's. Planted more sweet-Williams, & some Columbines under the rod-hedge against the shrubbery. Planted 8 Lau:rels, with a sweetwilliam between each two, on the bank of the Bastion behind the seat. Planted Columbines in the Orchard-walk.

5. Raked down, & weeded the Asparagus-beds the first time.

7. On my return from Chilgrove, & Hart:ing I found the Cantaleupe-bed come to a very fine degree of Heat. Turned out the Cantaleupes into their Hills: the plants

are healthy, & well-rooted; but a little drawn by the large rambling runners of ye Cucumbers. The three nearest hills are 80 Waverley; the six farthest are Armenian Cantaleupes. Six pots left, which I plung:ed in the great boxes.

Sowed about 40 seeds of the great White-Dutch-Cucumber, saved last Year.

Six pots of Waverley, & Armenian-Canta:leupes just coming out of the mould, by way of supply, if wanted.

8. Vast rain from the East: & all day on ye 6th.

9. Cut first Cucumber: it had a good flavour, & smell. Several more set. The seeds were put into the Ground 10 weeks, & two days ago.

Unusual heavy rain for 29 hours.

11. Vast rain great part of the day, & night.

The lining the Cantaleupe-bed between the frames with weeds cut from the orchard filled the bed with snails. Forced to take the weeds away, else the snails would have devoured all the plants. The water stands in the lining of the Cucumber-bed almost shoe deep.

14. At a mark cut in the bark of the great Oak in the mead, between two & three feet from the groun[d] I measured that tree, with a design to see how much the body may swell in one summer. It girted seven feet 5 inc:

April 12. Sowed about a peck of old bacon-salt in middle of the great mead.

Made half Hogsh: of raisin wine with an Hund: of Smyrnas, & half D^o. of Malagas: put to them in the tun-tub 27 Gallons of water

13. Made an Annual-bed for the biggest one-light frame with 6 barrows of hot dung, & one of weeds: laid on the mould six inch-es deep. Finished-off, & raked very smooth the bastion, & sowed it very thick with rye-grass, & white clover. Sowed ye bare places in the fields, & orchard with the same. Planted two rows of slips of a very fine sort of double-bloody-wall-flower from my Dame Scot's of Harting. Made the ground very mellow with lime-rubbish. Sowed a plot of Holy-oak-seed, & leek-seed. Planted some rose-campions, & Columbines in the new Garden.

A perfect summer's day, that fetched ye
beds finely to their heat after such gluts
of rain.

Saw seven swallows, the first this year,
playing about James Knight's House.
My great Dutch Cucumbers come up in
one of the Cantaleupe-boxes almost
every seed.

14. Sowed the annual Bed with African, &
French Marrygolds, purple, & white Asters,
and pendulous Amaranths.
Planted a potatoe-bed with fine large
potatoes cut in pieces, which came from
Swarraton: three rows a yard from each
other.
Put half barrow of loam into
each Cantaleupe-light.

16. Cut brace of Cucumbers: the second time
of cutting.
Sowed everlasting pease, & wild-Lathyrus
from the Hythe; soaked the seeds in water two
nights, & a day: Dwarf-sunflowers; Nasturtiums; Tree-primroses; Rhubarb; Boorcole,
red, & green; & savoys.
Dressed Artichokes.

~~16.~~ April 16. Earthed Cantaleupe hills for the first time: examined ~~xx~~ into the hills, & found the bed unexpectedly warm: no loam burnt, but very hot. Gave a pretty deal of water. Plants in general thrive, & throw-out runners. The turfs at bottom very useful.
Very cutting, March-like weather.

17. Cut brace more of Cucumbers.
Very stormy, cold weather.

16. Heard the first nightingale in my fields.

On my return on the 28 from Oxon I found the Cantaleupe-plants in good Condition; several of the runners had three or four Joints apiece. The three hills of Waverley-plants much more gross, & strong than any of the Armenian: tho' the last are in a promising way. Stop'd down the runners, & cut away some plants, where very thick. The bed very hot. One hill quite destroyed by a Grub: John destroyed the Grub, & trans:planted out a fresh pot in the Hill.

~~IIII~~ IIII Cut this day the twentieth Cucumber: many more growing in succession.
Cutting east wind for some days.

April 30. Made five hills in the new Gar: 17.
den for Hand-glasses, three with two bar:
rows of hot dung apiece, & two with two 82
piece, for the large white-Dutch-Cucumbers.
Some of the Cantaleupes have a shew
for bloom: their hills have been earthed
twice. Sowed more balsoms in
pots: the first sowing sadly drawn.
Stuck the dwarf-early-pease with sticks
out of ye faggots.

Feb: 12. From Farmer Kelsey 3 loads
------ of Dung . p.d

of my own
one : 1. l

From F: Berriman 4 loads. p.d

March 13. From Farmer Parsons p.d 3 load..

14. Farmer Berriman 5 loads p.d of my own sev..

--- Farmer Kelsey 3. loads. p.d

April 2. Farmer Kelsey 3. loads. p.d

--- Parsons --- 3 loads p.d of my own two..

---- Berriman --- 2 loads. p.d

June 1. Kelsey --- 4. loads. p.d of my own 3..

5. Berriman 5 loads. p.d --

18

83

Garden · Kalendar:
May 1st 1759.

Garden Kalendar:
May 1: 1759.

Garden-Kalendar.
1759.

May 1st Pulled-away the Hedge round the
ir-quincunx, & hoed the Ground-clean.

2. The Hanger out in full leaf; but much
angled about by the Continual strong east-
ind that has blown for many days. The
Leaves, & blossoms of all trees much injured
y the wind. The ground parch'd, & bound
ery hard. The cold air keeps the nightin-
ales very silent. No vegetation seems
o stir at present.

Disbudded some of the vines: the buds are
about an Inch long.

3rd Made second annual bed with 6 barrows
f Grass; & weeds only; no dung.

Planted-out the five hand-glasses with
he great white-Dutch-Cucumbers; 4 plants
n a hill. The plants are pretty much drawn.

This evening the vehement east-wind
eems to be abated; & the air is soft, & cloudy.
Ground bound like a stone.

♃. May 4. Sowed a pint, four rows, of small dwarf white kidney-beans in the lower field-garden.

Earthed the Cantaleupes the third time found all the plants in a very flourishing way, & the fibres extended to the very out sides of the hills. Cut away the plants to one in some of the hills; & left two in some stopping down the worst plant very short towards the bottom of the runners, for experiment sake, to see what the small wood about the stems will do. Some of the plants offer for male bloom.

Saw the first Redstart, & Cherrysucker.

Sowed about two doz: of the large white Dutch Cucumber-seeds for ye latter handglasses: the first sowing got full tall, & big.

Delicate soft rain all the afternoon, & all night, which soaked the Ground well to the roots of all vegetables.

5. Fine Growing weather.

Several of the Cantaleupes have male blossoms fully expanded.

May 7. Disbudded all the vines according to Rit. Almost every shoot shows bloom. 86 Housed 21 barrows of the last prepared Cantaleupe loam: by means of the late rains in is in most delicate order, & crumbles quite to dust.

9. Berriman sowed Baker's Hill with Barley, & after it 8 pounds of Clover, & two bushels of white-seed, or Rye Grass. The Ground cold, & cloddy, & pretty full of daisey-roots, & grass, & not in very fine order. Added since 8 pds more of Clover.

10. Several Cantaleupe-plants shew fruit, & grow away at a great rate. Pricked out the annuals into the second hot-bed. Fine showery, growing weather.

12. Gave the Cantaleupe-hills a full barrow of loam each: the fourth time of earthing. Cut away the plants to one on a hill.

14. One Cantaleupe-fruit in full bloom. Made three hills for large white Cucumbers in Turner's Garden.

May 15. Sowed the second pint of french-beans, large white Dutch: soaked them in water over night.

18. Sowed a Crop of white, green, & black Coss-lettuce.

All my Savoy-seed, & Boor-cole fails this year not one plant appears.

20. Strong sun-shine for many days, & a sharp east-wind. Cold white dews in the mornings. Our clay ground as hard as a stone. This burning Sun, as usual, makes the Cantaleupes not look quite right most of the fruit, as soon as it appears, turns yellow. The single fruit, that is out of bloom, not likely to stand.

The Dwarf french-beans are come-up pretty well.

The lettuce that stood the winter are finely loav[ed]
This unkind weather stops the setting of ye Cucumbers.

21. Earthed the Cantaleupes the last time within their boxes. Finding the Cantaleup[es]

much exhausted, & dryed by the fierce heat of the Sun, & the dry air, I watered them all over, leaves & all, with one 87 small pot of water. The leaves all hang down, & have a dry, paper-like feell, & look woolly; & the fruit all turns yellow. I remember they had all just the same appearance at this time last Year, the sun-shine & east-wind being as vehement.

Planted 100 of late Cabbages.

26. The burning, sunny weather continues. The Gardens suffer much by the drought.

29. Frequent showers.

The watering the Cantaleupes twice over ye leaves seemed to refresh them very much; but has occasioned one of Mr Hunter's plants to grow ~~ill~~ ~~lik~~ a little mouldy at a Joint on one of the leaders near the stem. So that water, tho' never so much wanted, is dangerous near the stem.

The Armenian plants in general have small leaves, & vines: & one in particular is

6. so fine, & wire-drawn, that one would imagine it would never be able to carry an fruit to perfection. The rest are healthy & are disposed very regularly in their frames; & are full of fruit. No fruit set yet.

Took off the Glasses from ye early Cucumbers, & annuals to give them ye benefit of the showers.

28: 29. Housed four loads of peat in most excellent dry order. The uncommo dryness occasions some waste by making the bats crumble.

Gathered two scarlet strawberries.

The early beans have large pods: the early pease are well blown.

30. The rain on the 29th: very heavy for some Hours; so as to make the Cart-way run. Raked all the rough-dug ground that was, till moistened, like an heap of stones. Prick'd a plot of Celeri.

31. Sowed a pint more of large French-

beans. The first sowings strangely devoured by snails. Full gathered a bowl-dish 88
three quarters full in one evening; &
still the plants were almost covered
with them ye next. Cold winds, & frosty
nights since the rain.
Hoed the strawberries that were planted
last Autumn, & filled-up the vast cracks
in their beds. At least half the Autumn
planted pine-strawberries are dead.
The scarlet will have some fruit; &
so will the few plants of Collison's. The
Nova Scotia will not bear this year.
Stringed the bearing pine-strawberries,
which are full of bloom.
The Autumn-sown Capuchin, & Brown-
Lettuce, now in high perfection. I have
a very poor Crop of Coss-lettuce this
Spring.
June 1. Distant thunder, & fine showers all
the evening, & part of the night.

May 31st. June 1st: 2nd: John tacked all the vines for the first time this Year according to Hitt. Those vines that were dressing in that method last Year, are now full of fruit: those that have been trained only this Year have little, or none.

Frequent good showers. The ground is now finely soaked.

Continued picking vast quantities of slugs from the french-beans, which are in a poor way.

June 3. Continual heavy showers all night, & all day. The Ground is now well soaked.

5. Lined out the Cantaloupe-bed with twelve dung-carts of hot dung. The bed is now 12 feet broad, & 40 feet long. Continual showers all day: so that no loam could be laid on ye bed, but what was already housed in the earth-house.

The Fig-tree has plenty of fruit, which grows apace.

June 5. Such a violent Rain, & wind
all the evening, & most part of the night
that they broke down, & displaced all the
pease, & beans, & most of the flowers; &
tore the hedges, & trees, & beat down sever:
al of the shrubs.
6. Continual rain all day. The lining
of the Cantaleupe-bed, which is not yet
earthed, in danger of losing it's Heat by
being so thoro'ly soaked.
8. Earthed the lining of the Cantaleupe-
bed, & raised the frames to the top of
the earth. The Waverley plants had
filled the frames with their roots: the
fibres of ye Armenian sort had not
extended themselves so much.
Sowed a pint more of dwarf-kidney-
beans in the room of those that were
devoured by snails. Fine summer weather.
Turned down the three forward basons
of Cucumbers from out their Hand glasses.
. Gathered first beans, a large Mess.

10. Fine soft weather for some days; now a soaking rain.

11. Finished off the borders in the new Garden, by cleansing, raising, & laying a good coat of fine peat-dust, finely sift in order to make them light, & dry. Sowed the first plot of Endive; & a plot of Lettuce, green & white Coss.

12. In the Evening began a vast storm which continued all the night, & tore & destroyed the things in the Gardens wo than the former: it broke down vast boughs in the Hedges, & had like to have overturned the Limes in the Butcher's yard. If the Annuals had been planted out they must have been quite whipped to pieces. The hedges look bare, & unsig:ly by being lashed, & banged by the wind; & the Ground is ~~littered~~ strawed with leave

13. The middle Waverley-Cantaleupe has some decayed, rotten ~~run~~ runners: Quæ if occasioned by those two waterings all

over their leaves in that scorching wea:
ther in May 90

The leaves of the Armenian Cantaleupes have a much blacker aspect than those of the Waverley.

14. Planted the empty basons in the field, & two borders in the New Garden with annuals, French, & Afr: Marry:golds, Sunflowers, Nasturtiums, pendu:lous Amaranths, & China Asters.

Hot growing weather: vast showers about

15. Planted 150 savoys from Alton.

16: 18. Lined out the Cantaleupe bed with loam very deep quite down to ye Ground on each side: the fibres may now, if they please, extend themselves 16 feet. The plants look in a most thriving way, & are loaded with fruit; but they hold off from setting strangely: no one set yet. Cut off a great branch of ones of the Waverley Cantaleupes, that was quite rotten.

June 19. Planted out Crop of leeks; &
some late Coss: Lettuce.

Furious hot summer weather.

20. To be planted pint of french-beans;
& an early row of Celeri to be trenched.

All the former Crops of french-beans lik
to come to nothing.

23. Called in upon Mr Miller at Chelsea,
& found he had 18 lights of Armenian-
Melons in excellent order. There were
about two brace, & half of fruit to a
light, full grown, & very rough, & black:
He pushes his lights, it seems, quite dow
in dry weather: & says the defect of male
bloom is owing to ye seeds being of some age.

30. On my Return from Sunbury I foun
my Cantaleupes in very bad plight in:
:deed: two of the Waverley plants were
quite rotten, & corrupted at the stem;
& one of the Armenians, the day after
I came home, withered away, tho' perfect

ound; & dyed as if eaten-off at the root;
ho' upon search no grub could be found
n the mould. And what is stranger, no
ne fruit was set upon any plant; tho'
hundreds have dropp'd away. There
certainly is a want of male bloom in
he Armenians to a degree: but then
he Waverley plants over abounded, &
et cast all their fruit.

I found a vast crop of pease, thro
he dripping season; & green pease soup
every day. The first hand glass cu:
umbers are in full bearing: I intend
o save 4 more (the large white Dutch)
for Seed. The small forward beans
have an unusual Crop. The fourth,
fifth crop of french-beans like to
come to good.

July 2. Planted out a vast bed of Holy-
aks.

6. Not one Cantaleupe set yet.

~~14.~~ July 6. Planted out about 50 Poly:anths, raised this spring from Seed given me by Mr Hale.

7. Finished my Hay-rick in most excel:lent order. The weather has been so perfectly hot, & bright for these five days past that my Hay was all cut, & made in that time. The Crop was so great that Kelsey's people made 8 carryings of it: & the burden in the great mead was supposed to be consi:derably greater than ever was know[n]. To my own stock I added two tons from Farmer Lassam, which in all ma[de] a considerable rick.

Finished cutting the hedges round Baker's Hill.

July 21. On my return from Dene on this day, I found I had but one Can:talupe set, & that a fig-shaped one, no[t] likely to come to good. The plants are in uncommon vigour, & grow unaccountably, & are full of fruit still; but strangely deficient in male bloom. The void spaces in the frames are quite filled out with the remaining plants.

Mr Carr's Cantaleupes were all turn up, with a noble Crop on them, about ten days before the fruit would have been ripe. He had a fine Crop: but the intense heats scorch'd off all the fibres thro' his light, dusty earth.

Full planted out Endives, & lettuce in my absence; & pronged up the bulbous roots against parsonss, planting annuals in their room. John trimmed & nailed the vines in a very handsome manner according to Hit. Those vines that have been managed in that manner for two years, have a noble crop of

~~16.~~ fruit very forward. My Crops of beans, & pease are very extraordinary this Year. The annuals against the broad walk in the new Garden are un:commonly large.

July 23. Gathered 36 Cucumbers. Earth up the Chinks round the hand-glasses with melon-loam.

Unusual hot summer-weath for three weeks past. Wheat-harvest is begun in some places.

26. Pulled-up an other of the Armeni:an Cantaleupes, which was rotten at Stem. So now I have lost four plants out of nine.

The fruit begins to set now at a vast rate on the remaining plants; as fast as ever they fell-off before.

The hot vehement season continues: the ground is wonderfully burnt.

uly 31. Now a great rain after sever: 17
2 weeks drought. 93

ug: 1. On Examination I found
bove 20 brace of Cantaleupes set:
bout 10 brace on one of the Armeni:
n plants; about 8 brace on the
nly remaining Waverly plant; about
brace on an other Armenian; 2
rage (one a full-grown fruit) on an
ther: & one Armenian is quite barren.
The Waverley plant is infected with
he rot that destroyed the rest, which
endeavour to stop by wiping, & dust.
It is observable that those plants
hat bear so prodigiously are those
hich (their fellows being rotten) have
he space of two or three lights to
un in. Had the fruit set in this
anner a month or six weeks ago (when
it all droppid-off) there had been a noble
early Crop.

~~18~~. Aug: 10. The first set Cantaleupe, th
unpromising at first, now a fine, beautiful
large fruit just like Millers. The rest of
later date come on apace. Prodigious
hot, sunny weather.

Sowed half pound of spinage mixed with
Capuchin, & Dutch Lettuce, & white-turn
Radishes. Trenched four rows more
of Celeri: & planted out 150 more Savo
Tyed about 20 of the Endives
Sowed a little more Endive-seed.

14. Lost the third, & last Waverley Can:
taleupe with a Crop of 4 brace of fruit
on it. I have now lost five plants out of
nine. The four ~~[illegible]~~ Armenians no
remaining have 10 brace of fruit likely
to come to good. Pulled off two brace &
half ~~out~~ of fruit, some ~~so~~ of a considerable size.
Hot dry weather still.

Aug: 16. Sowed a Crop of Coss- 94
Lettuce, & Endive to stand the winter.
Trimm'd the side-shoots of the vines
for the last time. The Clusters are
unusually large, & forward.
Perfect Summer-weather, but cooler.
27. Cut a vast Quantity of White-
Dutch-Cucumbers. One that was young,
& eatable weighed 2 pounds 5 ounces,
& measured 12 inch: & half in length.
The Canker continues to spread among
the Cantaleupes, & is likely to destroy
plants full of beautiful fruit within
a fortnight of being in perfection.
28. Planted on the bank several
large white Lilly-roots, Crown-Im:
perials, & double white-rockets.
Cut the first Endive.

70. Septem:r 4. Planted some tree primeroses on the bank.

It has been very wet, blowing weather for several days past.

8. Tyed-up about two doz: of the best bunches of Grapes in Crape-bags.

11. Cut off first Cantaleupe: it was finely emboss'd, & weigh'd 3 pds 11 ounc: but when it came to be cut-up, it had hardly any flesh, & was rank, & filthy.

Tyed-up more Endive.

Uncommon sunny, sultry day.

15. Tyed on 18 more Crape-bags on the best bunches of Grapes.

Fine, dry weather with pretty cold dew

29. All the Cantaleupes cut. Not one in perfection; tho' many were finely em:bossed, & looked wonderfully promising. The Canker, I suppose, had prevented

~~21.~~ 95

their drawing any nourishment, & getting any thickness of flesh.

Fine dry weather for a long time past, & the roads perfectly good.

The small bunches of Grapes are very good: the large ones not yet ripe against the wall.

Octob: 1. Tyed up last Crop of Endive.

The largest Cantaleupe was finely embossed, & tho' almost all rind, weigh'd 4 pounds 2 ounces.

3. Now a vast rain after many weeks fine Autumn weather.

5. Gathered the two first bunches of bag'd Grapes: they were a little mouldy; but the sound parts of the bunches were perfectly ripe, & sweet.

~~22~~. Octob.^r 8. Now perfect summer weather again after one wet day. The Grapes in the bags unusually fine; & both ~~[illegible]~~ bunches, & single Grapes are as large again as usual. It is to be observed that as this new Culture swells the berries so much; they are apt in this Cluster-sort to press too hard on each other, & prevent ripening, & occasion mouldiness: therefore if the grapes were thinn'd out the beginning of the summer with the points of a pair of scissars, it would certainly prove an advantage.

10. Planted two rows of Crocuss along the borders under the dining-room windows: both borders, especially that that hath the vine in it, were made very light, & mellow with an abundance of

sand, & blacksmith's cinders.
Weeded, & cut down the leaves of the strawberries; & mended out those beds that failed with the pine sort.

Now very dry, & warm: but there are great tokens of rain.

11. Now great rains, & wind.

Tunn'd three quarters of an Hogsh: of raisin wine. The Quantity of raisins in the mash vat were 1 hund: & half quart: of Smyrnas, & 3 Quarters of an hundred of Malagas. The Quantity of water put up was 18 3 gallon buckets; which made sufficient Quantity without any squeesing. The Colouring was 14 Quarts of Elder syrop. The weather was so hot that it stood but eleven days to ferment in the vat. The elder Juice was boiled up with 14 pounds of sugar.

 Octob[r]. 16. Finished off the bank in the new Garden, & planted the front row of the additional part with pinks both red, & pheasant-eyed: laid it with turf some days agon.

On measuring the great oak in the meadow which was measured in y[e] spring, I found it to be encreased in girth about one inch.

18. The mornings begin to be frosty, yet y[e] Grapes continue in high perfec:tion.

19. Finished a broad brick-walk thro' y[e] new wicket at the end of the dining-room & carryed a narrow one up by the side of y[e] pitching to the orchard-walk: rectifyed the broken pitching, & turned the gutter at the brew-house door, so as to get a 12 inch border four feet long

-for a white muscadine-vine.

22. Planted a row of Coss-lettuce touch-
-ing the wall along the vine-border un-
-der the dining-room window to stand
the winter. Planted a row of Holyoaks
against the boards of the wood-house.

24. Planted the irregular slip without
the new wicket in the Garden with first
two rows of Crocuss; a row of pinks;
several sorts of roses; persian Jas-
-mine, & Yellow D°. several sorts of
Asters; French-Willows; a curious sort
of bloody wallflowers; Double Campa-
-nulas white, & blue; double daisies; &
a row against the hedge of good rooted
Laurustines. Planted the back
row of the part of the bank newly length-
-ed-out with blue, & white Double Campa-
-nulas; & the border under the dining-room

26. window with the bloody-Double-wallflowers. Planted a bason in the field with french-willows.

Planted many dosens more of Coss-let:tuce against the buttery-wall, & down ye wall against the Yard.

Octobr 25. Planted a large layer of the musk-rose from Mr Budd a:gainst the boards of the old barn. Wet season after very dry weather.

26. Trimm'd, & tack'd the bottoms of the vines according to Hit: the lower parts of those under the Dining-room window are deficient in wood, till more can be got from ye stems. Began curving two shoots in order to reduce two of the vines to regular shapes from the bottom by degrees.

ovem:r 5. Planted my Hyacinths,
rcissuss, Ranunculuss, Tulips, Crown
perials, & Anemonies in the border
ainst Parsons's. It had been trench'd
ry deep with a good Quantity of
tten tan, & was in perfect dry
rder when the roots were put in.

Planted a small thriving larch
t the east Corner of Baker's hill;
wo well-grown Provence-roses in
e field-shrubbery; & two Monthly
oses in the orchard walk; all
rom North-Warnboro'.

Fine dry sunny weather.
Planted two rows of hardy lettuce
nder the filbert-hedge against
Parsons's.

6. Trimm'd & tack'd the fig-tree, leaving
leading bough in the middle to fill
he wall by degrees quite up to the eaves,

28. This tree is full of young wood, & fills the wall well; & may be carry'd by a second stage according to Hitt up to the tiles.

Planted a number of Goose-berries & Currans from Mr. Johnson, good plants, in the orchard-walk, & among the rasps.

The Grapes lasted in good perfection 'till the beginning of Novem^r: those that were hung-up in the study are very sweet, but shrivelled-up like raisins, not :withstanding a grape was stuck on the stem of each Cluster.

12. Plunged the seven pots of Pyram: Camp in the border against Parsons's under ye Filbert-hedges. Planted a nursery-border of small bulbous-roots. Dug-up a decaying Cluster-pine, & parsley-elder in the shrubbe & put a two-thorned-Acacia, & Judas-tree in their room. A most delicate summer-like day.

~~89~~ 99

Nov.r 14. Transplanted the striped-
pilobium into a fresh bason. Planted
bout 20 fraxinellas, seedlings from Mr.
udd, in a nursery. Planted several
aurels in the gaps of the Hedges round
aker's Hill.

The potatoes, raised from about 14
arge ones cut in pieces, turned out a
ine Crop of about 3 Bushels: several
ingle ones weigh'd about a pound.
ut by about 30 of the finest as a sup:
ly for a crop next year.

Planted some cuttings of parsley-elder,
with some Cuttings of fine white Currans.

5. Planted in the new garden two stand:
rd Duke Cherries; an espalier Orleans
lumb; an espalier green-gage plumb; a
uke cherry against the north-west wall
f the brewhouse; & a standard muscle
lumb in the orchard. These trees came

30. from Forster of North Warnboro; &
seemed to be good in their kind; were pla
ed the day they were taken out of the nur
sery, in basons, which being prepared
before, were in excellent crumbling ord
Nov: 16. Planted 3 pints, 7 rows of small
early beans in the lower field-garden.

2°/

Garden-Kalendar
for 1760: & 1761.

May 17: On my return this day (after six months absence at Lyndon, & London) I found my Garden in general in very good order, considering the long drouth this spring.

The Cucumbers in full bearing, but stunted in their vines. The Cantaleupe-melons in good Condition, & just shewing fruit; & the Succados very stocky plants. The Asparagus-beds are got stronger & bore wonderfully this spring. All the kitchen-crops are in good plight: & the Coss, & hardy lettuce that stood the winter, very fine. The Bergamot-pear, & knobbed-russet grafts like to take.

May 18. Fierce storms of Hail, which batter'd the vine-shoots at the end of the Dining-room very much. They were ~~early~~ very forward this sunny spring: the leaves were cut full of Holes, & several shoots were beaten quite off the trees. The persicaria-plants in the border under suffered much.

28. Dame Turner, & Girls weeded all the brick walks. Prick'd-out first Celeri, & prick'd-out, & planted a good many Savoys.

June 4. Furious hot weather for several days. The pease, & beans kept back for want of moisture. Some Cantaleupes in bloom. Covered all the inside of the boxes with wheat-straw to keep the sun from drying the mould; & to prevent much watering. Full employed in cleansing the garden from weeds. The vine-shoots grow in a most extraordinary manner, & are full of fruit.

5. Planted some persicarias in the new-garden border.

Out of one vine-shoot, which was procur'd from the old stem of a vine last summer; & being exceeding strong was laid-in five feet long, arise as many shoots this spring as produce 14 bunches of Grapes.

Fine, rain all night.

6. Planted-out all the persicarias; & about 2 doz: of the slips of the double bloody-wall-flowers.

Moist, hot, growing weather.

7. Lined-out the melon-bed very strongly, more than three feet on each side, with eleven loads of dung, & a large Quantity of weeds. Planted out a plot of late Cauliflowers.

4.

June 9. Gather'd first strawberries, scarlet, & Nova Scotia.

Cut the crop of rye-grass, & clover in Baker's-hill: a good Crop.

10. Planted 22 basons in the field with annuals, french & Afr: Marrigolds, China-Asters, pendulous Amaranths, & sun-flowers.

11. The vines at the end of the dining-room in bloom; about three weeks sooner than usual: occasioned, I suppose, by the very sunny season.

12. Housed the Baker's-hill-hay in excellent order: there were three decent loads.

14. John finished his second tacking & thinning the vines: those against the Yard shew prodigious strength; but are not yet blown.

Dry, settled weather.

June. 14. Planted annuals in the home Garden.

15. Wood-strawberries came-in in plenty.

16. Set Tull to earth the Cantaleupe-bed all over to the Ground very thick.

The Cantaleupes are full of fruit in bloom; & now shew a tolerable share of male bloom.

The vines begin to blow against the Gard.

Stopp'd-down the shoots of the vine over the entry-door.

17. Sowed first endive-seed.

A fine rain after scorching weather.

Three vine-layers (last year's-shoots) have produced between them 39 bunches of Grapes.

19. It being dripping weather, planted & pricked-out plenty of Savoys, & Celeri; trench'd-out one row of Celeri; & tyed-up several spring-sown Coss-lettuce. Those that stood the winter are

6. are all gone to seed.
Cold frosty air.
The muscadine vine-cuttings in the gutter thrive well; & so do the cuttings of the same sort, & of the cluster-vine in the nursery.
The grafts of the Bergamot-pear, & knobbed-russet from Ringmer take well.
This cold, windy weather likely to injure the vine-bloom at the end of the Dining-room.
The Cantaleupe-bed earth'd all over down to the Ground in an unusual thick manner.
The Nova-Scotia-strawberry a good bearer, & ripe even before the scarlet.

June 20. Planted-out leeks, & Boorcole; & sowed a plot of turneps. Continual showers.
21. On looking over the Cantaleupes, found one fruit set, & more in a promising way.
Some few bunches on the dining-room end have some Grapes set on them. Showers.
23. The Succado-melons (of which I have

three basons in the space of two lights) have got several fruit in full bloom.
Vast rains from the East.

June 26. Great rains.

27. Sowed a small plot of Coss-lettuce.

28. Agreed with John Wells to purchase the upper part of Dassam's orchard.
Stopp'd part of the vines against the yard, which are in bloom.

July 1. Finish'd stopping the vines.

2. Sowed second Crop of Endive, & more lettuce.

3. Sultry dry weather for three days: vast rains, & thunder in the night.
Planted-out two rows of seedling-polyanths all along the orchard-border.
New-planted two basons of the cold cucumbers: all the cumbers are in a strange way, have no vines; & are likely to come to little. The complaint is general.

July 6. Vast rains, & a flood.

7. Clear'd out the melon-frames that were quite choak'd with vines: not above 4 or five Cantaleupes set: the biggest fruit about the size of a hen's egg: the Succades shew no disposition for setting yet. Rain still.

Finish'd cutting the tall hedges.

Some grapes as big as young pease: all the bunches in bloom, & yeild a smell that may be distinguish'd at many yards distance.

14. Cut both the meads; a decent Crop. The weather was so hot, & sunny that we carry'd most of the Hay the next day; & finish'd the rick in excellent order the third.

18. Planted out endive, a large plot, in the field-garden.

20. The vehement sunny weather for these 8, or 9. days past has brought on the annuals strangely; & forwarded the white Cucumber plants sown in the middle of May so much that they seem likely now to come to good.

July 21. Trench'd out a Crop of Celeri
in Turner's Garden.
The first hand-glass white Cucumbers all
perish'd with the blight.
Melons make out lamely: one Cantaleupe
full-grown: no Succade set.
Trimm'd the vines the third time. The grapes
swell this hot weather.
The tree-primroses in full bloom; & are a
showey proper plant for large outlets.
August 1. Returning from Dene I found the
melons in a poor way: but two Cantaleupes
full-grown, & those small; & only five or six
more just set; & only one Succade set.
The late-sown white Cucumbers begin to bear
a little; the first are quite wither'd away.
An universal blight has this summer more
or less affected all the vegetable world.
The grapes to the Yard are very thinly set:
those to the South-west are thick set, & very
forward; but the Bunches are small.

10. Full in my absence trench'd four rows of Celeri in Turner's Garden; & planted out a Crop of Savoys. No rain for three weeks & three days 'till Aug: 1: & then showers

Aug: 4. Sowed a box of Mezereon-seed.

7. Planted out a Crop of Coss-lettuce to come in in Septem:r

Continual showers; & the Corn begins to gro

9. The Succade-melons now set apace.

The white cucumbers bear but poorly.

10. Vast rains.

11. Cantaleupe-melons set now; but are seemingly too late for ripening.

Sowed Coss, & Dutch lettuce to stand the winter. Sowed a quarter of a pound of spinage mixed with white turnep-radishes.

Put the bulbous roots in paper-bags, & hung them in the lumber-garret. They are vastly increased, especially the Hyacinths.

ug: 14. Trimm'd the side-shoots of the vines
fourth time: the fruit thin on the bunches.
ine harvest-weather for several days past,
ith cold drying north winds.
he white ~~[illegible]~~ cucumber-plants, which
oduced one fair large fruit; now show no:
ng but spotted, sickly ones. The early bed
ars pretty tolerably still.
th Cut more than half the second Crop of
lover on Baker's hill, which by reason of ye
ripping weather could not be housed till ye
rd There was one good load in pretty good order.
. Some of the Clusters of Grapes against the
d of the dining-room begin to change colour.
Cut Miller's first Armenian-Cantaleupe: by
means a curious fruit.
Brought three plants of curious Celeriac from
altham: the leaves are jagged like curl'd parsley.
pt. 1. Housed the remaining Clover in Baker's
ll; which, considering the showery season, was
t in good order.

17. Septem:r 2. Found several large Canta:
:leupes in a neglected frame.
Tyed-up the first Endives, & some late Coss-
-lettuce; & earth'd-up the early row of Celeri
quite to the top.
8. Gathered the first bunch of Grapes from
the end of the dining-room, which was ~~[illegible]~~ quite
ripe: those on the Yard-side are but just turn-
-ing colour. My Grapes in general are but
thinly set.

Plenty of figs in good ripe order.

Curious summer weather for many days.
11. Gather'd the first Mulberry that my tree ever
produced: it was very sweet, & good, but small.
There are some more on the tree.
18. Cut the first Succade-mellon; it was very
weighty for it's size, which is always small. It
proved very fleshy & high flavoured, & seems a
valuable sort.

Cloudless skies, strong sunshine, & strong
East winds for many days, which rise & fall
with the Sun. Fruits ripen at a vast rate,
& the roads are perfectly dry.

[Se]p: 12. Tull & John are busy every day in [g]rubbing, paring & burning the new-purchased [g]arden; & harrowing out the couch-grass. 10]
[T]he weeds & turf have produced already many [b]ushels of ashes; & will soon be burnt-up if [t]his dry weather lasts.

The Persicarias are vastly large, & fine.
[A]ll the annuals are come to a good size.

[1]3. Tyed-up 20 more Endives.
[G]ather'd two bunches of Grapes, which were [p]erfectly sweet & ripe. Very sunny weather still.

[1]6. The Succado-melons now come apace.
[V]ast rains, thunder, & lightening for 8 or 10 [d]ays; & a likelihood of great floods.
Grapes in great plenty, & perfection.

[2]9. Cut a brace of Succado melons.
Gather'd the Cadilliac pears, about half a bush: [e]l: three parts in four were blown-down.
[V]ast rains, & storms.

[O]ctob[r]: 1. Used the first Celeri.
Cut the last Succados, & a good-looking Canta:[l]upe. Continual rains; & frequent thunder still.
[T]he labourers work at the Haha when the weather [p]ermits.

44. Octobr. 14. Continual wet weather for a month: so that the fallows are full of wate[r] & no corn can be sown.

15. Transplanted six Geraniums into six penny-pots to stand the winter.

The new part of the Garden quite cleared from trees, & stools of trees.

Grapes in plenty, & perfection.

18. Turned out seven pots of Pyram: Campan:las into a mellow, sandy Border.

22. Transplanted a White Muscadine vine of Mr. Budd's sort into the border under ye Dining-room window. John annointed it with Dr. Hill's mummy, & planted it ~~as~~ a Cutting last March; & now it was a strong plant, & had a quantity of long fibres. In the summer it ~~shoot~~ made a shoot of abo[ut] four feet, & was now headed down to 4 or 5 bu[ds]. No frosts yet.

24. Put the whites of 8 eggs, shells & all, with a little sand, to 3 quartrs of an hogshead of raisin wine, which would not draw fine. Put Quart of b[randy?]

Grapes continue very good.

Octob^{r}: 25. Received from Mrs Snooke a basket of swans-egg, Doyenne, White Buree, & Colmar-pears for a specimen: also some Crasans, & Spanish Boncretiens.

27. Took-up from the Laurustine-hegde about 40 layers: laid-down about as many more.

Nov: 8. Began dressing the vines: found plenty of new wood in most places.

There have been a few smart frosts this autumn: but in general ~~there has been~~ a continual run of wet weather for these six weeks past; & great floods.

10. Widened the grass-plot towards the wall-nut-tree.

The farmers have been greatly hindred in their wheat-season by the rains; & will hardly be able to sow all their fallows.

12. Removed 8 black-cluster, & 6 muscadine-vines (which were planted cuttings last April) into the sandy bed at the end of the Asparagus. most of them were well rooted, & had made good shoots. Set the Geranium-pots in ye Garret-Window.

Nov:r 15. Continued to curve the leading shoots of the two vines against the end of the Dining-room, which in one year more will be at their full length, & may be reduced to a single stem.

The vines against the yard abound in young wood of a vast length, & will have fresh Horizontals every where, without bending back any shoots.

18. Planted in between the rows of Crocuss round the dining-room 100 Scotch-Crocuss, & 50 double Snow-drops.

19. Planted the new bank with perennial sunflowers, rose-campions, tree-primeroses, & several sorts of Asters.

Planted a bed of tulips, Hyacinths, Ranunculus, Anemonies, in a plot well-mellowed with lime-rubbish. A tolerable dry season for four or five days, after a glut of rain for many weeks. Dug the walks at the top & bottom of the new garden in order to prepare ym: for leveling.

Novr 22. Dug-up the double white rock:
-ets under the back of the melon-screen, & plant:
-d them on the end of the bank next the dining:
-room: planted with them some double white
Campanulas. Planted 20 double daffodils
near the other bulbs. Laid a shoot of the
moss-provence-rose, binding it round very
hard in two places with wire twisted ~~the~~
very tight, in order to make it take root.
25. New-planted a bason of red-martagons:
planted some Crown-Imperials, red Martagons
& Jonquils on the bank: planted the offset.
bulbs, & roots in a nursery bed.

Finished the vines.

Decem^r: 8. Sent 30 Coss-lettuces to M^r
Etty's little wall'd Garden to winter.
16. Brewed half Hogsh: of milder strong-beer
with only five bush: of malt, & two p^{ds} & half
of Hops: made at the same time half hogsh: &
12 gallons of small beer.
17. Trimm'd & tack'd the fig-tree, which is full
of young wood; & laid a long tender shoot from
the stool to the Corner of the House to supply

18. that part of the tree with fresh wood.

Very mild growing weather yet for the time of Year.

Decem^r. 19. Made half Hogsh: of raisin-wine with one Hund: of Smyrnas, & half Hund: of Malagas; & put to them 13 buckets of water, each bucket containing three Gallons.

31. The Year went-out, as it had continued ever since winter began, in a very mild way. There have been scarce more than two smart night's frost, & those early in Autumn: so that the Grass in pastures has kept springing the whole season; & the early, & hardy flowers, & plants are very forward. There has been a pretty deal of gentle rain; & now & then soft sunny days like April, which brought the flies, & other Insects out of their lurking holes.

Garden Kalendar
for 1761.

Jan: 1. Transplanted a polyanth-Nar:
cissus, many of whose Cups were in bloom,
into a large pot to set within doors.
2. Finish'd a new wicker melon-screen, &
lin'd it well with straw, & made a border about
four feet broad under it, & dosed the earth
well with sand, & some ashes, & dung; intend:
ing to make it a border for early Crops, & to
plant some Espalier pears along it, & to run
a narrow brick-walk by the side of it.
3. Brought in two loads of hot dung for
the seedling-Cucumber-bed; & many loads
of stones for the Haha. The ground treads
sadly for want of frost.
Sowed a long row of persicaria-seed under ye
dining-room window. The wall-flowers begin
to blow. Put some Cucumber-seeds in a pot by

the parlour fire.

Jan: 5. Made the seedling Cucumber-bed. Warm foggy weather, with a very high Barometer.

6. Tunn'd the wine: there did not run out sufficient to fill the barrel by one bucket full which was squeesed out of the Chaff.

8. Earth'd the Cucumber bed with mellow, sanded mould. The bed in fine moderate order.

10. Sowed about 40 Cucumber-seeds. The bed promises well.

10. Put seven bottles of rasp: syrop to ye raisin-wine.

12. Tunn'd 8 gallons of good small raisin-wine in the vinegar-barrel. What vinegar is bottled, is very fine, & good.

14. Plenty of Cucumbers up in the Hot-bed; & in the pot by the fire side.

Planted a row of Laurel-cuttings in the field-garden.

Hot-bed goes on well: sunny weather for ye plants

15. Sowed a Crop of radishes, lettuce, & Carrots

n the sanded border under the melon-screen.
Transplanted some Cucumber-plants that
came up apace.
7. Smart frost; which enabled me to plough
he new garden after waiting the whole winter.
Put more Cucumber-seeds into the bed.
19. The frost continues: carted into the new
garden 20 loads of marl well dissolved; 7 loads
f lime-Rubbish, & soot from the Malt-house;
a load & half of ashes. The ground began
thaw towards noon, & was much trodden, &
readed before the Job was done. Put the
bbish & ashes on the two lower Quarters,
the marl on the four upper ones.
4. Long the mason finish'd the dry wall of the
aha in the new garden, which is built of blue
ags, so massy, that it is supposed to contain
ouble the Quantity of stone usual in such
valls. Several stones reach into the bank 20
nches. The wall was intended to be 4 feet & an
alf high: but the labourers in sinking the ditch
n inclining ground mistook the level, especially

about the angle: so that at that part to bring it to a level it is 5 feet 8 inch: high, & 4 feet 6 inch: at the ends: an excellent fence against the mead, & so well fast'ned into the clay bank, that it looks likely to stand a long while. The workman-ship, exclusive of carting the stone cost £ s d 1:8:10.

Jan: 24. Cucumbers thrive well, & shew a rough leaf. Misty, still weather with an high Barometer. John finish'd Mr Etty's wall-trees in 4 Jobs.

26. Sowed about 14 Succado-melon-seeds to plant an early melon-frame, if they succeed.

Cucumbers look finely; & begin to shew a second rough leaf.

Sloped, & finish'd off the ditch of the terrass, & levell'd most of the terrass.

Spread the marle, & rubbish on the new garden; there is a good Coat of each.

Smart frosts for three or four days.

29. Frost continues very smart. Finished cutting all the Alleys thro' the new Garden; & levelled all the terrass ~~are~~ as far as it can be, 'till it settles. Cleared away the roots of trees in the meadow.

0. Frost smarter than ever. Wheeled the
dung that was left after paying the farmers
ut of the melon-ground. Trench'd a well-dung'd
lot above the earth-house for melon-loam;
burned some old melon-loam.
The heat in the Cucumber-bed declining, order'd
he bed to be lined with 15 barrows of very
ot-dung.
Beautiful rimes for several mornings on ye
Hanger. It froze within to night.
31. Carted in 10 loads of Hot-dung for the
earing Cucumber-bed.
Succado-melons begin to appear.
Dug out all the under-ground dung in ye melon-
Ground, & levell'd the Area.
Feb: 2. The over-fierce lining scalded all
he plants. Sowed more seeds.
. Potted the Succado-plants that were not
much damaged.
Very high barometer, & settled fine weather.
Sowed more Succado seeds.

~~6.~~ Feb: 5. Made the bearing Cucumber-bed with 10 loads of good dung: it is, I think, too deep; being four feet odd inch: behind, & 3 feet odd inch: before. The bed is made full ear[ly] as the plants are but just peeping out of [the] ground: but the dung being brought-in for the forward plants would not keep wi[th]:out making-up.

6. Planted seven rows, about 7/8 of a Gallon of Winsor-beans in one of the middle quarter[s] of my new Garden. This is the first crop in my new purchase, which ~~is~~ was in so wet a con:dition as only to be fit for beans.

7. Last sown Succados, & Cucumbers come-up-apa[ce]

9: 10. Levelled the terrass, & new walks so far that they will want but very small amendment before they are turfed. Fierce March-like winds from the west for many days, that ~~h~~ had quite dry'd the Ground.

12. The wind turning suddenly to the north, last night was the fiercest frost this winter. Dug one of the lower new Quarters, which came up pretty well. Snowed hard all the

Afternoon, & rain'd at night.
Feb: 16. Put the mould on the Cucumber-bed, which seems now to be pretty mild.
Continual showers.
The first Succados have a perfect rough leaf.
The second sowing are potted, & look pretty well.
19. Planted out the Cucumbers in their bearing beds, five plants in an Hill: each plant has a fair rough leaf. The bed seems very mild.
Heavy showers.
23. Sowed a dung-cart, & an half of ashes in the great mead. There was a very strong wind while they were sowing, which seem'd to carry away a great deal into the Air.
Sowed more Succados for fear of accidents; & some small early Cucumber-seed.
24. Made a seedling Celeri-bed with one barrow of dung, & covered it with an hand glass.
25: 26. Clear'd the meadow of faggots, & wood; & levell'd the Ground, where the hedge was grubbed.
March 2. Sowed 12 Waverley-Cantaleupe-seeds in one of the bearing Cucumber-frames.

~~8.~~ March 4. Carted into the melon-ground ten loads of hot dung for the Succado-fram

The Cucumbers thrive surprizingly, & have three Joints each. Earthed-up the hill a little to day. The bed maintains a fine gentle, genial heat. The Succado melons thrive; & the forwardest begin to shew a Joi

Continual stormy weather from ye west with small rain.

7. The Cantaleupes come up well; every seed.

9: 10. Long finish'd the brick-walk along by th melon-screen; & Tull sowed the border with rad-:es, lettuce, & Carrots. Long made a large stone-drein also at the bottom of the new-gar across the walk into Dassam's ditch: it is so placed that in great floods the waters from every alley must run with a swift descent towards it.

10. Cucumber-plants thrive wonderfully, & begin to throw-out wires. Some have five Joints, & are stopp'd-down for runners. Stopp'd some of the forward Succades in pots.

10. Sowed five more Waverley Cantaleupe seeds to supply in Case of accident. ~~9.~~ 114

Planted about 200 Cabbage-plants in part of one of the middle new-quarters.

An other levelling Job at the terrass.

Frequent showers.

11. Made the Succado-melon-bed with ten loads of dung for ~~a~~ one three light frame. The bed is very stout; full four feet deep behind, & near three before. The frame & bed are more than six feet high.

Planted some double bloody-wallflowers, from last year's Cuttings, in the border of the melon-screen.

Planted the 12 Cantaleupe-plants in six pots.

Frequent showers.

13. One of the plants that was ~~####~~ stopp'd down shows a Cucumber at the foot of a runner. The sun in a few minutes scalded part of a leaf that touch'd the Glass.

14. Mowed the Grass-plot the first time: there was a vast deal of Grass, which lined the Cucumber-bed.

~~10.~~ March 14. Planted the following fruit-tree
sent me by Murdoch Middleton: on the north
side of the first lower quarter of my new Gar
:den one Crasan-Burgamot pear; on the
South side one Swan-egg Do: on the north
side of the second lower Quarter one Vir:
:goleuse-pear; on the south side one Doyenn
at the two middle ends of the same Quarters
two Green-gage plums: & in the border of
the melon-ground one Colmar-pear. All
these trees are espaliers, & in good Condi:
:tion, except the Doyenne-pear, which has
a miserable tap-root with hardly any
fibres. Some of the pears shew a little
tendency to canker. Put a large quantity
of stones, & rubbish at the bottom of every
bason, & planted as high as possible.
Proved bad, & are changed.
Sowed a Crop of Carrots, parsneps, Coss-lettuce,
Onions, radishes, & spinage, in the first lower
Quarter of the new Garden; which raked, &
crumbled in pretty good order.
16: 17: 18. Finished leveling the terrass, & new walks,
& dug the new borders, & Quarters. Fine

still, settled weather, with a rising Barometer, & wind to the East, & North.

The stopp'd Cucumbers have side-shoots with three Joints.

The five Cantalupe-seeds all up.

March 18. Sowed a gallon of dwarf marrowfat pease in one of the middle Quarters: they made just 9 rows at four feet apart, & exactly fill'd the quarter. The mould was hardly mellow enough to drill them; & they were covered in with difficulty.

19. Dug the border at the back of the melon-screen, & planted a row of Holy oaks at five feet apart.

20. Earth'd-down the succade-bed; & put the hills into each light. Raised the Cucumber-frames. The plants are very large, & have rast leaves.

21. Sowed six large basons in the field with double upright lark-spurs.

The sun at a few minutes neglect scorches the Cucumber leaves.

~~Ap.~~ 23. Turned the Succades out into their bed, which seems very mild. The best plants are forward, & show runners. Planted beside one or two very stocky plants in each hill, which never have been potted.

Cleared the Cucumber-bed of all pots; rais'd the frames, stopp'd the plants, & earth'd the bed out to the frames.

Fine sunny weather.

Four pots of succades left.

The Cantaleupes are very strong in their pots, & show a rough leaf.

Strong'd & raked the Asparagus-beds.

Watered the Cucumbers over ye leaves the first time.

25. Finish'd turfing the terrass, & new walks, which took-up 8 loads, & an half of turf, being each twelve feet wide; beside the slope of the terrass. Hot, dry, sunny weather, which makes the turf stare, & chop.

First cucumber blowed before any male bloom.

Transplanted out forward lettuce from ye wall.

Dress'd Rasps.

March 25. The Succade-bed was beginning to ~~[illegible]~~ burn it's mould a little: put some fresh mould round the bottom of the hills.

26. Cast 18 loads of dung for the Canta-leupe-bed.

Planted some Catchflies on the end of the bank next the house.

Planted four rows of fine large potatoes cut to pieces: each row ~~[illegible]~~ three feet apart; & each piece one foot.

30. Grafted the tall peaked pear-tree in the orchard with Doyenne-Grafts; & the standard pear in the new Garden with Crasan, & Chau-montelle Grafts. The Cions came from Ringmer; & the two latter sorts were canker'd & bad. Put an handful of salt in the loam. Hot sunshine with a drying east wind.

Cut vent-holes in the front of the succade-bed to prevent burning.

31. Planted some wild, & Garden Lathyruss in the bank at the back of the melon-screen between each two Holyoaks: they were two

years old in the seedling-bed, & had long tap-roots between 2 & 3 feet long running into the carrion. The seed of the wild La:thyrus was gathered from a plant observed by my Bro: Tom to flourish most beautiful:ly in the midst of a bush in the short Lythe.

April 1. The Succade-bed continuing too hot, I ordered a pole to be thrust quite thro' the bed under each hill, so that one might see thro: One hill being more furious than the rest I had the plants (top of hill & all) taken-off in a shovel, & the hill new: made-up with cold earth. The plants grow, & are not yet injured.

1. Grafted-in two cuttings of Mr: Middleton's espalier-Crasane, instead of the Ringmer ones, which were canker'd, & bad: left one Ringmer one.

Planted 6 basons of double larkspurs in the new-garden borders.

2. Sowed in the seed-bed in the melon-ground Battersea Cabbage-seed, Savoys, borecole, leeks,

Holyoaks, stocks, carnations, & sweet
illiams. Bright sunshine, with an
ast-wind, & very high barometer. The
round is bound like a stone.
Hoed, pronged, & cleans'd all the home garden,
& borders, during this parching season.
p: 3. Planted a Garden Lathyrus on the
ew bank between every two asters, & p: sunflowers.
Stopped up the vent-holes in front of the
uccade-bed; left them open behind. Most of
he plants look well.
owed a great Quantity of Cucumber-seeds
or the neighbours.
4. Sowed tree-prime-roses, beet, & some seeds
f a red Cowslip in a pot.
Sunny, burning weather.
Dress'd artichokes: in that hot weather
he beginning of December they sprouted thro'
heir ridges, & continued growing very much
he winter thro'; & have now vast greens.
Hoed & cleansed the grubb'd ground in
he meadow.

16. April 6. Made the Cantaleupe-bed for
two three-light frames with 18 loads of dun
It is about 14 Inches wider behind than ye
Succade-bed, & about three feet deep.
7. Turn'd out a fine pot of Succades into a
hill joining to a former. The succades were
in great danger of being burnt by the hot
weather's setting the bed in a rage again: but
by cutting & boring vents, & frequent openi
the hills all seems now to be safe. These pla
have long runners that have been stopp'd ag
8. The Cantaleupe-bed is in a great fury, &
comes very early to it's heat. Frequent still
fine showers after near a month's dry weathe
Cucumbers blow a great pace.
Made the annual bed with 7 barrows of dung
for the biggest one-light frame.
9. Sowed one of the upper quarters of the new gar
:den with 3 quarts of marrow-fat dwarf pease,
which made eleven rows at 3 feet apart, &
just fill'd the ground. The ground, which has
laid rough all the late dry scorching weather
being slack'd with the rain, raked, & fell to pieces in

very good order; the marl seeming to do a
great deal of good.

Apr: 11. Put a finishing hand to the new Garden by cutting the edges of the turf round the
water-tables, & terrass, & mending any patch
of turf that was wanting.

Planted 24 cuttings of the fine bloody-
wall-flower. Those planted the beginning of
last June, came to little.

Sowed the annual-bed with dwarf sunflowers,
marvel of Peru, Pasoms, China Aster purple
& white, Fr: & Afr: marrigolds, Pendulous
Amaranths, & Convolvulus minor. Sowed
some China pinks, Convol: minor, & dwarf
sunflowers in the cold Ground.

15. Planted a row of Laurels of 25 pr. Hund:
from the filberts against Parsons's down by the
wood-hedge to the new part of the Garden; with
a Laurustine between every two Laurels.

Fine gentle rain for 12 or 14 Hours.

Planted some laurels at the lower end of
the new bank. The fine rains make the
new turf take kindly to the ground, & close up
it's Joints.

18. April 17. Planted half hundred more cab:bage plants; & some forward coss lettuces from under the melon screen.

Sowed the part of the meadow where ye hedge was grubb'd, & the Haha with rye-grass: some white Clover in the Haha.

18. Made a low circular mount round the great oak in the mead, & Turfed it.

Earthed-down the Cantaleupe-bed, & hill'd the lights: found the bed very hot still.

Sowed more China-asters on the end of the Cantaleupe-bed. Perfect summer.

16. Measured my new-purchased piece of Garden which contained forty two rods of Ground; & the old part fifty six: in all half an acre, & ~~sixteen~~ eighteen rods.

18. Planted some cuttings of the black Cluster, & Muscadine Grapes.

20. Made a frame, or cradle for annuals of rods & pease-haulm about four feet wide, & eight feet long; & put into it about 16 barrows of dung, & grass-mowings.

Dung borrowed 1760.

Jan 10. Of Berriman pd 2 loads.
Feb: 8. Of Berriman pd 2 loads.
Of Kelsey pd 2 loads.
Kelsey carried out for us 2.

Feb: 15. Of Parsons pd 2 loads.
March 16: Of Parsons pd 5 loads.
Of Berriman pd 6 loads.
Of Kelsey pd 7 loads.
Kelsey carried out for us 2.

June 3. Of Kelsey pd 5 loads.
Of Berriman pd 3 loads.
Kelsey carried out for us 3.

Dung borrowed 1761.

Jan: 3. Of Kelsey dung pd car pd - 1 load.
He carried of ours 1 load. pd

31. Of Kelsey dung pd car pd ------ 6 loads.

Feb: 2. Of Parsons pd car: dung pd - 4 loads.

March 3. Of Parsons pd car dung pd. 5 loads.

4. Of Kelsey dung pd: car: pd - 4 loads.
carried 1 of mine. pd

March 26 Of Berriman pd car: 2 loads.
Of Parsons pd. car: dung pd 3 loads.
Of Kelsey dung pd Car: pd 10 loads.
carried out of mine 3. pd

1761. 1762.

Garden-Kalendar: for 1761.

April 20. Made a small hot-bed for the small one-light frame to raise white-cucumbers in.

Set-up the urns.

21. Turn'd-out six pots of Cantaleupes in the six hills: there were two plants in every pot except one. The plants are strong, & stocky; but seem to be somewhat injured by staying so long in the pots. The bed now seems safe from burning, having been made sixteen days.

Sowed some white-Dutch...Cucumbers in the one-light frame.

Cut the first Cucumber, which might have been cut some days before. More fruit were lost than usual: but now there are abundance set. The bees frequent the frames much.

Planted 12 cuttings more of the double wallflower.

4. April 28. Planted five rows of dwarf white french-beans pretty thin in one of the new Quarters: used just a pint of beans.

Finding some of the Cantaleupe-plants look a little amiss, I prick'd two seeds into each hill. Cutting N:E: Winds for many days.

Cucumbers sett at a vast rate: there are now about three brace fit to cut.

Sowed more white-Dutch-Cucumbers in the one-light frame: & a few large dark-green.

May 12. Fine rain after a long dry fit. Sowed a small crop of Roman-Broccoli. Cucumbers in vast abundance, & very large. The Succades offer fine fruit.

14. Hot summer weather: the Succades swell & seem several of them to be set.

Began building my fruit-wall.

15. Disbudded the vines for the first time: great quantities of fruit especially at the end of the dining-room. The figtree shows about 140 fruit.

Finish'd a forest-Chair on the bastion; & a plain seat under the great oak. Hot burning weather.

May 19. Vast rain with a very stormy wind, which hinders the masons in their wall-building; & damages the vines, shrubs, flowers, & trees of all sorts.

20. Made six holes for the large white Dutch Cucumbers, with one barrow of dung to each hole, & planted three plants under each hand-glass.

20. My Brother Tho: & I went down with a spade to examine into the nature of those animals that make that chearful shrill cry all the summer months of ~~May~~ in many parts of the south of England ~~the short Leythes~~. We found them to be of the Cricket-kind, with wings & ornamented Cases over them, like the House kind. But tho' they have long legs behind with large brawny thighs, like Grasshoppers, for leaping; it is remarkable that when they were dug out of their holes they shewed no manner of activity, but crawled along in a very shiftless manner, so as easily to be taken. We found it difficult not to squeese them to death in breaking the Ground: & out of one so bruised I took a multitude of eggs, which were long, of a yellow Colour, & covered with a very tough skin.

~~4.~~ It was ~~We~~ easily ~~easily~~ to discovered ~~distinguished~~ the male from the female; the former of which is of a black shining Colour, with a golden stripe across it's shoulders something like that of the Humble-bee: the latter was ~~of a~~ more dusky, ~~[illegible]~~ & distinguished by a long terebra at it's tail, which probably may be the instrument with which it may deposit it's eggs in Crannies, & safe receptacles. It is very likely that the males only make that shrilling noise; which they may do out of rivalry, & emulation during their breeding time; as is the Case with many animals. They are solitary ~~animals~~ Insects living singly in Holes by themselves; & will fight fiercely when they meet, as I found by some which I put into an hole in a dry wall, where I should be glad to have them encrease on account of their pleasing summer sound. For tho' they had express'd distress by being taken out of their knowledge; yet the first that had got possession of the chink seized an other with a vast pair of serrated fangs so as to make it cry out. With these strong tooth'd Malae (like the sheers of lobster's claws) they must terebrate their curious regular Holes; as they have no

eet suited for digging like the mole-cricket.
I could but wonder, that when taken in hand,
hey never offer'd to bite, tho' furnish'd with
uch formidable weapons. They are remark=
bly shy, & cautious, never stirring but a
ew inches from ye mouth of their holes, & retir=
ng backward nimbly into them, & stopping short in
heir song by that time you come within sever=
l yards of yr caverns ~~most~~: from whence I conclude
hey may be a very desirable food to some
nimals, perhaps several kinds of birds.
They cry all night as well as day during part ~~the~~
the month of May, June, & July in fine weather; & may in the
till part of the night be heard to a consider=
ble distance; abounding most in sand-banks
n the sides of heaths, especially in Surrey,
& Sussex: but these that I caught were in
 steep, rocky pasture-field facing to the
fternoon sun.

21. Frequent showers, & a strong wind.
Sowed a Crop of large white French-beans.

22. There are about 12 brace of Succade=
melons set; the largest of which are about the
size of a pullet's egg: & two Cantaleupes, which
seem to be secure.

6. May 27: 28: 29. Vast rains, with black, cold weather for many days.

June 1. Went thro' with tacking the vines for the first time.

Cold black weather still, with a norther:ly wind, very unkind for all vegetation.

3. Great rain

4. Planted out & hand-glasses of the large green Cucumbers; & a large plot of Savoys, & late-raised Cabbages.

8. Cold black weather, which makes the Cucum:bers pale, & ill-flavoured; & hurts the melons.

Drew first Carrots under the melon-screen.

The Rooks are perchers: there are but two; & one of the old ones was some how destroyed as soon as they were hatched.

9. Sowed the first Crop of endive.

17. Great rain: rak'd-down, & planted the winding-border over-against the fruit-wall, with tall annuals behind, & a row of China-asters before.

Cut-off a large Succade fruit that was rotted at a joint just by the stem of the fruit. It had firm seeds in it, & would have soon been ripe.

June 19. Limed the vine-borders round the house. Black weather without a gleam of sunshine for many days. Prick'd-out more Celeri. Planted more Savoys.

21. Discovered a curious Orchis in the hollow shady part of Newton-lane, just beyond the Cross. It is the Orchis alba bifolia minor, Calcari oblongo; grew with a very long stem; & has been in flower some weeks. I brought away the flower, & mark'd the root, intending to transplant it into the Garden, when the leaves are wither'd.

22. Hot summer weather. Cut my Clover-hay. Cut the first Succado.

Hot burning weather, which grew more & more vehement 'till the 25; & then a great deal of thunder, & lightning all night.

23. Cut a brace more Succades.

25. Cut another Succade.

The annuals are sadly scorch'd by the heat. The Succades, considering the long shady season they grew-in, & the early season of ripening, are good, & well-flavoured.

~~8.~~ June 25. Put-up two loads of Clover-hay on the rick, & covered it well with straw.
26. The vines begin to blow very fast.
July 4. Rick'd-up the meadow-hay in good order.
6. Planted-out leeks, savoys, & two plots of endive.
10. Most of the Succades being cut, I ordered the plants to be watered in order to try for a second Crop. The finest Succades weigh'd about 20 ounces, & were very good.
There are two Cantaleupes only which are just near cutting: the rest are only now set:ting in great plenty.
Cut the first white-Cucumber.
Took-in the Cucumber-frames. The early Cu:cumbers are now ~~in~~ full of fruit.
Saved seed from two fine Succades.
Perfect fine summer-weather.
The Succades have some second fruit in bloom.
12. Cut the first Cantaleupe: it was a fair, well-emboss'd fruit, & weigh'd one ounce short of two pounds; but was pale-flesh'd, & not in so fine perfection as the best Succades.
16. Cut the second Cantaleupe, a small one.

July 16. Trench'd three rows of Celeri.
Raised the melon-frames to give the roots a little
room. There are plenty of Cantaleupes; & a
good second Crop of Succades.
Large white Cucumbers in great plenty; &
plenty still on the old forward bed. Stewed
20 for dinner.
The Succades have some second fruit
as big as hens eggs.
25. Finish'd my fruit-wall, coping the two
returns at the ends with stones of a sandy
nature out of the old priory. The coping-
bricks were full of flaws, & cracks, being
made of earth not well prepared, & instead of
over-hanging the wall, came but just flush
with it: however, by using six that were broken
ended, we had just enough, & they may lie
on the wall many years.
Began delving the fruit-border which
was trod very hard.
Finish'd peat-cart; the spits were in excellent order: housed four loads; & brought in
all my wood: & two loads of sand; one for the
fruit-border, & one for the hot-bed earth.

July 25. Hot, ripening weather for a long time.

Inoculated five budds of the double Haw=thorn on a common one: the budds were poor coming from a sickly tree, & did not part well from their wood.

27. Look'd over the melons, that were run pretty wild. There are about ten brace of well-grown Cantaleupes; & not more than two brace of second Succades; their haulm being damaged by over dryness.

Sprinkled all the plants within, & watered the boxes round; as the mould is uncommon=ly dry, & burnt, & the weather very scorching.

Large white Cucumbers bear vastly.

30. Dress'd the fruit-border the second time with lime, & sand.

Trench'd the next year's melon-earth, & dress'd it with a good coat of lime.

The earth very dry, & parch'd.

Aug: 28. On my return from Ringmer after three weeks & four days absence, I found Tull had cut nine brace of melons. The continual sunny weather had brought on the Cantaleupes before I expected them, & made them come al: :most all in a week. They were divided among our Neighbours, & were much commended.

I found the annuals very handsome & very strong; the Savoys strangely grown; & the Endives very large. Full had planted out rows of Sweet-Williams, & Stocks in my absence. The vines were grown very wild; & have no fruit yet turn'd in Colour, notwithstanding the heat of the summer. The best Canta: :leupes weigh'd about two pounds & an half.

Aug: 29. Cut a Cantaleupe, which prov'd a very fine one. Weigh'd the largest of the great white-seed Cucumbers: it's weight was three pounds & 14 ounces; & it measured 14 inch: & an half in length.

Full has dug the fruit-border twice, & levelled it: but there has not been rain enough yet to moisten the stubborn Clods, so as to make them fall well to pieces.

29. Sowed a small Crop of Coss-lettuce for plants to stand the winter.

Aug: 31. Pruned the vines, that were much over-run with shoots, for the last time. The Grapes just begin to turn Colour. Tyed-up about 20 endives, which run very large this Year. All the buds of the double Hawthorn seem to be dead.

Septem.r 2. Cut two Cantaleupes, very fine fruit. The Cantaleupes run to a fair size, notwithstand:ing the bed is very little wider than the frames. The Succades produced about 6 brace of good second-crop fruit, which ripen'd well, & are almost all cut.

4. Cut a fine Cantaleupe; the last of any size or value. It prov'd a very curious one.

Mark'd the best, & most double annuals for seed.

5. Dug the fruit-border the fourth time after a great rain: it fell well to pieces, & seems to be well-mellow'd with sand & lime: 'till this rain it lay in great Clods as hard as stones, being so much trod by the masons, & harden'd by a hot, sunny Summer. It has three coats of good mould on it, & must be

full two feet deep in good soil.

Septr: 8. Earth'd-up the Celeri for the first time. Cut the two last Succades: good siz'd fruit. Cut in the whole about 30 brace of melons of both sorts; many were very curi: fruit. It is to be observ'd that, as my frames are so wide, a crop of melons succeeds better when the bed is little broader than the boxes, than when the bed has been lin'd-out, & earth'd down to the Ground. Because when the bed has been made so extensive in my strong soil the more delicate sorts of melons have collected more moisture than was proper, & have been liable to mouldy & rotten bines: but now with a narrow bed there has been no decay in the plants, notwithstanding there have been frequent great showers the summer thro'.

9. The grapes now turn a great pace.

12. Hous'd the lights, & took the melon-frames to pieces. Hot sunshine with cold dews.

18. Dug the ~~wall~~ fruit-border for the last time, & levell'd it for planting. It is in fine mellow

order, & falls very fine, having been dug five times; & dress'd with three Coats of sand, two of lime, & one of morter rubbish. It now lies up within four inches of the upper Joint of the stone-part of the wall.

Sad wet black weather for a long time; & some very heavy rains. The Grapes come on but poorly.

Septemr: 28. Planted Sweet-Williams, & pinks alternately on the new bank.

Earth'd up the Celeri the second time.

Fine settled weather after above a month's cold wet ~~[illegible]~~ season.

Some little Succades, secured under handglasses, still continue to ripen.

28. Made 18 quarts of elder-juice, & put to it 36 pounds of 4d sugar, which made 29 Quarts of Syrop. Mem: two gallons & half of pick'd berries, moderately squeesed, produced about a gallon of Juice.

Octob: 7. Planted out in a bed to blow 60 Carnation-plants, & 80 stocks: the best are to be removed into borders.

Octob: 14. Now the Grapes are good, not: withstanding the vast continual rains.
The drein that goes from the bottom of the new: garden under the walk, & fruit-wall runs apace.
21. Dry, fine weather.
Planted 130 of Cabbages in the new Gar: den at two feet apart to stand ye winter.
22. A very white-frost with thick ice.
24. The ground being very dry I planted my bulbs; a row of Hyacinths above 60, & a few Tulips, & polyanth-Narcissuss on the edge of the fruit border: a row of tulips, & polyanth-Narcissuss, Cornflags, & Jonquils next Parsons's: & two rows of Crocuss under the buttery-window. Planted a large bed of Nursery-ofset-bulbs in a bed by themselves.
Planted-out against Parsons's, & under ye Buttery-window several of my fine bloody-double-wallflowers. Just before I finish'd came a vast rain.
Nov: 2: 3. Planted two standard-golden-pippens in the old orchard; & 12 small

~~16.~~ crab-~~grafts~~ stocks in the nursery. Took-up & removed the things in the nursery, & planted them in regular lines three feet apart. Dug-up & planted 6 pear-suckers for stocks.

Sanded, dung'd & trench'd the next year's melon-earth a second time; it was dress'd once with sand & lime, & falls now very mellow.

Dry, soft, delicate weather. Grapes continue very good still.

5. Planted four rasp-plants from Chidbury-hill Wilts at the nearest end of the rasp-border & several slips of pyram: Campanulas in a Nursery-bed.

7. Planted one Quart, three rows, of small early beans in a Quarter of the new Garden

A smart frost with Ice.

Dress'd the basons for the espalier-pears with mortar-rubbish; & laid some rubbish at the bottom of every bason.

13. Planted a quart more of early beans.

Decemr: 15. Brewed half Hogsh: of moderate strong ~~beer~~ beer with 5 bush: of Rich: Knight's malt, & two pd: & half of hops. What was brew'd in the same barrel last Decr: was excellent.

Decemr: 17. Made half hogsh: of raisin-
-wine with hundred of Smyrnas, & half
hundred of Malagas: & put to them 13 buck-
-ets of water, each bucket containing 3 Gal:

22. Wheel'd-in 20 wheel-barrows of hot dung
to cast ready for a seedling-Cucumber-bed.

Vast quantities of rain have fallen the
autumn & winter thro': & as yet there have
been but a very few days of hard frost.

23: 24. Vast rains, & floods.

26. Made an hot-bed for the biggest one-
-light frame, with the 20 barrows of dung.

Planted a Dutch-medlar, & a Service
in the old orchard; & a mountain-ash
in one of the basons in the field.

Vast rains.

30. The bed not coming to it's heat from the vast
wetness of the Dung, I order'd in a load from
Kelsey's; which with 10 barrows of my own made a new one.

By the negligence of Murdoch Middleton my
wall-trees never came 'till the 26: they are in
general good trees, & were planted (consider-
-ing the wetness of the season) in good ~~order~~ condition; &
in the following order, beginning from the terrass:

Breda-Apricot; ~~Red Hamburg vine~~ Sweet-water vine; Roman Nectar.
- - - - Mr. Snooke's black-cluster vine; Roman Nect:
- - - white Muscadine vine; Newington Nectar:

Decem:r 30. Planted two Cistus's in ~~my own~~ Mr Etty's dry garden; & a Phlomis, & an Halimus in my own. Planted some cuttings of the American black Poplar, & the Groundsel-tree in the Nursery.

Garden-Kalendar
for 1762.

Jan: 1. Put about 20 Cucumber-seeds into the Hot-bed before it was come to it's heat: it has been made only two days.
4. The bed comes to a bold heat. Exceeding wet weather; & the ground full of water. There has been no settled dry weather since the end of August.
5. Tunn'd the Half Hogsh: of raisin wine: there were about 3 gallons too much without any squeezing. Coloured it with 17 pints of Elder Syrop. The wine tastes very sweet. Added two more pints.

Mur: Middleton's Sweet-water vine; Noblesse peach;
Mr Sn: ~~[illegible]~~ White Muscadine vine; Noblesse peach: John Hale's
& Passion flowers, one at each end of the wall.

Jan: 5. Cucumber-plants begin to appear: the bed is very warm.
11. 12. A violent storm with vast rains, & floods.
14. The bed, when covered much from the great rains, too hot still. Obliged to keep the light tilted a nights. The plants a little da:maged by the steam, & heat. Continue to sow more seeds.
14. Bottled out the barrel of vinegar, which was very fine, & extreamly keen; & put-in 8 gall: more of strong small-wine.
20. Cucumber-plants have a rough leaf. Shut the light down quite close to night for the first time. The mercury mounts very high.
26. Brought in ten loads of hot dung for the bearing Cucumber-bed. Bright sunny weather & dry pleasant frosts for many days. Trench'd my flower-bank, & some of the Kitchen-ground.

~~20.~~

Feb: 1. Sowed 8 Succade-seeds.
The Cucumber-plants look finely.
Frequent rains with a very high Barome:
:tre; & the Country in an unusual wet con:
:dition. The cast dung heats furiously.
5. Cold, dry, March-like weather for a few
days, with a very high barometer. The
ground being a little dry for the first time
since last August, I sowed a small Crop
of Coss lettuce, Carrots, & radishes in the
upper part of the melon-screen border, which
was but in very poor cold Condition, not:
:withstanding the quantity of ashes, & sand
that have been put on it. As to the lower
part, the water appeared in the Clods while
it was digging-up rough.
7. A strong N: W: wind all night, which
occasioned much the fiercest frost that has
been this year, with ice full an Inch thick.
The paths are now dry, & white.
Lin'd the seedling Cucumber-bed (which
begins to abate of it's heat) with seven bar:
:rows of dung. The plants look well, & show
a joint.

Still'd & earth'd down the bearing-bed; &
as it comes but feebly to it's heat lin'd it
round with pease-haulm. High barometer,
& a strong freezing wind.
A good part of my new garden has been dug
since these dry days: the marl has done
great good in the Quarters, & makes
them crumble well. Dung'd the flower-
bank well, & the opposite border. Covered
the roots of the new-planted trees with straw.

Feb: 10. A violent fierce frost.

11. Finding the fruiting-bed by great covering-
up was much improoved in heat, I planted the
hills with seven or 8 of my best plants each.
The plants have a large rough leaf, & some
of them a joint; but have stay'd full as long
in the seed-bed as will do them any good.
The new bed is at present warm enough; but
the danger is whether such moderate heat
will continue long enough to set the fruit
well; & 'till the sun gets strong enough to
make the fruit grow. There are many fine
plants left in the seedling-bed.

12. Sowed 14 Succade-seeds in the fruiting-frames;
those that were sown in the seed-bed included, which

never vegetated.

Strange sudden alterations from fierce frosts to heavy rains, & so back again.

Feb: 15. The bed seems to be come to a good heat. Succades begin to appear.

18. The bed advances in heat, & rather draws the plants. Potted the Succades.

Nasty, wet, blowing weather.

19. Sow'd 10 more Succade seeds.

Sow'd a box of Polyanth seed.

The sun, which quite forsakes the upper walk of the new garden about the end of Octob:r begins now to shine full along it about half an hour before it sets. The Hepaticas, Crocuss, snow:drops & double daisies begin now to make a very agreeable appearance as the first promise of spring. Warm moist weather, which makes the grass spring sensibly.

A shoot of a white vine, which I lately short'ned, bleeds pretty much.

The ground has never this winter been once covered with snow.

20. Made an hot-bed in the rod-frame with 16 barrows of dung; &, after covering it pretty thick with mellow mould, sowed it with radishes.

Feb: 20. Sowed two basons of Persicarias in the border against Parsons's.

21. A most violent N: E: wind all the evening, & all the first part of the night, with a small, dry, drifting sort of snow, which drove thro' the tiles, & every cranny in a most extraor:dinary manner. The ground is but just covered except in drifted places. A very hard frost in the morning. Many people froze to death.

24. Severe frost with heaps of drifted snow on the Ground. A high barometer.

The Cucumber-bed steams very much; & it has been so very cold lately, that there has been very few opportunities of giving the plants sufficient air. The plants look the worse for their Confinement.

25. Finding the bed full hot, I pull'd off the pease-haulm-lining at the back.

Sowed the Clover in Baker's hill all over with two dung-carts of Ashes.

27. Sowed 8 basons of double upright-larkspurs along the border of the Garden-door walk, & in the border between the Cherry-trees.

Cold black weather: the snow has now laid a week in shady places.

The forward Cucumbers look very poorly.

~~24~~ March 1. Fierce frosts a nights, & strong cutting winds a days with storms of snow.

Murdoch Middleton's pear-trees of last year prooving canker'd, & distemper'd, he changed them; & I added some more sorts. They stand now as follows in the new Gar:den, beginning from the first quarters on the side next the wall, then going down the middle quarters; & then by the side of the terrass.

N: Side of the Quarters next the wall:
Chaumontelle, & Virgoleuse:
S: side of D^o: Crasane, & Doyenne:
The middle quarters:
St Germain, Brown Bury, Doyenne:
Up the side of the terrasse:
Autumn Burgamot; & Swan's egg.
There are also at the inner ends of the wall-quarters two Green-gage plums:
One Crasane-pear in the border of the walk facing the Garden-door: & one le Royal, & one Queen-Claudia plum in the melon-screen border.

March: 2. Planted a plot in Turner's with five rows, three pints & half of early pease at four feet apart. 133
Very strong frost with thick ice: freezing air all day with flights of snow.
6. This is now the 14 day since the snow fell; & it lies in great Heaps still under the Hedges. There have been every day since cold cutting winds with a dark cloudy skie, & strong frosts every night.
The want of sun, & freezing air make the Cucumber-plants look very poorly, & quite stop their Growth.
Sowed a Gallon, 11 rows of dwarf-marrowfats, which at 3 feet & half a part just fill'd a quarter.
Sowed two ounces of spinage.
The dug-ground is quite dusty.
10. Pull'd up the forward Cucumbers, which have never thrived since the fierce weather began; & planted some from ye seedling-bed which are better.
Sowed a Celeri-bed with seed from London, & some seed of a jagged-leaved sort from Mr Missing.
Planted some Spanish-Chestnuts from Mr Roman, & some variegated Sycomore-keys from bro: Tom.
Sowed a bed of Leeks. This is the 18th day of the frosty weather: very thick ice last night; & the snow still lies in cold-shady places. A freezing wind.

Dung borrowed for 1762.

	Of Kelsey - Dung pd. - Car: pd. - - - -	1 loads.
Jan: 26:	of Kelsey - D: pd. - Car pd. - - -	7 loads.
	Car: 3 of my own.	
March 15.	Kelsey - Dung pd. - car: pd. - - -	5 loads.
- - -	Parsons Dung pd. - Car pd. - - -	5 loads.
April 8.	Kelsey - Dung pd. - Car: pd.	8 loads.
10.	Parsons - Dung pd. - Car: pd. -	9 loads.

Garden-Kalendar.
1768.

March 11. This the 19 & last day of the fierce weather.

13. Cut down all the wall trees, & all the espalier pears. The two peaches seem unsound at the pith; all the rest are healthy trees.

Widened the walk down Baker's-hill, & turfed it. Planted several sorts of Asters in the new garden.

Soft spring-like weather for the first time.

15. Carryed in ten loads of Hot dung for the Succade-bed.

26. Sowed Holy-oaks, sunflowers, Cullumbines, China asters, & savoys.

27. Planted four rows of Potatoes; pieces from fine large roots.

April 6. Sowed a bed of onions.

7. Planted the succade: bed, that has been now made a fortnight, with some good potted plants, & some plants raised in the bed. The

bed is full hot. Sowed the first Cantaleupe

Sowed three rows of broad-beans.

Apr: 7. The forwardest Cucumber about as big as the top of one's finger. The plants now grow away. Fine summer weather.

Planted holy-oaks, asters, & peren: sunflowers up the garden-hedge in Baker's hill.

8. Sowed five rows of marrow-fat pease.

9:10. Brought in 17 loads of hot dung for the Cantaleupe-bed.

Sowed some white Broccoli-seed from Bp's Waltham.

The Succade-bed is very hot; but the plants by being tilted a nights, & shaded a days look very well, & have runners.

12. Sowed the Cantaleupe-seeds, & some Succade

16. Sowed some common Cabbage-seed, & some Roman Broccoli.

Made one hand-glass-bed to raise the large white Cucumbers.

Made the Annual-bed.

Potted the Cantaleupes.

17. Sowed the annuals.

19. Made the Cantaleupe-bed with 17 loads
of dung: it is of a very proper thickness.
20. Dress'd the Artichokes.
24. Earth'd the Cantaleupe-bed, & hill'd it.
made six hand-glass beds, with one barrow
of dung to each, for the large white Cucumbers, & planted them.

The fruit-wall & espalier-trees are
all alive, & begin to shoot.
26. Cut the first Cucumber. There are
plenty coming on.

Fine hot summer weather for these
twelve days past, which has brought every
thing on in a wonderful manner.
27. Planted the Cantaleupe-bed, the two first
Hills with Waverley plants, & the rest with
plants from my own seed; all save the last
Hill, which is planted with Succades to keep
up a Succession. The plants are beautiful
& thriving beyond Common; but the bed
is very hot & wants watching.
Very hot weather with the appearance
of thunder.

April 27. The first Succades fill the hills ~~with all~~ their fibres, & have runners with several joints:

The fruit-trees against the wall push apace. I disbudded them to day. The vine also are all alive.

May 3. Sowed 6 rows of white Dwarf-french beans. The seed looks but poorly.

8. The Succades begin to shew fruit.

Hot sunshine with very cold winds.

11. The Succades have male bloom full blown

17. The Succades have now fruit in bloom

22. Some Succades seem to be set.

Brought some Geraniums, & a Sedum fro. Bp's Waltham.

Shady moist weather: prick'd out plenty of Savoys, ~~&~~ Celery, & Celeriac.

25. Tack'd the vines, & disbudded them for ye first time: the appearance of an abundance of fruit. Hot sunny weather for many days.

June 4. Vehement hot dry weather for many days (a fortnight past) so that the fields &

Gardens begin to suffer greatly. The early
Cucumbers hardly bear at all tho' constantly 136
water'd: & the melons swell very slowly.
Turn'd out the white Cucumbers from
under the Glasses.
June 8. This long hot sunny season has
forced some of the vines into bloom. They
did not blow last year till about the 26.
Cut my Clover-hay.
The forwardest Succades nearly full grown:
the Cantaleupes have abundance of fruit
in full bloom, but hardly any male bloom.
A long dry hot season: the Corn begins
to suffer.
16. Cut first white Cucumbers from
the hand-glasses. Hot burning weather
still.
Began stopping down the vines.
They are all in full bloom.
The Cantaleupes begin to set.
17. This morning a valuable shower for an
Hour & half that made the Cartway run.
Cantaleupes & Succades now set at a vast
rate.

6. June 18. Sowed four rows of white dwarf french beans: soak'd the seed in water.
Sowed a small plot of Endive.
26. Dry & hot weather yet.
Some bunches of Grapes, that used in general to be only just in full bloom, now so forward, that they are grown pretty well to the third part of their full size.
An abundance of Cantaleupes set: the vines are in good health; & some fruit are the size of a large apple. The Succades have but a scanty first crop, which is near cutting: but promise well for a second.
We transplant the annuals only a few at a time as they can be watered. They are stocky in their nursery bed.
The fruit-trees against the wall, by being sprinkled over the leaves two or three times aweek during this burning season, have been kept in a constant growing state, & have not one curled leaf.

A fine shower on June 20.

28. A fine rain. Planted out some Savoys; & more annuals. The pine strawberries bear well.

30. Hot summer weather.

July 3. Cut first Succade.

5. Set out for Tidworth. During that week Tull cut 4 brace of Succades.

About the 10th Mr Carr began to cut his crop of Cantaleupes, which were extraordinary delicate, & of a good size.

On my return to Selborne the 24 I found 3 brace & an half of Succades cut, & ready to cut in the early box. The late & hill of Succades are not come; & the Cantaleupes are small & not very rough; but the vines look healthy. People are in the midst of wheat-harvest, & have cut some oats. Not the least rain since wednesday sevennight. The Country is burnt up in a most deplorable manner, beyond what any middle-aged person remembers; all the ponds & many wells are dry.

The grapes are uncommonly forward, & flourishing; & the vines have made vast shoots.

~~8.~~ July 28. Cut the first Cantaleupe at
six weeks from the setting: it was, I suppose
hurried by the vehement hot summer; but w
not very curious.

29. Cut second Cantaleupe.

Cut the first Succade of the Hill in one
of the Cantaleupe boxes; which came not
till after two Cantaleupes, tho' planted at
the same time. There usually is a fortnigh
difference in their ripening.

31. The Succades of the latter hill come apac
Those in the first box have been well watered
& shew a pretty good second Crop.

Vehement hot weather still.

August 3. Cut all the Succades of the farther
hill, which came a great pace this very
hot dry weather. Watered the hill well, to
try for a second Crop. They were excellent.

4: 6. Frequent showers with a strong wind tha
blew down many apples & pears. The first rain.

The rain improved Mr Etty's wallfruit visib
in a day or two.

Cut a large delicate Cantaleupe.

7. Planted out Savoys; & sowed half pd of spen

rge, & some radish-seed.
The ground is moisten'd in but a little way.
Aug: 4. Cut my field of oats.
10. A fine rain. Sowed a plot of ~~of~~ turnep-seed; & trench'd out the first Celeri, four rows in Turner's Garden.
12. A fine rain with some distant thunder.
The Grapes begin to turn Colour.
Planted in the new garden two trenches more of Celeri; & two of Mr Missing's parsley-leaved Celeriac. Mr Etty's Nectarines, & peaches begin to shew their fine ripening Colours.
13. Frequent heavy thundershowers with hot growing weather.
14. Hot moist weather. The Succades have plenty of new wood, & shew several brace of promising second-crop fruit.
The grass-walks have in ten days quite recovered their verdure, tho' they were so deplorably burnt.
Planted 12 stock-gilliflowers from Mr Etty.
Eat a very curious Cantaleupe: it weigh'd two pounds, & an half, & was very dry, & thick in flesh.

~~10~~. Aug: 16: Cut the last Cantaleupe: Many were very delicate, cracking both at Eye, & stem.

21. Planted three rows of Polyanths on the bank next the Alcove: planted two plots of backward Savoys.

Septem^r: 8. The wasps (which are without number this dry hot summer) attack the grapes in a grievous manner. Hung up 16 bottles with treacle, & beer, which make great havock among them. Bagged about fifty of the best bunches in Crape-bags. Some of the forward: :est bunches are very eatable, tho' not curi: :ously ripe. Mr Snooke's grapes were eat naked to the stones a fortnight ago, when they were quite green.

There are about 3 brace of second-crop Succades, which will come in good time if the weather proves good.

Frequent showers since the 4th of Aug: now a promise of dry weather. The fields abound with grass as if there had been no drought this summer.

Septemr. 18. Delicate Autumn weather for a fortnight. Began eating the grapes, which are good, but not curiously ripened yet.
By means of bottles & birdlime I have prevented innumerable swarms of wasps from doing the grapes any considerable damage. They are reduced now to a very moderate number; not more than appear in common years. Gather'd some nonpareils & golden rennets, which are very fair, & ready to be laid up, being a fortnight at least earlier than common.
Cut a decent second crop succade.
Walnuts & apples are innumerable this year; but there are no small nuts.

20. Tyed up a large parcel of endives: they are but small this year.

21. Cut a succade.

23: 24. Exceeding heavy rains with tempestuous winds, which blowed down an abundance of apples.
Gather'd in the Cadillac pears: near one third were blown down.
Cut up a very good flavoured Succade.

12.

Octob: 5. Trimm'd & tack'd the wall-fruit trees for the winter. They are all alive, & health[y]. Planted out some Coss-lettuce to stand the wint[er] under the fruit-walls.

13. Grapes very curious. The wasps begin to be very troublesome, so that we caught 200 of a day. Eat two very good Succades within these few days. Dry weather, with white frosts.

15. Supply'd the row of Hyacinths on the fruit-border with several double blue, & a few very double flat-blowing flowers.

Very dry seasonable weather.

16. Dug-up the Crown-imperials on the bank, & took-out a large basket-full of roots, & planted only two roots in each bason.

Grapes very curious.

17. First very great white frost.

23: 24: 25. Vast floods. Vast damage in many parts.

26. Plenty of Grapes, & very curious.

29. A flight of snow for a few hours.

Nov: 1. Grapes very fine.

3. Gathered the last Grapes, which were above thirty curious bunches, from the vine over y[e]

Entry door. 140

Planted four curious gooseberry-trees from Waltham, & two basons of ragwort from Fundington.

Nov: 11. Great snow.

Planted some very small Coss-lettuce against the fruit-wall.

Shut up the Alcove ~~room~~ with straw-doors for ye winter; & took in the urns.

13. Severe frost with very thick Ice.

Eat the last Grapes.

19. The frost still continues very fierce. Bearing Ice for many days. Uncommon early frost.

The fierce frost continued eleven nights.

24. Trimm'd & tack'd the vines, whose shoots are both smaller & shorter than usual: perhaps owing to the vast Crop, & very burning year. However there is wood enough to fill the walls.

29. Planted the border by the necessary full of tulips, Polyanth-Narcissuss, Double daffodils, & Jonquils. Moved the the two plum-trees from the melon-border to the rasp-border: they had taken poor root.

Decem^r: 5. Planted one hundred & a Quarter of stocky Cabbage-plants; to stand the winter. Made a strong rod-hedge against Parsons's yard.
10. Sowed three pints of small early beans. The ground was in fine order; there having been hardly any rain for a month past.
18. By the favour of the long dry weather I pre:vailed on Parsons to set about cleansing the river course, from Gracious-street to Wells-bridge which was quite choak'd, & in great rains occa:sion'd a very troublesome flood. We threw out about 50 loads of mud, & have open'd so free a channel, that the road is quite dry, & the water will have an easy passage as fast as it comes to those parts.
Finish'd a paved foot-path from the Butcher's shop to the Blacksmith's, above 70 yards: it cost just one pound.
27. Very hard, still frost. Pleasant weather, & no rain for several weeks.
31. Extream severe frost with a cutting wind.

Garden-Kalendar
for 1763.

Decemr: 24: 1762. Made a seedling Cucumr: bed with two dung-carts of hot dung, which was in fine order, & had never received any wet since it was thrown-out.
Jan: 1. Sowed about 20 seeds: the bed is in very fine order. Very fierce frost indeed, which begins to reach things with:in doors. The wall-flowers seem to be much damaged.
There has been no fall now, except a trifling shower, since the 11th: of Novemr: when there was a pretty deep-snow. The ponds begin to get low.
4. Extream hard frost still. The Cucumrs: begin to appear.

7.

Jan: 11. Fierce frost still, but not very windy. The sun has scarce appeared for many days: so that the paths & roads have been hard & dry all day long. The Thames, it seems, is so frozen, that fairs have been kept on it; & the Ice has done great damage to the ships below bridge.

Covered the bulbs with straw, & the arti:chokes, & some of the most curious Asters: & put straw round the bloody wall-flowers. Lined the Cucum: bed a little: the plants look pretty well.

This frost began on Xmass-day.

15. The frost more fierce than ever with vast rimes in the night, & sunny days. No snow yet. I have covered the wall-:trees, & all tender things with straw. The frost has been three weeks to day.

17. Carted in & cast 10 loads of good hot dung for the bearing cucumber-bed.

Most severe frost still. There has been no

rain since Nov: 11.th The Country is all in a dust, & many people are obliged to draw water for all their Cattle.

19. Vast rimes all day long for these two days without the least thaw.

20. To day is 10 weeks since there was rain.

21. Vast rimes still day & night.

22. To day the frost has been a month.

24. Made my bearing cucumber-bed with ten loads of very good dung.

The first-sowed cucumber-plants look very well for such a severe season, & have a rough leaf, & another opening. I keep sowing more seeds every week. Very bright still weather.

25. I measured in a new-dug grave in Faring:don Church-yard, & found the frost had enter'd the ground about 10 inches. Vast fog.

27. This day the dry weather had lasted eleven weeks.

28. The frost begins to slack.

Jan: 29. Strong south-wind with rain & a mild thaw. The frost began this day five weeks.

31. A thoro' thaw with strong wind, & a great rain.

Feb: 5. After ten days absence at Ring=:mer I found the Cucumber-plants in pretty good order; but the bearing-bed too hot to plant in.

8. Planted my Cucumber-plants in the bearing bed, which seems to be pretty mild. The plants are of different ages: the forwardest have a joint, & a broad rough leaf.

Wet blowing weather for several days.

9. Feb: 9. Brewed half Hogsh: of strong-beer with 5 bush: of malt, & two p:ds & half of hops. Used only rain-water to try the difference. Added one bush: of malt, & made an hogsh: of table-beer.

12:13. Heavy snow for 14, or 16 hours.

14. Deep snow notwithstanding the ground

was so wet; & a pretty hard frost, & bright sunshine.

The cucumber-plants grow, & look very well; & some of them have two joints.

15. A second deep snow in the night, which goes off to day with a swift thaw, & rain.

15. Made half an Hogsh: of raisin-wine with one hund: of Malagas, & half an hund: of Smyrnas. One basket of ye Smyr:nas were pretty much candyed: the rest were pretty good. Put to the raisins 12 buckets of water, each bucket contain:ing 3 gallons.

19. Frequent rain, & dark weather in general since the thaw.

Sowed 12 Succade-seeds in the Cucumber-bed. Lined the bed round with hay to keep in the heat. The plants look very green, & thrive. The bed seems in fine gentle temper.

21. Sowed two Jobbs of ashes of my own making; which with what few more I may make

6. will manure the great meadow allover.
22. Constant rains.
23. The Succade-plants come: up well.
The Cucumbers thrive.
A very soft spring like day.
25. Sowed 8 rows of marrow-fat pease: the first crop on account of the frost & rain.
Planted a white muscadine-vine from Ringmer at the end of the Dining room: a moss: provence-rose from a layer in the border opposite the fruit-wall; & a monthly-rose in the same border. Mended the Laurustines against Parsons's.
Sowed ten more Succade-seeds: eleven of the former sowing look well.
Dry sunny weather for three days.
26. Potted the first Succades, which are fine plants. The Cucumbers begin to fill the Hills with their fibres, & to want earthing.
26. Sent a small flitch of bacon to be hung in Mr Etty's smoke loft: it lay in salt six weeks

but two of them were fierce frost.
Layd several small twigs of the Moss Pro: vence rose: the larger shoots do not root kindly.
March 1. Planted about three Quarts of broad beans in the room of the small ones which were all kill'd by the frost.
Vast rains still. We are now entred into the 5:th week of the wet weather.
The last sow'd Succades are coming up.
2. Great rains for several days past: to day stormy wind & thunder.
There are vast floods about the Country: & incredible damage is said to be done in the Island of Ely by the breaking of the banks. It has been a very wet season now for near five weeks.
The ground is so wet that nothing can be done in the Garden.
5. Tunn'd the raisin wine, which held out exactly, leaving about a gallon for filling up. Coloured it with twelve bottles of

8.

elder-syrop; & put to it one quart of brandy. I have usually put but a pint at the beginning.

March 5. Made the Succade-bed with ten cart-loads of dung, brought-in the same day. The bed & frame are full seven feet high behind: somewhat the higher for it's being made by mistake full scant for the frame.

Several of the best Cuc: plants are just ready to burst into male bloom. They & the melon-plants thrive well, & have been earth'd twice. Potted to day the second-sown Succades.

Fine, sunny weather for two days.

The Passion-flowers at the ends of the fruit-wall appear to be much injured by the great frost, tho' they were in appearance well covered with straw.

6. Two of the Cucumr: plants have male bloom full-blown. Beautiful weather.

7. Sowed a Crop of Carrots, radishes,

Coss-lettuce, & parsneps altogether in 9.
part of one of the lower quarters of the
New-garden. The ground is in good order.
Planted a standard Orleans-plum, &
a standard Autumn-Bergamot-pear
in the Orchard next Baker's Hill.
Beautiful weather.
Cucumbers blow male-bloom apace.
The Succade-bed begins to fume.
10: Sowed a row of parsley.
Sowed an Ounce of Onion-seed in one
of the new Quarters: the ground in excel:
lent order. Fine sunny weather for a week.
12: 13.. Furious N: E: winds with so very keen
an air, that things froze within doors in not
much less degree than they did in January.
14. Fierce clear frost, but a still air.
Sowed carrots, radishes, & Coss-lettuce under
the melon-screen.
The Cucumber-plants first began to disco:
ver some fruit on the 13.
15. Fierce still frost, & strong sunshine.

~~10.~~ These frosts cut down the wallflowers & Polyanths in a sad manner just as they are coming into bloom.
The Succades are stopp'd down, & thrive vastly.
March 17: Earth'd, & hill'd the Succades, the bed being very moderate in appearance.
Soft, spring-like weather.
Sowed a spot of Polyanth-seed on a border facing to the South: the seed was saved in 176
19. Planted the Succade-bed with two pots of plants in each hill. Each pot contain'd two fine stocky plants, that have each two large rough leaves; & have been stopp down, & show for runners. The bed seems to be mild; & has been made a fortnight to day. Matted down the bed with three of my 9 new London-matts; & trigg'd the lights a little.
A stormy west wind.
22. Found several Cucumbers in bloom this morning. Wet windy weather.

24. Sowed 18 Cantaleupe-seeds in the Succade-frame. They were saved from a fine fruit in 1756, & are very plump, & large; & are the same with those from which Mr Cane raised such fine melons last year at Tidworth.
Set several of the Cucumbers in bloom.
The bed rather declines in heat.
The Succades begin to grow, & extend their roots in their new hills.
Some of the young Nectarines are in bloom; & one peach.
The Hyacinths under the wall are blowing apace: some are blown.
25. Gave the Cucumber-bed a strong lining of hot dung to set, & forward the fruit.
The plants had extended their fibres quite without the frames.
Planted 20 good Cauliflowers from Hartley in a well-dung'd spot, & covered them with hand-glasses, & pots.

~~12.~~ March 25. Transplanted into a go
mellow plot of Ground those few Coss-lettu
under the fruit-wall that survived the
severe winter.
26. Planted five rows of Potatoes qui
across one of the middle quarters of
the new-garden in well-dunged deep moul
The pieces were cut from large firm roo
that had been well-preserved from ye frost
If the pieces had not been planted 15 inc:
apart, they would not have held out.
Sowed a good large plot of Savoys; &
a plot of leeks.
Fierce frosts with very thick Ice.
28. Sowed London-Celeri, & Mr: Missing's
Parsley-leaved Celeriac under an Hand:
:glass with two barrows of dung.
Earth'd the Succades (which had pretty
well run their hills) for the first time.
The middle hill was hot; but there were
no tokens of burning.

The young Cucumbers begin to swell, & seem to be set.

29. Earth'd the Cucumber-bed for the last time. One of the forwardest fruit is gone off. Removed the Cantaleupe seeds, that did not come up so soon as they should do, into a warmer part of the bed.

30. Moss'd the Cucumbr. bed all over to see if, that will promote the swelling of the fruit by keeping the bed moist & warm. It is a practice much in use among Gardeners.

April 1. Sowed in the borders round the Garden 21 little basons of double upright larkspurs; from an ounce of London seed. Sowed a plot of stocks from seed of my own saving: they came first from Ringmer. All my stocks were kill'd last winter. Sowed 18 more Cantaleupe seeds: the last now come up pretty well. The Succades extend their fibres a second time without their hills; & have runners four or five inches long. Delicate soft dry weather. The ground works well.

~~4~~ April 2. Sowed a bed of Sweet-Williams.
Earth'd Succades the second time.
Beautiful soft grey weather.
Sowed a few more Bentworth Cantaleupes
& a few Succades.
Put a bottle of brandy at the time
of tunning to the raisin-wine; & now
an other to prevent it's working too long.
4. Planted several sorts of curious Asters
& Golden-rods sent me by Mr Gibson in
the borders, & field-basons.
Potted the first-sown Cantaleupes, ten good
plants.
5. Cut the first Cucumber, a good fruit;
to carry to London. The rest, several
brace, are swelling away; but are yet of
no size.
The Hyacinths are blowing out apace.
7. Sowed second crop of marrow fats.
8. Carted in 17 loads of hot dung for the
Cantaleupe-bed.

9. Made the Cantaleupe bed. 149

11. Sowed a plot of white hellebore seed: & potted the Succades.

13. Made 1 hand-glass bed, & sowed it with white cucumbers.

13. Cut 13 large, well-grown Cucumbers, which were sent me to London by the coach when they were two shill: apiece in town.

16. Planted half-hund: of Cabbage plants.

18. Sowed more savoys.

21. Earthed the Cantaleupe, & annual beds.

22. At my return from London found the Cucumber-bed full of fine fruit; & the Succade plants well-grown; but not yet in bloom: The Hyacinths are now in high beauty: there are many curious ones in the nursery that must be mark'd for transplanting.

25. Earth'd up the Succades for the last time: the plants are very stout; but do not shew any bloom or fruit.

~~16~~. April 25. Sowed the annual-bed wi[th]
Alton, & London Balsoms, China-asters
African & French Marrigolds, Pendulou[s]
Amaranths, Marvel of Peru, & dwarf Sun[f]
26. Stak'd & tack'd the espalier-pears, &
plums; & eased, & disbudded the fruit-wa[ll]
trees. Dry cold weather.
27. Planted five ~~&~~ hills with Cantaleupe-
-plants from Seed of my own: & in two hills
where there were only two plants to a pot
I put in one more from Mr. Acton's seed
Planted the first Hill with Succades to keep
up a Succession. The bed has been made
18 days; but yet is hot, & must be tilted
when covered; & well-watched in very hot
sun-shine. Mr. Acton's plants (from hi[s]
seed which I gave him first) are in the firs[t]
& second hills.
The Cucumbers bear wonderfully, & larg[e]
well-grown fruit.
30. There have been cut this month from
four lights only above 40 well-grown Cu-
(-cumbers.

Sowed some of Gordon's Celeriac (much commended) between the Cantaleupe boxes.
The Cantaleupe-hills by tilting a nights, & frequent waterings go on very well.
Tyed those Hyacinths that are white with a pink-eye with a piece of scarlet worsted as a mark to save offsets from. Mark'd the blue Hyacinths with a blue piece of worsted tyed to the sticks that stand before them.
May 2. Sowed six rows (about three fourths of a quart) of white dwarf french beans in Patner's Garden. The Ground is very mellow.
Extreme sharp wind with hail for these two days past.
Stopp'd down the Cantaleupes, which are settled in their Hills, & seem past all danger of burning.
Layed down several branches of the fine bloody wall-flowers. Many of the wallflowers were kill'd last winter: as the Artichokes seem all to be.

~~18.~~ May 4. Several smart claps of thunder, which appeared extraordinary in the midst of such cold weather.
Very white frosts every night.
6. Made a row of Standglass-beds, with one barrow of dung to each, for the white cucum:rs
White frosts, & sunny days.
The succades begin to shew fruit.
7. Planted the Stand-glasses with white Cucumber-plants
Weeded the brick walks in the Garden.
The Cantaleupe-plants take well to their Hills, & begin to shew runners.
8. A strange tempestuous day, with violent thunder, storms of hail, & gusts of rain. very cold weather before, & since.
10. Observing that some of the Cantaleupes were a little of a yellowish hue, I examined the hills, & found that notwithstanding the cold black weather, & that the bed had been made a month, yet the mould began to be a little burnt. Upon which I gave them a good watering, & a second earthing, which

will soon bring them right. The vines were run thro' the hills; & most of them shew good runners.

∴ One imperfect male blossom of the Succades is blown out.

11. Added a pint more of brandy, in all five pints, to the last raisin-wine, which still hisses pretty much.

13. Lined & earth'd out the Succade bed, which seem'd to be declining in it's heat. Several male blossoms are open. Hot summer. The grass grows apace in the meadows.

14. The Succades have now a fruit in bloom. The Cantaleupes, which seem'd a little injured by too much heat, by watering are pretty well restored to a good Colour.

15. Planted about 40 late Cabbages in the new Garden.

Prick'd about 200 fine Savoy-plants from Mr. Etty's in the Garden near the tub.

25. The Succades blow pretty well; but no fruit is set yet.

~~20~~. One Cantaleupe has a male bloom, & a weak fruit blown: the rest are in good healthy order.

One of the Newington-Nectarines has three fruit that seem likely to stand. The vines on the House shew well for fruit. the Muscadine vine (which was planted a cutting April was three years) promises to have 31 bunches of Grapes.

Continual cold N: E: Winds.

26. Observing that the Succades were back:ward in setting, & went-off soon after blow:ing; I examined into the mould that lay on the lining, & found that it was so over:heated by a thick coat of mowed Grass as to be scalding hot, & quite unfit for vege:tation. Took-off the grass, & trod-down the earth close to the bed, where it was sunk away, watered it very stoutly, & fill'd it up to the frames with good fresh earth.

27. Planted six rows of dwarf white french beans in the new garden. The first crop are come-up pretty well.

27. Earthed the Cantaleupes quite out, & raised the frames.
Cold, black, dry weather: no rain for a fortnight.
28. Prick'd out the first Celeri.
Added about half a pint more of brandy, in all five pints & an half, to the last made wine, which hisses still pretty much.
Cold, bright weather.
June 4. The weather has been dry, except one trifling shower, for these three weeks to day. No Succades set yet.
The Cantaleupes thrive, & show fruit.
Water'd the Succades well at their stems.
Sunny, dry weather: rain is much wanted.
5. The Succades now begin to set. The Cantaleupes have some fruit that promise for setting. The Succades this very dry season wanted more water at their hills.
The fields & gardens begin to suffer by the long dry season.
Cold, dry weather with an high Barometer.

~~22.~~ June 6. Tack'd up the vine-shoots.
11. It is exactly a month to day since there has been any rain except a trifling shower or two that did not half lay the dust. The fields & Gardens begin to suffer; & there is but a poor prospect of a crop of hay; & most people's old stock is quite spent. There have been great showers about for this week past; but we have had none of them yet.

The Succades have now many brace set; & there are a brace or two of Cantaleupes secure. The Succades have lost a fortnight for want of more water this severe dry season. Widen'd out the Cantal: Bed before & behind, & laid on a good depth of earth.
Heavy showers now about.
13. Only a few showers that did not lay the dust.
14. Hot burning weather again.

14. Potted two curious Styrax: Camp: one has 23 stalks, the other 17. They were so large that no garden-pot would hold them; so were planted in large butter-pots with holes bored in the bottom. Several large roots were broken off in the removal; but possibly that loss may not affect the blowing.

15. Vast rain at Alton; but only a small sprinkling here.

The Cantaleupes set apace.

16. Small showers that refresh the fields & Gardens a little.

The Cantaleupes set all their first fruit, & promise for a good Crop. Some of the Succades are pretty well grown, but they are all on second & third wood.

Planted out the annuals, which are backward & weak.

Sowed Endive, & Coss-lettuce.

The vines are beginning to blow.

~~24.~~ To day compleats the fifth week since there was any rain here except a few small showers lately, which never laid the dust. The grass-walks look rusty. There have been fine rains round the Country.

20. Raised & earthed the melon-frames for the last time: the boxes are now even with the tops of the hills, & the beds are earth'd down with a great depth of mould. The Cantaleupes continue to set well; & the single Hill of Succades: hardly any of the first fruit has been lost. But they have had a deal of water this burning season. Prick'd out some of Gordon's Celeriac, & some Common Celery in the shady end of the melon-border. Planted the bank in the new-garden, & part of the back of the melon-screen with annuals. China-asters run very scanty this Year. Some of the Succades seem to be full grown. Trod down the mould on the melon-bed, & spread some loose earth over it.

June 25. This is now the sixth week of the dry weather. A small shower this evening that has not laid the dust.

Watered the Cantaleupes well, round the frames, & laid some short hay over the mould to keep it moist.

The Cabbages begin to look blue.

27. Gather'd first marrow-fat pease.

The Corn begins to suffer by the long dry weather. ~~[illegible]~~

I continue to water the melon-beds often.

The Grass-walks look exceeding rusty.

28. Cut the grass in the meadow, & slip.

29. Just as all the grass was spread about came a great rain all day from the east: the only rain to do any good for six weeks, & three days.

30. Vast showers with Thunder & hail.

Planted a plot of very forward Savoys; & a plot of later-sown ones.

The thunder-shower damaged the zigzag a good deal. The rain has thorowly soak'd the ground down to the roots.

~~26~~. July 4. Tyed the Succades that are but a midling Crop. There is a second Crop coming on.
Took off the frames from the early cucumbers, which bear still vastly.
Half the hay is housed on waggons in barns: the rest is in Cock.
Soft, showery, growing weather.
The Cantaleupes come on unequally; some scarce swell at all, & some are full grown.
5. Rick'd the hay ~~in very~~ moderate order: the load that stood in Kelsey's barn was strangely damp, & heated; & was spread & dry'd over again.
6. Finish'd stopping down, & tacking of vines: they are in full bloom.
Planted a good plot of leeks in Turner's.
Showery, growing weather.
8. Put a quarter of a pound of hops to the strong brewed in Feb: which promises to be good.
9. Showery weather still.
Putty'd the melon frames to keep out the wet: housed the cucumber frames. The plants that were in full bearing are much check'd by being exposed at once

to the open air: but their fruit is not much wanted, now the hand-glass-hills are in full bearing.

14. Trenched-out four rows of stockly Celeri in one of the lower quarters of the new garden.

Showery weather.

13. Mr Tho: Mulso, & Lady, & Mr Edw: Mulso & Miss Harriot Baker came to visit me.

19. Finished planting-out 6 trenches of Celeri, & a second plot of Endive.

Cut the first Succade.

Very wet weather.

26. Succades come very fast. Cut some tolerable Cauliflowers. Succades weigh 24 ounces, & are very dry. Continual showers, & a quantity of hay damaged.

Planted two rows of Gordon's Celeliac.

27. Divided-out, & planted round the new garden Mrs Snooke's fine double Pheasant-eyd-pinks

28. Drank tea 20 of us at the Hermitage: the Miss Batties, & the Mulso family contributed much to our pleasure by their singing, & being dressed as shepherds, & shepherdesses. It was a most elegant evening; & all parties appeared highly satisfyed. The Hermit appeard to great advantage.

July 29.. A vast rain. The hay lies about in a miserable way.

30. Cut the first Cantaleupe, which, considering the wet season, proved a good one.

Aug: 1. Wet weather still.

2. Took up my Hyacinths under the fruit-wall: they have many offsets, & seem not to be damaged with the wet season.

3. Terrible rain, & my neighbour's hay in a deplorable way. The rainy season has lasted just five weeks to day.
Cut a fine-looking Cantaleupe, & sent it by the Ladies (who left Selborne this day) to Dr Battie. Cut several Succades: they want Sun & dry weather.

4. Vast rains still. The wet has lasted five weeks yesterday.

5. Eat an extraordinary fine Cantaleupe notwithstanding the rains.

9: 10. Two fine days: during which my neighbours got in their Hay rather better than was expected.

11. Sowed a crop of spinage. Dry weather for three days; but distant thunder.

Aug: 15. Sowed a plot of turneps.
Dry weather for some days.
16. Showers again. Cut some fine Cantaleupes.
People are just entering on wheat-harvest.
22: 23. Showery weather, & very little wheat
housed: it begins to grow under the hedges.
Finished cutting my Cantaleupes, & Succades.
The grapes are very backward & small, having
seen nothing but black showery weather
for these eight weeks.
25. Mr Mulso's family left me.
26. Now a long rain after two fine days. The
wheat grows pretty much.
Septemr: 4. Now frequent showers after some
fine days. There is a good deal of wheat still
abroad.
7. Now wet weather after some fine days. Much
wheat abroad still.
10. Tyed up endive. Showery, bad weather.
13. Many days black wet weather.
The Grapes begin to change Colour.
Planted a row of stocks on the fruitwall border,
& under the dining room window.
18. Black wet weather.

Dung borrowed in 1763.

Kelsey - pd: Car: Dung pd - - - 1 load.
Brought in of my own 1 load.
Jan: 17. Kelsey pd - Car - Dung pd - 5 loads.
- - my own 3 loads.

Parsons Dung pd - - - - - - - - - 2 loads.
Jan: 18. Pd Kelsey his last five loads
- - of dung by allowing him to take
- - three loads from the dung-hill in
- - the orchard.
March 5. Kelsey - Car pd - Dung pd - 5 loads.
- - my own 2 loads.
Parsons Dung pd - - - - - - - - - 3 loads.
Apr: 8. Kelsey - Car pd Dung pd ——— 10 loads
- - my own 2 loads.
Parsons Dung pd ——— 5 loads.

The rainy season continued 12 weeks; since which there has been some delicate weather in the latter end of Septemr & Octobr that has made the grapes better than could be expected.

Octr: 18. Planted an hundred of Cabbages to stand the winter. 15]

24. Dug up the potatoes which are large & fine. Trimm'd & tack'd the fruit-wall trees: the wet summer had forced most of them into too much large willow-like ~~w~~ wood, which will not blow so well next year as smaller. The vines against the wall have got well-ripen'd shoots, & promise for plenty of fruit next year. The garden abounds with good Celeri, & spinage, & a very fine sort of Savoys. Toletable grapes in plenty. Hares or some vermin have gnawed almost all the fine Pheasant-eyed pinks, & the new-planted cabbages.

30. Now rain, & stormy wind after just three weeks soft, still, dry, summer like weather.

Nov: 4: 9. Vast rains, & floods. Very fine grapes still: there have been no frosts to any degree.

16. Serene, beautiful weather for several days, with the Mercury within half a degree

of settled fair. Planted my Hyacinths in two rows all along the border opposite the fruit-border: dug in first some well-rotted dung. Put the blue & best pink-eyed intermixed in front. Planted my Tulips, narcissuss, & Jonquils in the border opposite the bank. Dug & cleared the banks, & dining-room shrubbery this fine season.

18: 19: 20. Most severe frost indeed with thick bearing Ice, & a very cutting wind: a small snow. There has been a very mild season till now.

Decem.r 19. Planted some Hepaticas, fritillarias, & winter aconites from Ringmer. & some fine persian Jasmines, & cob-nuts. Vast rains & floods of late.

21. Brewed half Hogsh: of strong beer with 6 bush: of ~~[illegible]~~ coal-dry'd malt, & 2 pds & an half of hops; the water all from the well. Continual wet weather.

1763.

1764.

This year begins as the former concluded with continual heavy rains, & vast floods. There has indeed been little else but wet weather (a few short intervals excepted) ever since the 29th of June.

Jan: 5. Made a seedling Cucumber-bed with dung that had been very much wash'd.

9. Finding the bed come to a pretty good heat I sowed about 20 seeds.

13. A most violent storm all night, that must have in all appearance done great damage: vast rains at the same time.
The Cucumbers are come-up & look well.
The wind blew-down the hot-bed screen.

23. The second sowing of Cucumbers are come-up very well.

28. Very stormy weather still, with great showers. The Crocuss begin to blow.

31. Vast rains, & storms of wind. Prodigious inundations all over England, Holland

~~N.~~ & Germany. Lined the Cucumber-bed with many barrows of hot dung.

Feb: 7. Brewed 45 Gallons of strong-beer with eight bushels of malt dryed with Welch-coal & three pounds & three quarters of good hops. The strong-beer was closely covered down with sacks, while infusing in the mash-vat: & the yeast was beat into the beer several times, 'till it was put into the barrel. Made with the same malt Half an hogsh: of ale, & an Hogsh: of small. The strong-beer was made entirely with rain-water. Tunn'd the strong beer the third day.

10. Made a bearing Cucumber-bed with between eight & nine loads of good hot dung for two two-light frames.

Vast rains, & high winds still.

Sowed the great mead all over with about 30 bushels of my own ashes; & the little mead with 12 bushels bought of Mr. Etty.

13. Bottled-out half an Hogsh: of Mrs. Atherley's port-wine. It had not, I think, quite so good a smell & flavour as usuall; & seem'd always to shew a disposition to mantle in the glass.

Feb: 17. Put the Hills of earth on the Cucum.r Bed: the earth by means of the long wet season was not in curious order. 3.
160

18. Planted the Cucumber-plants on their Hills. The plants are grown to two Joints, & are stopped down. The bed seems to be in good order.

20. It has been now pretty dry ever since the fifteenth day. There have not been so many dry days for some months. The weather-glass is very high, & the wind N: E.

21. Sowed 10 Succade-seeds in the Cuc.r bed. A very white-frost & bright sunshine. The snails after so mild a winter are very numerous, & get into the bed & eat the plants.

26. This is now the eleventh day of the dry weather: the roads are finely dry'd. A strong North E: wind, & a sinking Glass.

27. A considerable snow on the ground. A severe frost this evening.
The snails continue to annoy the Cuc.r bed; & have destroy'd all the plants in one hill, & damaged several others.

~~4.~~ Feb: 29. Very hard frost, & snow on the ground. The hot-bed goes on but poorly: the plants don't grow, the snails damage them every night, & the succades don't come up.
March 1. Gave the hot-bed a good lining of hot dung. In general the plants don't grow; but one begins to shew a runner. Blowing black weather, & snow on the ground.
5. The frost has been so bad for a day or two past that the plants in the bed seemed in a very poor way, & the bed almost cold: but now the lining begins to take effect, & there is some warm sunshine that will set y^m to growing again. The snails continue to gnaw the plants tho' we kill numbers.

Sowed 12 Succade-seeds. A mouse devoured the first: indeed the bed would not bring them up. The frost has been now a week last saturday. The rose-trees, Crocuss, Hyacinths, & polyanths are much pinch'd by the severe weather.
10. Very severe, black cutting weather for a fortnight past, ~~which~~ with several pretty large falls of snow, that do not lie long at a time. The hot bed succeeds very poorly.

March 12. Sowed five rows of marrowfat
pease, the first crop; & some radishes &
Coss-lettuce under the fruit-wall: the border
is very mellow.
Planted a row of laurels against Parsons's
behind the filbert hedge.
There has been now no rain for these three
weeks: the landsprings are much abated.
15. Gave the hot-bed a strong lining.
Planted six rows of broad beans.
Planted a row of Laurustines before the
laurels against the street.
16. Sunny, summer-like weather, & the ground
in good dry order.
The Hot-bed comes into good Condition again,
& the Cucr: plants throw out runners. Mossed
the bed round the hills. The second sowing of
Succades come up well at last: there are only
four plants of the first sowing.
Dress'd the border next Parsons's, & new-planted
the perennials; & planted a row of sweet Williams
in the front. Dress'd the Rasp bed.
The Crocuss, that seem'd to be so much coddled
with frost, now make a great shew again.

March 17. Planted half hund: of Cabbadge plants; the second planting.

18. Very bright sunny weather with a vast white frost after several grey days. During this late dry weather the Garden has been cleared & put in pretty neat order.

19. Now rain after a fit of dry weather that would have lasted five weeks, had it held out till tomorrow. The long fit of wet that occasion:ed such floods & devastations all Europe over, lasted, with very few Intervals of dry between from Iane 29: 1763: to Feb: 15: 1764.

One of the Cucr. plants has got a male bloom full blown. The Cucumrs. now thrive, & the melons plants come up well.

Potted all the first sown Succades, which were a little drawn, in three pots. The last sown come up very well. Soft, showery weather.

20. Made the Succade bed (the dung brought in the same day) with eight loads of dung: it proves full stout enough, but is made rather too narrow, & longer than needs be. Blowing March weather. Mowed part of the grass plot for the first time: there was a great swarth of grass, that made a

good living for the Cuc.r bed, which now works well: Several plants have male-bloom.

March 22. Planted five rows of potatoes in a mellow rich part of the garden with pieces from very large sound roots that had been very well-preserved. The ground had been well dunged, but no thatch was used.

Sowed a deep, well-dug plot with a Crop of Carrots, Coss lettuce, & parsneps together.

Planted a row of pine, & Nova Scotia straw-berry-plants: the bed is run to ruin & must be destroy'd.

Raked down the Asparagus-beds.

Planted some basons in the field with Sweet-Williams. The garden is now mowed all round. Blowing cold weather with some showers in the evening.

The Cuc.r bed heats well, & the plants keep throwing out male-bloom.

Made a hill with one good barrow of dung for an handglass, & sowed it with Celeri-seed.

24. Earth'd the Cucumber-bed: the plants extend their fibres very fast.

Sowed four pots with fraxinella-seeds.

8.
March 28. Sowed a Crop of Onions, & a plot of leeks. Planted Horsechestnuts in the nursery.
29. Earth'd the Succade-bed: & sowed some white Cucumbers.
April 3rd Lined the Cucumber bed again.
5. Planted out the Succades. Two Cucumbers in bloom. Sowed sixteen Cantaleupe seeds, & 6 succade seeds.
7. Planted the second Crop of pease.
13. Potted the Cantaleupes: they are fine plants. The Succades come up poorly. The Succades in the hills are fine stocky plants, & full of runners. There are two Cucumbers of some size; & more setting.
16. Sowed about 18 basons in the best garden with Larkspurs, one ounce of seed.
17. Rain & snow
19. Suddain transitions from hard rains to fierce frost, & ice.
21. Cut a brace of Cucumbers, large fruit, the first this season.
Made the Cantaleupe-bed for six lights with sixteen loads of dung.
Many Cucumbers are now set, & coming on.

All the wall-trees had each a little bloom. 9.
Planted about three doz: of wall-flower cuttings.
27. Made the annual bed, & sowed it with 163
African & French-marrigolds, marvel of
Peru, Iroquois-Gourds, Pendulous Ama:
ranths. Sowed Dwarf-sunflowers in the
cold ground.
Sowed a crop of Savoys: & a little plot of
burnet.
30. Earthed the Cantaleupe-bed, & made the
hills for the plants.
May 4. Sowed four rows of white-dwarf
french-beans.
Planted out the Cantaleupes in the Hills.
May 5. On my return from Oxōn I found the
Succades in great vigour, with their wood of
some length, that shewed the rudiments of bloom.
The Succades take well to their Hills, & look very
green. The Cucumbers are full of fruit.
Many of the blue, & white Hyacinths are very
beautiful indeed.
Bright summer-like weather; & all things
in a very growing Condition.

May 7. Earth'd-out the Succades.
Disbudded the wall-fruit trees, that were grow. very rude. In all appearance they will have no fruit this year.

Open'd, & painted the Alcove.

Cut the Laurustine-hedge in the yard down to the Ground.

12. One Succade-fruit is blown before any male bloom.

15. Great showers for several days with a S: W: Wind that damages the flowers & trees. The Ground is well soak'd. The grass grows very fast, & the spring-corn comes up well. Many of the double-stocks are very beautiful. The Cantaleupes throw-out good runners.

17. Hot weather: things grow very fast after such fine showers.

Planted out 4 Iroquois-Gourds against the fruit-wall. The Cucumbers bear well. Finished weeding the brick-walks. The Succades are full of male-bloom, & begin to shew pretty good-looking fruit.

21. Lined the Succade-bed with two loads of hot dung, one before, & one behind. The plants now

throw out plenty of promising fruit; some of it is in bloom. Tacked the vine-shoots against the wall for the first time. The vines round the House shew for fruit; but not in such Quantities as for some years past.

May 26. The weather for some days very sultry: to day was thunder & rain; & in some places very heavy showers; but not at Selborne.

June 2: On my return from Fifield I found an abundance of Succades set; & some as large as Goose-eggs. The Cantaleupes (tho' the Haulm has not half-filled the boxes) are setting very fast. The very hot weather has drawn the stalks of the fruit pretty long.

4. Earth'd-out the Cantaleupes & Succades to the full; & brought the mould in front quite down to the Ground: raised all the melon frames quite above the mould.

Planted 100 of Savoy-plants from Ludgershal in a nursery-bed: but was forced to water the ground very much before it would plant. The ground by means of the wet winter & late drying winds is as hard as a stone; so that there is no sowing or planting any quantity till rains come. On account of the hardness of the Ground the Tent-corn begins to want rain very much. The fine double stocks are still in full bloom.

Very cold, black, drying weather for these ten days past.

June 6. Sowed a Crop of Endive: watered the Ground to make it rake.

7. Prick'd-out a plot of Celeri.

8: 9. Now fine rains, after the Ground had been bound-up like so much stone for some time. Thinn'd-out, & tack'd the peaches, & nectarines in a very regular manner, so that the shoots will have the benefit of the sun & air to ripen them. There was not one fruit to be found. The trees are kept open in the middle, but make a very regular appearance on the sides.

14. Sowed second crop, a pint of white dwarf-french-beans in five rows. The ground is still very hard, & dry; the late rains were not plentiful enough to make it work well. The first sowing of french-beans are tolerable.

Some few of the Burnet-plants have escaped the fly, & are got pretty large.

June 13: Very hot summer weather.
15. The vine against the fruit-wall from Mrs
Snooke's black sort is now in bloom before any
of my black Grapes against the House; which
confirms me in my suspicions that her
sort was earlier than mine.
Turn'd out the white Cucumbers from under
the Hand-glasses: they are full of fruit.
Hot weather; & the garden requires a deal
of water. Finish'd tacking the vines.
18. Mowed the greatest part of the great mead:
but was deterr'd from finishing the whole
by a vast tempest of thunder & lightening
that lay along to the N: W: N: & E: all the
afternoon. It thundered loudly for hours
together; but not one drop fell with us.
The heat, being reflected from white thunder-
clouds, was unusually severe. The weather
cock stood all day plumb S: but the storm
came up from the N: W: There is a very
fine crop of Grass in the meadow. This day
has burnt & scalded things in the Garden
in a strange manner. Gave the Cantaleupes
a good watering within the frames: but gave

14. no water to the Succades, as many brace of them, at least ten, are full grown, & near ripene

June 19. The thunder-storm, which threatned so hard, sunk quite away in the night. A fine sunn day with a brisk wind at E:

20. The same weather; & the hay makes at a vast rate. Carry'd four Jobbs to the rick.

21. A Continuance of hot sunshine with brisk air. Carry'd four more Jobbs, all my hay in most curious order without one drop of rain. This is now the ninth day of hot sunshine: so that the ground is greatly burnt; & the grass walks look very rusty. Nothing can be done in the Garden, which is like an heap of stones. Laid pease-haulm, & straw round the outsides of the melon-beds to keep out the fierce heat. Water'd the Cantaleupes well round the extremities on the straw. They have several fruit about half grown; & several that never moved at all after setting: they now begin to throw out fresh shoots, & fair fruit. The succades have had no water all this fierce sunny weather. The cucumber-frames are beat out of bearing by the

Heat. The hand-glass Cucumbers are shaded all day, & yet are injured by the intense sunshine. There has been no weather to plant-out annuals: they are damaged by the hot season. The self-sown Larkspurs all turn out single: the basons of double seed never came up.

22. Thunder in the morning; & a little shattering of rain, being the skirts of the storm: clear burning weather the rest of the day.

23: 24. Little soft showers: but heavy rains at Farington, & all round us. Such gluts of rain near Odiham as did great damage to the Corn & hay. Vast damage in London, & round Reading.

25. The grapes of Mrs Snooke's black-Cluster fairly set. The black Hambro', Sweet-water, & Muscadine but just coming into bloom. My own black-Cluster on the House but just blow-ing. Prick'd-out more Celeri: the ground is very little moistened. Stopped-down the vines against the wall. Began planting-out the annuals: & tyled the Succades; which are a fine plentiful Crop.

26. Finished planting-out the annuals; & sowed a Crop of turneps mixed with Coss-lettuce. Frequent soft showers: but the Ground yet but little moistened.

~~16~~ June 28. A good lasting rain that moisten'd things well down to the roots. Rak'd-down the rough ground, & planted-out a large plot of Endives, & a plot of Savoys; & a plot of leeks. Potted-out two Pyramidal Campanulas, one with 14 stalks, & one with two.
The Martagons make a vast figure.
Cut the first white Cucumbers.
Sowed a row of curled-parsley.
The Grapes of Mrs Snooke's sort quite large: some of my own just set: the other sorts just coming into bloom.
29. Several showers. Planted more Savoys.
30. Planted half hundred of common cabbages. Cut the laurel-hedge against the necessary very neatly with a knife.
July 2. Hot, burning weather for two days. Cut the first Succade; but a small fruit. Housed my Cucumber-frames, & Glasses.
3. Cut the second Succade. Very hot weather.
4. Cut a brace more Succades. Stopped-down, & tacked all the vines against the House: they are now in full bloom, & smell very sweetly. Fine soft showers. Dug-up the tulip-bed; & several Hyacinths from an old nursery.

July 5. Planted some stocks from Mr Budd's 17. 167
in a nursery bed. Stopped down, & trimmed
the Laurel's against parsonss Yard, & the
street. The Cantaleupes run vastly to bine;
but do not fruit well. Some few Canta:
:leupes in every light are almost full-grown,
& look very black, & rough.
6. The first stout shower, that soaked the
Ground well.
7. Cut a Succade, that was crack'd very deeply
at the eye. The Cantaleupes usually crack
so; the Succades never before. Sunny weather.
Cut two brace more, the most choice fruit of
the whole Crop.
9. Cut all the crop of Succades, three brace &
an half, tho' they were not crack'd at the tail, to
carry them to Fifield. Hot sunny weather.
Ordered the bed to be well-watered for a second
Crop: Saved the seeds of a very delicate
Succade, that grew close to the stem.
The Succades proved good at Fyfield.
21. At my return from Fyfield, I found the
Cantaleupes greatly over-run with haulm, but
no more fruit set. There will be a slender crop;
not more than a brace to a light, & those but
small. The Grapes on the fruit-wall are

18 large (especially those on Mrs Snooke's black Cluster) & much forwarder than those on the walls of the house. The peaches, & Nectarine-trees grow too much, & run into willow-like wood. Showery, hot weather for a fortnight past.

22. Cut the first Cantaleupe: it proved a very good one, tho' under-sized.

Put some hops, & sand into the strong-beer brewed in Decemr: to fine it down.

The Iroquois-Gourds are very peculiar in their growth: they are short stocky plants without any runners. Some of them have variegated leaves. The Pyram: Camp: are drawn by standing in the brewhouse: put them in the Alcove. The white Cucumbers bear plentifully.

27. Trenched three good long rows of Celeri in Turner's Garden. The Ground is in good order. Showery weather. Planted a plot of Savoys from Hartley.

28. Cut two fine Cantaleupes, that crack at the eye; but they are undersized.

Aug: 1. Cut a fine black Cantaleupe: it was crack'd at the eye. Sowed a large plot of Ground with prickly spinage, & Coss lettuce.

Showery weather with a strong wind that
damages the Garden. Cleared the vines of
their side shoots.

Aug: 2. Planted three more rows of Celeri
in Turner's garden: the six rows make a
large stock. Black, windy, showery weather.
The black Cantaleupe proved a curious one.
Thinn'd the leeks in the seedling-bed, & left
the largest to stand as part of a Crop. Dress'd
the bank, & borders. The Iroquois-Gourds
shew pretty large fruit; but have no runners.
The grapes on the fruit-wall are much larger
& forwarder than those on the House. Saved
a little Polyanth-seed. Trimmed the side-wood
from the shoots of the wall-trees, & tacked them
down close as they grow.

There will be a small ~~m~~ second Crop of Succades:
2 brace of small succades of the single hill are
not yet come.

Many people have just began Harvest.

7: 8. Two dismal wet days: vast quantities
of water fell.

11. Tyed-up 25 endives; the first tying.

12: 13: 14. Showery, bad harvest-weather.

20. Aug: 15. Put a pint of brandy to the Half hogsh: of raisin wine made Jan: 1763. In the spring it was got fine, & in good order: but now it is in a great ferment. I have beat up the bung, & left it open.

Very wet weather still.

17. A pretty fine day with a brisk drying wind. Many people were housing wheat all day, which went in in better condition that could be expected.

18. Vast heavy drowning rains. The white Cucumbers were in full bearing; but are da:maged by the rains, & long cold black weather. The annuals are injured by the wet. The Grapes on the House are small, & backward; those on the wall are much before them. The first-sown french-beans bear vastly: the latter don't come on.

24. No rain since the 18: & this is the fourth most beautiful harvest-day that ever was seen; during which the farmers in these parts have quite finish'd their wheat-harvest. Those that had the most patience will have by much the best corn.

Planted two offsets of a fine sort of Lychni:
:dea, given me by Mr Gibson, in my flower 169
border; & a sucker of a fine purple lilac
in the nursery.
Planted half a doz: of my fine bloody wallflowers
on the fruit-border: they are fine plants.
Cut a Cantaleupe-melon, that is much cracked
at the eye. Figs are large & good.
The grapes on Mrs Snooke's black-cluster-
vine just begin to turn: those on the house
are small, & backward.
The vine Murdock Middleton sent for Warner's
black Hambro; seems, by it approaches towards
ripening, to be some ordinary sort of white
Grape. The barometer is very high.
25. Beautiful weather still; but the Glass
falls. The Cantaleupe, tho' it had but little
smell, was very fine.
Put a bottle more of brandy to the raisin-
wine, which works much.
Made & housed the second cutting of the shrubbery,
& orchard in fine order, without a drop of rain.
Housed two of the melon-frames, & put a few fruit

~~22.~~ under the hand-glasses.
Tyed-up the second Crop of Endive: they are very large.
26. Cut a brace of every fine-flavoured Cantaleupes, the last of the season: they were not large. Housed the last frame. The wasps were got to be very troublesome at the melon-bed, gnawing great holes in ^the^ fruit. Set bottles of treacle, & beer.
27. Very hot, summer-like weather: the glass after sinking a day or two, is now going up again. Mrs Snooke's black Clusters change Colour apace; & the white sorts begin to grow transparent. The wood of the vines ripens apace. The wood of the peaches, & Nectarines ripens well; & begins to shew ~~their~~ ^its^ blowing budds surrounded with three leaves.
There are two brace of pretty good Succades under the hand-glasses.
29. Sowed some more Coss-lettuce: those among the spinage, as well as the spinage, come-up but poorly. The grapes against the yard just begin to turn. A soft rain after ten hot, dry days.

Aug: 31. Very hot sunny weather. Cut the first tyed endives, they are delicately blanched. The barometer is now very high.

Septemr: 1. Got a stone-mason to fix the stone with my name & the date of the ~~#~~ wall in the middle of the fruit-wall. When the mason came to chizzel a hole for the stone he found the wall perfectly sound, dry, & hard.

3. Returned the raisin-wine (which had been drawn into a tun-tub two days) into the barrel again, & put in one ~~ne~~ more pint of brandy: there is left behind near three Gallons of grout. Hot sunny weather still. The wine frets a little still.

7. Tyed-up more endive: the third tying: the endives are very large, & fine. Earthed-up two rows of Celeri for the first time. Beautiful weather still: it has now lasted three weeks. Harvest is finished in general; except some vetches, & barley that are not yet ripe. The Grapes on the fruit-wall ripen very fast. During this sunny weather fresh Cantaleupes, & succades set very fast since the frames have been taken away.

~~24.~~ Sept.^r: 12. Now a great rain after three weeks, & three days delicate weather.

16. Cold, windy weather still. The annuals are much damaged.

18. Gathered the sweet-water grapes on the front wall which are ripe; & some of Mr Snooke's black-cluster-grapes, which are very eatable but not highly flavoured.

In the night between the 16: & 17: my melons & Cucumbers were pulled all to pieces; & the horse-block, three hand-glasses, & many other things were destroy'd by persons unknown.

22. Fine settled weather: the Grapes are now good, but not delicate. The wasps are not very numerous; but have damaged some bunches.

24. A very white frost, & Ice in some places. Gather'd a plate of Grapes from the wall of ye House next the yard: these are the first that have been perfectly fine.

25. A second very white frost. Beautiful sunny still weather with a very high barometer. The annuals are much cut-down. Took-in three of the Iroquois Gourds, which are very peculiar

fruit: those from the variegated plants
are of a yellowish Cast; those from the
green leaves of a dark-green Colour.
The succades that ~~we~~ were taken in before they
were ripe, & hung to the beam over the Kitchen-
fire, have ripen'd well; & proved of a good
Colour & flavour; but are some what moist
& flabby. Dug the border of the fruit-wall,
& took away all the gourds, & annuals. Tyed-
up ~~more~~ endives: they are vastly large; but
some what damaged by the frost. There have
been a few good mulberries; but they ripen too
late. Earthed up all the rows of Celeri; &
two rows for the second time. The Mich: Dai:
seys covered with butter-flies, & other gaudy
insects make a very gallant appearance in
the sunshine. We have continued to catch
the wasps, & hornets, which are not very nu:
:merous, with birdlime. The late Cabbages,
& savoys are in great perfection: the french-
beans are quite cut down, & destroy'd. The
potatoes are good, but not very large.
Sep: 30. A very sharp March-like wind from the
N: many days with frosts & Ice. The ground is
very dry; & the Clays have a fine season for wheat.

~~26~~. Sep: 30. Wind & rain, & a low glass.
Octr: 1. Now a brisk wind, & sunshine.
Planted out several double bloody wall-flow:
:ers under the fruit-wall, & melon-screen.
Planted several offsets from the potted Cam:
:panulas. Sent a basket of Grapes, & Ca:
:dillac pears to Lady Stuart.
6. Gather'd in a moderate quantity of all the
keeping apples: they are well-coloured, but small, being
vastly thick on the trees.
The Grapes are now delicate, both white & red.
Fine, serene, summer-like weather: except now &
then a small shower: the dry season has lasted
seven weeks to day.
7. Beautiful clear weather.
20. Fine soft weather intermixed with some gentle
showers. This delicate weather makes most cu:
:rious Grapes. The farmers put their wheat into
the ground in fine order.
23. Dry sunny weather with an high barometer.
Earth'd up the Celeri for the last time: made
use of some, which was well-blanched, & well-
grown.

Octr: 24. Bright, cold weather. Grapes in the greatest perfection.
26. Planted 100 of Cabbages to stand the winter. Planted my Coss-lettuces, some very large some very small, against the fruit-wall to stand the winter. The farmers carried out their dung from the melon-bed in a fine dry season. The weather very dry & cold. Gather'd 6 medlars, the first fruit that ever the tree produced.
28. Very bright, cold, sharp weather with considerable Ice. Gather'd in a considerable part of the grapes, which are very curious. The dry fit has lasted ten weeks to day.
Novr: 1: Planted out some stocks from Mr: Budds & a few from Ringmer. Dry still weather; but thick Ice in the morning. The ground is dry like summer. The ponds, & wells are exceeding low: many wells are quite dry.
Novr: 5: 6. Put the tulips, taken up in Summer, into the ground; & made a nursery of the best offsets. Dug up the Polyanth-Narcissuss, & Daffodils, that had stood two years, & transplanted them: they were greatly encreased. Mrs Snooke's tulips are planted in the border where the two

~~28~~. Cherry-trees stand. My own filled out the Border towards the alcove, & made a bed near the tub for water. Planted a row of Jonquils on the fruit-border near the Staka.

The rain that has fallen yet is very trifling, only just enough to make the ground slippery. To day, the 6th a stormy wind, & sinking glass.

6. Now a very heavy rain with a violent stormy wind.

7. Gather'd-in a large basket of Grapes, the last of the season: they are in fine order.

8. A very great rain: so that the dry season might be said to last just eleven weeks ~~from~~ from the 19 of August.

8. Bottled half an hogsh: of elder-raisin wine, made in Feb: 1763: it took a second fermentation last spring; but is now very good except a little smatch of the brandy which I put-in to stop the working.

Novr: 6: 8: 10. A great deal of rain.

14. Trimm'd & tack'd all the trees against the fruit-wall. The peaches, & nectarines all promise to produce bloom: some have made shoots too gross & willow-like. Dug & laid down the border in curious order. Tack'd the vines some perpendicularly, some horisontaly. A smart frost in the morning.

Novr: 22. Eat my last Grapes.
23. Planted a Golden-pippin, & a Queen-Claud-plum, both standards, in the orchard: & a Portugal-Laurel in the shrubbery. The golden pippins planted in the orchard two or three years ago are both much annoy'd with the Canker, tho' they were planted on Hillocks to avoid the wet.

Dung borrowed in 1764.

Feb: 8.	Of Kelsey Dung p:d Car: p:d — —	5 loads.
	Of Parsons Dung p:d Car: p:d —	2 D:o
March 1.	Of Kelsey (no Car: to pay for this)	1 load.
19.	Of Kelsey Dung p:d Car: p:d — —	5 loads.
20.	Of Parsons Dung p:d car: p:d —	3 loads.
Apr: 11.	Of Parsons Dung p:d — car: p:d —	3 loads
	Of Kelsey Dung p:d car p:d — —	4 loads
	car: out two of my own. car p:d.	
	Of Beariman Dung p:d waggon. loads	2 car p:d
19.	Of Kelsey Dung p:d car p:d —	3 loads
May 21.	Of Kelsey Dung p:d car p:d — —	1 load.
	— — — car: of my own one. car p:d

Garden-Kalendar for the Year 1765.

1765.

Jan: 4. Made half an Hogsh: of raisin-wine with one Hund: of Malagas, & half an hund: of Smyrnas: one of the half hund: of Malagas was very indifferent, the rest were fine.
Put to the raisins eleven buckets of water containing three Gallons each. The Smyrnas cost 32^{s}: pr Hund: the Malagas 30^{s}.
From the eve of last Xmass-day to the eve of New-year's day was a very dry, severe frost: it went off with a very mild thaw.
5. Received a ten gallon barrel of mountain-wine from my Bro: Thomas.
12. Great rains, & strong winds for several Days.
8. Made an hot-bed for the one-light Cucumber seedling frame,
14. The Cucumrs come up very well; but the bed is full hot. Moist, foggy weather.

Jan: 19. Tunn'd the half Hogsh: of wine: it ran the barrel full, all save about one Gallon that was squeezed. Put to it 14 bottles of elder-syrop for colouring. Put up on the raisins four buckets of water to make vinegar, & raisin-wine. Put one pint of brandy to the wine.

22. Wet mild weather since new-year's day. The snow-drops are in bloom; & the Crocuss swelling.

24. Press'd out the second ran of raisin-wine, four buckets of water having been put up after the first wine was drawn off. Fill'd the vinegar-barrel about three parts full: & there remained about 8 gallons for present drinking.

30. A high barometer, & N: E: wind, with some dry days: but frequent fogs, & some sunshine. The first sown Cucum[rs] have now a rough leaf. There is now a good Quantity in the earth-house of mold for the bearing: cucum[r]. bed, consisting of some old melon-mould, some from the bottom of the faggot-stack, & some earth cast up by the moles on the Common; all well turned & blended together. The Hepaticas are well blown: & some

Crocuss are blown-out.

31. Sowed my own ashes, which were sufficient for what used to be called the great mead. Bought ten bushels of Mr. Etty, which sowed the slip.

Feb: 1. Sowed a box with Polyanth-seed from Bp's Waltham said to be good. Dry but dark weather.

4. Carry'd into the melon-ground 8 loads of hot Dung for the bearing Cucumr. bed.

A very severe frost all day with a great rime. The ground was so very hard that the carting all day made not the least Impression. There has been some frost for several days.

Empty'd the dung hole.

7. Very hard frost still, with great white dews. Things begin to freeze within. The sun shines hot & strong all day. The glass fell much some days agon: but rises again. It is most probable snow fell farther north: here was a little scattering one morning. The sun now, just before setting, shines plumb into the Dining-room-Chimney.

9. A very swift thaw.

10. Rain all day: this second frost lasted just a week.

4 Feb: 12. Made the bearing Cucum: bed for two two-light frames of yᵉ 8 loads of dung The dung has never shewed any great Heat. The bed is of a good thickness, & is well made. The Cucum:rs have one broad rough leaf; & shew a second.

13. Sent down a large portmanteau full of all sorts of perennials to my Brother Harry at Fifield. Gave the flower-bank a large dressing of rotten dung. Dug up the bank at the end of the barn, to prepare it for planting.

16. Hard black frosts for many mornings. To day frequent flights of snow. The Cucum:rs have a joint, & two rough leaves. The bearing-bed begins to heat well.

17. A very severe frost with a scattering of snow. There has never yet been snow enough at one time to cover the Ground.

18. A very severe frost. Laid the Hills of earth on the Cucum: bed. The bed seems in fine temper. It froze hard all day in the shade. Stopped down the Cucum: plants.

19. A very severe frost; & the ground as hard as Iron: strong sunshine, & a freezing air all day.

Turned out the Cucum:rs into their Hills: they were well-rooted in their pots.

20. A most severe frost, which came in a doors, & froze under my bed. Strong clear sunshine. The ice that was broken Yesterday, could not be broke to day without great violence. It is difficult to cover the Hot-beds enough.

Cut down two beechen stocks at Dawn-acre for boards, & planks. They yielded 593 feet of sawn stuff; out of which there were three planks for a manger; the rest were all boards. The stock out of which the planks were cut proved faulty: so that they were not so good as could be wished. Plunged the planks Yesterday in James Knight's pond.

Hung an Ham of my own making in a paper-bag in the Chimney.

Destroyed 24 bullfinches, which lay very hard on the Cherry-trees, & plum-trees, & had done a great deal of Mischief.

21. Hard frost & bright sunshine; but nothing near so severe as it was. The wind from full E: is turned full W:

Feb: 22. Sowed about a doz: Succade seeds. A thaw with a very sharp wind at S: E: the ground is still very hard under the surface, & the Ice very thick on the waters.

23. The mercury, which was very low yesterday, now rises again very fast; & the frost seems likely to go off without any fall at all. The ground would dig well, if the frost was out.

26. The Succades are come up extraordinarily well every seed. The frost went off on the 24th: with some rain. The Cucumrs: seem to be settled in their hills, & begin to shew runners.

27. Potted the succades in four pots. A good deal of rain & wet melting snow.

28. A great snow with a fierce driving wind from the West, which forced it into every cranny & opening so that the peat & mould in the houses were covered. It lies in very unequal depths on the Ground, being drifted by the strong wind: but would have been about ten inches in general had the air been still. The ever-greens were so loaded that they were weigh'd down to the Ground. The wind was so strong, & the snow so searching, that the Hotbeds were not uncovered above two Hours all day. The sun brok

out in the evening: but ye Horizon looked very threatning, being of a very livid Colour, & promising more fall. The Mercury fell very low indeed in the night; & was quite concave at the top when I went to bed.

March 1st A pretty smart frost in the night; but a swift thaw all day with some rain. The snow lies very thick still; so deep that I could not get out on Horse-back at the Northfield-lane end. The Glass very low still. The Cucumrs look well, & the bed is not injured by the bad weather. Sowed twelve more Succade-seeds: those in the pots look well.

2. A frost in the morning, & strong sunshine all day. The snow is still very deep, & melts only by the Heat of the sun. Newton-lane has been quite stopp'd up, & impassible. The Glass keeps rising, but is still very low. The lane towards Rood is not passable.

3. Exceedingly bright sunshine; a frost in the morning, & a rising Glass. I found on going to Faringdon that the snow had been much deeper than I was aware. Newton-lane below the Cross was barely passable. People more than 50 years old hardly remember such a snow.

March 4. A smart frost, & very strong sunshine all day. The bees work very briskly on the Crocuss amidst the banks of snow. The snow melts only where the sun shines. The blackbirds begin to whistle.

5. A great rain from the E: which melted the snow at a vast rate.

6. Great rains, & a flood at Gracious street.

7. The snow is all gone, except under some Hedges; &c. removed some of the Cucum^r. plants, & put in some from the pots, which have a better Countenance. The bed has been a little too hot.

8. Brewed half an Hogsh: of beer with six bushels of Rich^d. Knight's malt, & two pounds & three quarters of good Hops of the second year. When Hops were new 2 p^ds & ½ used to be sufficient. Made an half hogsh: of ale & ½ hogsh: of small of the same brewing. The water for the strong was all rain & snow water; which stood some days in tubs to mellow, & soften.

Put about a Quarter of a pound of Hops, & an handful of sand into the 45 Gall: barrel of strong beer brewed Feb: 1764. to fine it down for use.

8. Cast 8 loads of hot-dung for the Succade-bed.

Put a second pint of Brandy to the new-made wine: it is very quiet for it's age.

10. A vast rain & flood. The snow lies very thick still in some ditches, & hollow places.

11. Tunn'd the strong-beer, having stirred in the yeast two or three times a day while it stood in the tun-tub.

Hung the flitch of bacon in Mr Etty's Chimney.

14. Great storms of Hail, rain, & snow, with several loud Claps of thunder. The farmers are much behind in their season.

18. Vast rains; & nothing done in the Garden. The Cucum:rs have got male-bloom.

Sowed 12 more Succade seeds: those sowed last die in the pots: the first sowing thrives, & has a rough leaf. Turn'd the Succade-dung in the Yard: it was very hot.

19. Farmer Parsons brought 60 bush: of tan from Alton for the Cantaleupe-bed. Vast hail storms with some thunder.

21. 22. Continual heavy showers. The floods are much out. Cucum:rs thrive.

March 23. The Cucum:rs are full of male-bloom
No fruit shows yet.
24: 25. Vast showers. Gave the Cucum:r bed a lining
in front for the first time. Moss'd the bed.
The Apricot-tree has two blossoms blown-out; which
seem to be the only promising ones it is likely to have.
Some Peach-blossoms are just ready to open.
26. Made the succade-bed with the 8 loads of
Dung which has been brought-in ever since the
eighth of this month, & turn'd once. As it seem'd
to make but a shallow, weak bed, I laid about
twenty bushels of tan on it.
A very great rain. The Country is in a sad,
wet Condition.
27. One of the Cuc:r plants shews a fruit. A vast
storm from the west, which blow'd one of the melon-
-lights quite off the frame against the espalier-
-plum-tree; but without breaking any panes. The
Cuc:r lights were in danger of being blown-off, &
were secured by heavy slabs.
28. Mowed the grass the first time. A great rain.
The succades decay in their leaves thro' the dampness
& shadiness of the weather.

March 29. I Planted five fann'd Elms to screen Will: Carpenter's necessary House; & five large Laurels in a curve to screen my own, which I propose to move to the Corner next Parsons's yard: & ~~five~~ three elms in the corner of Parsons's yard to conceal my own from the street.

Continual rains still.

30. Put a little mould in the Succade-bed, & sowed sixteen Cantaleupe-seeds in it. The bed is yet full hot to lay-on the hills of earth. Raked down the asparagus-beds, & sowed five rows of pease; the first Crop of any kind put into the Ground this year. A stormy wind all day, & frequent showers.

31. & first of April. Stormy Winds, & great rains.

2. Earthed the Succade-bed, & put-on the Hills. The mould in a cold, clammy Condition. Planted three Dutch-Honey-suckles in the new-Garden. Sowed 16 basons of double-upright-larks-spurs. A very wet afternoon. A vast rain at night.

4. Planted three pots of Succades in their Hills: those that were forward were so damaged in their leaves by the long continuance of bad-weather, that the second sowing were preferable, which shew only seedling-leaves.

12. Sowed more Cantaleupe-seeds in the Succade-
bed: the first sown are just coming-up. Sowed more
Succade-seeds. Lined the back of the Cucum^r: bed
with one load of Dung. Planted seven rows of
Rasps in one of the upper quarters of the new Garden; three of white, & four of red. Planted five
rows of beans; the first planting.
Made a Celeri-bed for an Hand-glass with two
barrows of dung.

The peaches & Nectarines begin to blow-out.
Frequent showers still; & the Ground sadly wet.
Berriman brought 20 bushels of tan; in all 80.
The Cantaleupe-dung brought-in is 12 loads.
Set some boards a nights against the fruit-trees in
bloom. Sowed some spots of persicarias; & a drill
of parsley.

April 6. The Cucum^r: is blown-out to day. A vast
rain last night, & great wind to day. A very great
flood at Gracious-street. The springs are vastly
high; & the Lavants broke-out at Chawton.
Turn'd the Cantaleupe-dung.

7. Tempestuous winds, with vast rains, hail, & thunder.

8. 9. Stormy wind, & showers. The farmers are vastly
backward in their season. Very little lent-corn sown.
Frequent Claps of thunder, & a very cold air.

April 12. The first fine spring-like day, & no wet the whole day long.
Potted the Cantaleupes. Sowed a Crop of Carrots, parneps, Coss-lettuce, radishes, onions, leeks, & savoys; & sowed one long row of finochia in a drill with a little rotten dung mixed with the mould. ~~The~~ The ground worked as well as could be expected. The mercury is shot up very tall; but the skie threatens again for wet. Lined the Cucumber-bed with some grass-mowings: fruit blows every day. The Nightingales begin to sing. The Hyacinths begin to blow.

Planted five rows of potatoes in Turner's Garden, & put old-thatch in four of the trenches, & peat-dust in one for experiment sake. Exchanged roots with Mr Etty, as his ground is so different: his sort came originally from me.

13. Made the Cantaleupe-bed for two frames in the new Garden with 12 loads of dung that had been brought in just a fortnight, & cast once, & 60 bushels of tan on the top of it. It is a stout bed; & the tan lies at least six Inches thick. There have been three pretty fine days together, without any wind, & with very little rain. Some peaches & Nect: blow finely: some have little bloom.

~~14.~~ Farmer Knight is to fallow, & plow Baker's Hill in an Husband-like manner, this summer, & to sow it with wheat at Mich: & to allow me the straw of the Crop for the use of the Ground. The year following he is to sow it with oats, & allow me the straw: & I am to sow a Crop of St foin along with his Corn.

April 17. Layed down about 100 Laurustines; & grafted 6 crab-stocks with Cuttings from ye Lunning tree. Made a new bed for aromatic Herbs. A Little rain for a week past; but shady mild weather.

18. Bright, spring weather. Cut the first Cucumr: a small one: there are many swelling away.

19. Laid on the Hills on the Cantaleupe-bed. The earth is all prepared in the earth-house; be:cause the mould will not work at all in the new Garden. Now heavy showers after several fine days.

23. No Sun at all for several days: but black weather & frequent showers. It rains from all Quarters of the Compass. To day several Claps of thunder. The Ground is in a wet Condition. Something bites of the Cucr bloom, & gnaws the fruit. The grass grows very fast.

April 24. Turn'd out the Cantaleupes into their Hills: they are fine plants, & well rooted. The Succades succeed but poorly.
A soft, spring-like day, & some sunshine.
Caught the mouse that eat the Cucum^rs.
25. A very heavy rain.
26. Extraordinary foggs, & moist air without any Sun.
27. Cucum^rs come every day. Hot growing weather.
29. Made an annual bed, & sowed it with China-asters, Fr: Marrigolds, Dwarf-sunflowers, Chrysanthemums, & pendulous Amaranths. Sowed some large white Cucum^rs for the Hand-glasses. There have been two beautiful summer-like days together.
There are 99 considerable trees in Sparrow's hanger; 94 beeches, 3 ashes, & two oaks: there are also three large oaks in the pasture-field adjoining.
May 3. Sowed a second Crop of Pease in the ground where the turnep's stood; sowed four rows of dwarf white french-beans. Harsh, cold winds from the N: E: with an high barometer.
6. Cut down an Head of the Burnet, & gave it the mare. The Heads are very large, & just offering for Bloom. Very fine dry weather.

May 7. Planted half-Hund: of Cabbage-plants for a succession. Planted some slips of the double wall-flower. The melon-plants grow but poorly. Very dry weather; & the ground very much bound The fleas eat the Savoys.

Cut some Heads of Burnet, & gave it the Horses, in:tending to observe how long it will be before they spring again. Each root has a vast head.

8. Made four Hills for hand-glass Cucum:rs with two barrows of dung to each Hill. Very sultry weather; & showers about.

13. Hot burning weather: the ground is bound very hard. There has been hardly any rain for 18 days The peaches & Nect: by being sprinkled with water now & then this dry time, swell away. One Nect: tho' treated with the same care with the rest, is quite over-run with blistered leaves & shoots; & must, in all appearance, be taken away.

The Succades in one Hill have long runners that have been stopped down. The Cantaleupes seem not to take well to their Hills.

All the tulips seem to have run from their origina beauty.

May 14. Rack'd off half ~~an~~ hogsh: of raisin-elder
made last January, which was not quite free from
fretting. Let it stand one night in the River, & return'd
into the same barrel well wash'd; with half a ~~Gallon~~
pint of brandy. The wine is strong, & sweet enough
at present. There came out about a Gallon of
Grout; so that the barrel is not full.
No rain yet, but a sinking Glass.
The melons grow now.
Stopp'd down some of the most vigorous of the peach,
& Nect: shoots, which seem to threaten to run to Willow-
like wood. There is some fruit on each tree. All
the trees save one look healthy. The vines promise
a great deal of bloom.
15. A very moderate rain, that just moisten'd things.
18. Burning sunshine with a strong drying E: wind.
I have sprinkled the peach, & Nect: trees twice a week
during this drying weather. Most things want
watering. The melons, which have been earthed &
watered frequently, grow away. There has been rain
but once for these three weeks.
21. No rain yet; but strong sunshine, & a very drying
East wind. The Ground is much parch'd ~~at~~ on the
surface. The Succades begin to shew the rudiments of

18 bloom. May 24. Very harsh winds with some
flights of Hail. No rain now, save one little show
for a month past. The ground bound like Iro[n].
Earth'd-out the melons to the full in their frames
Put 10 field-crickets in the bank of the terrass: made
the Holes with a spit.
26. Several small showers from the N:
27. Now dry weather again with a very high Glass.
The Succades begin to blow, & to shew some fruit.
The Country is in great want of rain.
June 1. No rain yet: but drying scorching weather.
The corn, & Gardens suffer greatly. I do not remem-
:ber my Garden to be so totally overcome with hea[t]
& dryness so soon in the Year. The walks are burn[t]
up past mowing.
2. Thunder was heard at a distance.
3. Drying winds, & fierce sunshine.
The succades have fruit blown.
4. No rain yet: scorching, sunny weather. A sinking
glass, & some tokens of showers.
6. Thunder in the evening, & very black clouds to
the E: & S: E: a fine rain at Petersfield, but not on[e]
drop here.
7. Lined the succade-bed: as the dung was very stale

& dry we intermixed some layers of new-mown grass, & some weeds. The horses have been all so long at Grass that there will be no getting any fresh Dung.

8. The Succade-fruit begins to set. We water the melon-beds a good deal this scorching weather. The drought has continued six weeks from the 6th: & is now entered on the seventh week. The succade-lining heats furiously.

10. The weather continuing very burning, we water the melons ~~water the~~ largely. The Succades set apace, & the bines are of a good strength: the Cantaleupe-vines run rather weakly.

11. Earthed-out the Succades to their full depth, & extent; raised the frame, & found the roots were got-out very strong. Planted the basons in the field with annuals which are weak & drawn: there was no planting but by dint of great waterings: & no making melon-earth but by the same expedient. The stones & bricks are so extreamly dry, that the mason, who is facing my stable, is obliged to dip them all in water. The grass in the walks breaks & crumbles ~~[illegible]~~ under peoples feet as they tread. The lining of the succade-bed is very hot, & throws a good heat into the bed.

12. I set about five brace of promising Cantaleupes in the first frame: there are a few Succades about as big as pidgeons eggs.

~~20~~. Finish'd tacking the vines, which have an un-
:usual quantity of budds for bloom. Some shattering
showers; & some large ones about.

June 13. Sowed four long rows, one pint, of dwarf
white kidney-beans; & prick'd-out a large plot of
Celeri. The ground was well-watered before any
thing could be done. Planted annuals in the bor-
:ders of the Garden. Several very soft showers,
many times in the day; but not moisture enough
to lay the dust, or make the eaves drop.

14. Soft showers for four Hours this morning; &
showers again in the evening. So that Yesterday
the dry weather might be said to last exactly 8
weeks, beginning the day after S^t. Mark:
Turn'd-out the white cucumbers from under y^e
Hand-glasses: they are very strong, & shew fruit.

15. Sowed a Crop of Endive; two rows of fenochia,
& some vast white kidney-beans from Lima.
Hot, sunny weather.

17. Trimm'd-out the Succades, which were grown very
rude & wild: the fruit keeps setting here & there,
but not very fast. The bed is very warm, & has
been pretty frequently water'd. The Cantaleupes
seem to be setting; the bines are still but weak.
Some little shattering showers, which refresh the
leaves of things: but the ground is still as hard

as ever. Mrs Snooke's black-cluster
Grape is beginning to blow before any of the other
Vines, even the white-sweetwater.

June 19. Hot dry weather with an high Glass.
Cut my Grass: four mowers cut the great mead, ye
slip, & the shrubbery by dinner-time. Some of the
Succades are almost grown, some setting, & some
plants have no fruit swelling yet. Watered the
outsides of the Succade-bed this very dry weather.
Tack'd & thinn'd the Peach, & Nect: trees: there
is but little fruit. Some of the trees run to too
vigorous wood. The ground is strangely dry'd,
& burnt. My Crop of Grass is very well for
so burning an year.

21. Rick'd up my Hay without one drop of rain;
tho' the Clouds, a sinking Glass, & an hollow wind
threatned very hard: there were five jobbs.
Water'd the Crops very much.

22. A N: Wind, a rising Glass, & all tokens of
rain over for the present. Water'd the Canta:
leupes: there are a good many fruit set in ye first
frame; but a poor promise in the second.
Water'd the things again.

24. Gave the Cantaleupe-bed a good lining with two
waggon loads of dung; & some layers of Grass from the

22. orchard to set it in a ferment. The Cantaleupes now shew a good many likely fruit. Very hot dry weather & no rain yet. We are obliged to water very much to keep things alive. The melons have had an unusual share of Water.

June 28. A little rain; which was a noble watering at Fyfield for 12 hours

July 5. A little rain.

6. On my return from Fyfield I found a large Crop of Cantaleupes set; & some above half grown & a good many Succades coming on: the forward:est are full grown. The bed is well lined out, & very warm; & the fibres are running very strong without the frames.

There have been fine rains round Andover & Salisbury: the verdure on the Downs is very delicate, & the sheep ponds are full of water. But when I came on this Side Alresford I found all the ponds without one drop of water & the turf & Corn burnt up in a very deplora:ble manner; & every thing perishing in the Gardens. The peaches & Nectarines keep cast:ing their fruit. Cherries are now very fine.

The downs between Alresford & Andover are full of Burnet: so full in many places that it is almost the only herb that covers the Ground; & is eaten down very close by sheep, who are fond of it. The Case is the same between Andover & Sarum where in many places the Ground is covered with Burnet now in seed: a Child might in those places gather a considerable Quantity in a day. It is worth observation that this herb seems to abound most in the poorest, & shallowest chalkey soil. On Selborne Common (a rich strong piece of Ground) it has not been yet discovered.

Near Waller's Ash I rode thro a piece of Ground of about 400 acres, which had been lately pared by a breast plough for burning: here the bur:net was coming up very thick on the bare ground, tho' the crown of the root ~~was~~ must have been cut off of ~~cou~~ course along with the turf: this shews that it is a plant tenacious of life, since it springs from the severed ~~wounded~~ root like plantain.

Pd Will Dewey for 8 Doz: of young sparrows.

The drought has lasted 10 weeks last thursday.

The peaches, & Nect: have cast most of their fruit.

~~24~~. July 8. A gentle rain most part of the day: & in the evening a great shower for about half an Hour that moistened things well. The cartway ran with water, which is more than it has done before since the 25:th of April. This rain did not reach Faringdon or Empshot; so that it was of small extent.

9. Planted out a bed of leeks; & sowed a little spot with Batavian Endive; & a quarter with turneps.

10. Finished stopping down, & tacking the vines. The Grapes on Mrs Snooke's tree as big as small pease. Harsh drying winds. The garden quarters not moistened enough to plant. Dug up the Hyacinth roots, which seem very moist considering the very dry time.

12. ~~Pried~~ Tiled 8 of the forwardest Succades. Hot dry weather, with cold dews at night. My Cherries are now in high perfection. Large showers about yesterday; but a few drops only fell here. Some of the Cantaleupes swell very fast. It appears by the trial sticks that the bed has now as good a ground heat as most beds when made only five or six weeks; this must be owing to the lasting heat of tan. The Swallows & martins are bringing out their young. Young partridges that were flyers seen.

July 13. Farmer Knight, having plowed Bakers Hill twice before, stirr'd it across to day. The weeds are all kill'd, & the soil is baked as hard as a stone; & is as rough as the sea in an hard Gale: the Clods stand an end as high as one's knees.

14. Saw Pheasants that were flyers.

16. A good rain for about three Hours. A great rain at Haslemere, where I was then. Several fern-owls or Goat-suckers flying about in the evening at Black-down House.

18. Cut the first Succade-melon, a very delicate one; & deeply crack'd at the Eye: it had not one drop of moisture in it. Dry hot weather ever since the rain.

19. Rains about, but none here. Hot ripening weather. The dry fit has lasted 12 weeks yesterday. The wheat turns colour very fast. Added some earth to the melon-bed, where the lining was crack'd away from the main bed.

20. Gather'd a good quantity of Burnet-seed from my plants. This plant sheds it's seed as soon as ripe; & therefore whenever it becomes a field plant, it must be cut as soon as it shews any tendency to ripeness.
The melon-bed has still a moderate Heat.
Some shoots of the Laurustine are blowing, others budded for bloom

July 21. The Glow-worms no longer shine on the Common: in June they were very frequent. I once saw them twinkle in the South hams of Devon as late as the middle of Septemr.

The Redbreast just essays to sing.

Dry dark weather with an high glass. The garden dry'd up as hard as a stone: the Crops come to nothing; & no opportunity of planting out the autumn, & winter Crops. Cherries still very fine.

The haulm of the Cantaleupes (notwithstanding the continual drought) shews some disposition for rotting: in many parts it splits longitudinally & heals up again. There will be a very fine Crop of Succades.

23. Cut the second Succade, a small one. The field crickets cry yet faintly. Hot dry weather still. No rain coming we were forced to put out more Annuals in the dusty border, to shade 'em well, & to give them a vast quantity of water. The garden looks quite destitute of crops: no turneps will come up; no Celeri can be trench'd, nor endives, nor savoys planted out. The ponds in most parishes are quite dry'd up.

July 24. Succades come apace.
25. Some people have hack'd pease. Two most sultry days. Succades come by heaps. The wells in the street begin to fail. Turn'd all the large Cantaleupes.
This day the dry weather has lasted just 13 weeks.
Some of the Succades crack very deeply at the eye: those are always delicate.
26. Gathered a good basket of french beans; the first of the season. Put some tall sticks to the Lima-beans. Gave the Garden a good watering.
27. Housed my billet in curious order.
Abraham Low has got above 50 bunches of grapes on a vine of my Sort, which is but three years growth from a Cutting.
Many samples of new wheat were shown this day at Alton market: the Corn was said to be very fine.
28. The Martins begin to assemble round the weather-cock; & the swallows on the wallnut-trees.
Dry hot weather still, with a N: wind.
The Goldfinch, yellow-hammer, & sky-lark are the only birds that continue to sing. The red-breast is just beginning. The field-crickets in the Lythe cry no longer.
29. Eat a most curious Succade; & saved it's seed.
The beetles begin to hum about at the close of day.
Trench'd one row of Celeri to try if it can be saved.

July 31. Berriman began to reap in ye Ewel-close. The best of the Succades being cut, I gave the bed a good watering within & without: water'd the Cantaleupe-bed on the outside. Sultry weather. Wind S: for two days.

Aug: 1. This day the drought has lasted 14 weeks. Sultry, cloudless weather. Planted out four rows of loaf cabbadges, & two of Savoys between the Rasps in the midst of this burning weather, as there is no prospect of rain. The well sinks apace; we have watered away 26 well-buckets in a day. No Endives can be planted out yet. No rain at all since the 16 of July.

3. A plentiful rain for five hours & an half with a great deal of thunder & lightening. It soaked things thoro'ly to the roots, & fill'd many ponds.

4. Cut the first & the largest Cantaleupe, it weighed three pounds. The Succades keep coming. The Swifts have disappeared for several days. Newton-pond was just got empty; & yet there was a pretty good share of water in the pond on the Common. The Cantaleupe-bed by the trial-stick shews still a considerable Heat: it is owing no doubt to the tan. Laurustines cast their old leaves.

Aug: 5. Did a great stroke of Gardening after
the rain: sowed a quarter with turnep seed, & planted
it with savoys, the rows wide apart. Planted
out five more rows of Celeri; in all six long rows:
& planted a plot of endives. The endives seem to
be planted too late to come to any size: & the Celeri
& savoys probably will not be large. The ground
falls to pieces, & works as well as can be expected.
Gather'd the only & first Apricot the tree ever bore:
it was a fair fruit, but not the sort sent for; being
an Orange & not a Breda. Scarce any of Murdoch
Middleton's trees turn out the sorts sent for.
7. Dripping warm weather since the thunder storm.
8. The first Cantaleupe, growing on a faulty stem,
was not curious. Very showery weather.
Cut the second Cantaleupe: it is crack'd at the
eye. Great showers with distant thunder.
Mr Galden saw a single swift. Glow-worms appear'd
again pretty frequent; but more in the Hedges, &
bushes than in June, when they were out on ye turf.
9. Melons keep coming. Saw two swallows feeding
five young ones that had just left their nest: they
usually bring them out the beginning of July.

Dung borrowed in 1765.

Feb: 4.	Of Kelsey Dung pd ~~Car: pd~~	5 loads.
Do	Of Parsons Dung pd Car: pd.	3 loads.
March 8.	Of Parsons Dung pd Car pd.	5 loads.
Do	Of Kelsey Dung pd car pd	3 loads.
March 29.	Of Kelsey Dung pd car pd	3 loads.
– –	Of Parsons Dung pd Car: pd.	5 loads.
– – –	Of Berriman Dung pd C: pd	4 loads.
April 4.	Of Kelsey Dung pd car pd	1 load.
June 24.	Of Kelsey Dung pd car pd ~~waggon~~	2 loads

12

190

A Calendar of Flora, & the Garden from August 9th: 1765.

The distinction between ye Scirpi, & the Junci.

Scirpus, a bull-rush: this kind of plant bears stamineous flowers, & naked seeds gathered into a squamose Head; each scale holding a flatish triangular seed: the stalk is without any knots, round, & has a spongy pith.

Juncus, a rush, differs from ye bull-rush in having an hexapetalous Calix, & as many stamina as ye Calix has leaves; & many seeds contained in a seed-vessel.

Continued from the last page.

Novr. 25. Discovered the Ivy-leaved speedwell, or small Henbit (veronica flosculis singularibus, hederulæ folio, Morsus Gallinæ minor dicta) plenty in every garden & field.

Discovered on a bank at Faringdon Filex elegans, Adianto nigro accedens, segmentis rotundioribus; a beautiful fern about six inches high: Pilewort, or ye less Celandine (Chelidonium minus) in it's first leaves; it blows in March, & April: The greater Celandine in

it's first leaves (Chelidonium majus vulgare) & chervil
in it's first leaves (Cicutaria vulgaris; sive Myrrhis
sylvestris seminibus laevibus) called also wild Cicely,
& cow-weed. 191

Decr 6. Finish'd tacking, & trimming my fruit-wall trees: the peaches, & Nect: lie well to the wall, but seem not to be well-ripened in their wood this year. The vines, (which were contracted to make room for ye Peach: & nectarines) have large well-ripened shoots.

12. Found in a stubble in bloom, & pod the oval-leaved Turritis (Turritis foliis ovatis)

The flowers now in bloom are yarrow, Turritis, spurrey, butter-cups, viola bicolor, dandelion, dead nettle, hedge Do:

Put a finishing hand to my new stable by making my saddle cup-board, shelves, &c:

Discovered in shrub-wood Rough spleen-wort (lonchitis aspera) it is known from polypody by the tapering leaves reach-

14. An hard frost. (:ing down to ye bottom of ye stem.

31. A severe frost with an harsh E: wind, & cloudy skie: the Ground does not thaw in the middle of the day. Dug up melon-earth, & turn'd it up to the frost. Put some mellow earth in ye border under the melon-skreen.

Garden-Calendar for 1765.

Aug: 9. Planted a double row of Polyanths all along the great bank in the garden: they are all very small, being much stunted by the dry weather. Planted also some slips of the double Pheasant-ey'd pinks, which have very near blowed themselves to death.

Some hard rain, & distant thunder.

10. A beautiful dry day. Many people are hous:ing their wheat. The dripping week past has done a world of service.

Planted a large plot with savoys, & sowed it with turnep-seed. The last-sown turneps come-up by hundreds.

Cut a large Cantaleupe that was crack'd neither at eye nor tail.

11. Cut an other not crack'd.

12. Vast showers: very little wheat carry'd.

The rains have restored a fine verdure, to the grass-walks that seemed to be burnt to death for many weeks.

14. Great showers. The Cantaleupes come very fast, but do not crack well in general. Ten showery days restore a verdure.

♃. Aug: 14. Sent a brace & an half of Cantaleupes & a Succade melon to Bro: Benj:[n] at London.
Some small Cantaleupes, that were not at all crack are delicate. A very rising Glass. Penny royal, baum, sage, mint, thyme, rue, marjoram, & lavender in high bloom.
Baker's hill is harrowed down after these great rains: it was no easy matter to subdue the clods at all. Some of the old elders round the garden are ~~innumerable~~ almost leafless. Wallnuts are this Year innumerable. The white apples are fit to make pies. Grapes, peaches, nect: are very backward.
The Ground is now well soaked.
The yellow hammer continues to sing.
Wheat grows in the gripes.
Tremella abounds now on the walks; & the lichens encrease in size. The french beans are still lousy in some degree.
14. Sowed a Quarter of a pound of prickly seeded spinage, & some Coss lettuce to stand the winter. The ground was in good order, & fell well to pieces. A cold north wind.

Planted several slips of red pinks round ye borders, & some stocks, & bloody wall-flowers.
The burnet-seed, where it shatters on the Ground, comes up very thick.
The catkins for next year are formed on the Hasels.
Aug: 16. A cold N: E: wind, & rising glass. Much wheat has been housed to day. Some Cantaleupes, & Succades crack well at ye eye.
The stone curlues clamour. The mornings, & evenings are chilly. Plums, & figgs are very backward. The large Aster with yellow thrums, supposed to be Virgil's Amello, begins to flower.
Trimm'd the vines of second wood for ye last time: the grapes are very backward.
The yellow-hammer continues to sing.
The uncommon Aster with a black thrum blowing.
The variegated Epilobium in bloom.
17. Very cold weather for the season, with a N: Wind.
People house their wheat very briskly.
A very high barometer.
Melons continue in plenty.
The flea eats up the young turneps at a vast rate.
The weather so cold & dry, that nothing grows well in the Garden.

~~4.~~ Aug: 19. Cut all the Cantaleupes: they are not in general so well grown, & so ~~a~~ thick flesh'd as in former years, owing perhaps to the burning summer, which all the while was attended with N: drying winds not at all kindly to any kind of fruit, or Crops in the Garden. The bed maintains still a sensible heat.

20. Most beautiful harvest weather for several days the wheat will soon be all housed: that that was not ~~to~~ carry -in too hastily will be in curious order.

The wren whistles. A nest of young water-wagtails is just come forth. Tack'd the wall-trees: their tops are shrivell'd, & their fruit advances but poorly.

21. Took in all the melon-frames in very dry order. The bed has still some sensible heat in it. Very dry sultry weather with a falling glass. The night-moths, & earwigs, I find, feed on the flowers by night, as the bees & butterflies do by day this I found by going out with a candle.

22. Upon digging into the melon-bed down to the tan after the frames were taken away, I found that the tan maintained an heat equal to what is usual in a mild bed at first planting. From whence I con:cluded that the heat was too powerful this sunny scorching summer for the fruit by forcing them into

ripeness before they are full-flesh'd; in common Summers, when there is a good deal of shady wet weather no doubt the use of tan is of excellent service for Cantaleupes, as I have experienced.

Put some little melons remaining, under hand-glass:es. Hot sun-shine breaking out of a thick fog which lasted 'til eleven o' the Clock. A vast un:common dew.

Wild-ragwort, scabiouss, hawkweed, knap-weed, burdock, yarrow, rest-harrow, &c: in flower.

Put a Quartr: of a pound of hops to the strong-beer brewed in March, which has work'd afresh this Summer.

24. Wheat is housed in general; all the latter part of the Crop in most curious order. Barley & oats are beginning to be cut.

Haws begin to turn red: elder-berries from red to black. Most sultry ripening weather for many days. Some few of my black grapes just begin to turn; & some of the sweet-water begin to grow a little clear. Wasps encrease very fast.

Orleans-plums ripen.

Coveys of partriges are very large. Martens are grown very numerous at Selborne: they are much encreased within these few Years. Vast crops of hops in some Gardens.

~~6.~~ Aug: 25: 26. Most severe Heat, with a fall:
:ing Glass, & probably rain at a distance. People
are beginning to pick Hops. Black Grapes begin
to turn on the wall. Several Martens have now
second broods: quæ: if these late hatchings are not
rather in favour of hiding than migration.
27. Gathered my first figs. No rain now for 16 days.
My only Nectarine, & two only peaches begin to tend
towards ripeness. Mich: daiseys begin to blow.
Earth-nuts, & blue Devil's bit in bloom. Althæa
frutex in high bloom: Ladies bed-straw just out.
Yellow-hammer seems to have done singing.
28. Still, hot, gloomy days. Rain begins to be much
wanted by the farmer, & Gardener.
30. A moderate shower with a brisk Gale. The melons
left under hand-glasses keep coming. Full moon.
Yellow toad-flax, (linaria) great purple snap: dragon,
(Antirrhinum) (~~from~~ found in a lane at Empshot, &
supposed to be thrown out from some Garden) Eye:
:bright, betony; small spear-worth, (Ranunculus flam:
:meus) vervain-leaved-mallow, the common-reed, many sorts
of Epilobium; Scabious, purple, & deep blue; wild basil,
now in bloom. Wild Basil is a pretty flower, & a common weed.
Swallows feed flying, & water-wagtails running round

Horses in a meadow. The gentle motions of the Horse stir up a succession of flies from the grass.
The water-wagtail seems to be the smallest english bird that walks with one leg at a time: the rest of that size & under all hop two legs together.
The Alders have form'd their young catkins against next spring.
The Grapes change pretty fast.
Septemr. 5. Brisk winds, & showers for several days. The apples are pretty much blown-down in some places; & the hops received some Injury.
The winds beat-down many of my figs, & baking pears.
Since my melon-frames have been taken-in, & before the rains fell to moisten ye mould on the bed, there grew up at once a very singular appearance of the fungus kind, that seemed rather to be poured over the ground than to vegetate: it was soft & pappy, & about the consistence of thick milk, & of a very ill savour. Where I wounded it with a stick it sent out a sort of bloody Ichor; & soon hardened it into a dark substance; & is now turn'd into a fine Impalpable dust like that of the Lupi Crepitus. I have had them on beds before the frames have been taken-off; when they have crept in part up the side of the frame. To the best of my remembrance they have never appeared on any beds that

8. that have not been covered with tan. On con:sulting Ray's methodus I find no traces of any such kind of fungus. ×

On the Lythe I found a few days since in full bloom the Dentaria aphyllos, seu Anblatum; a peculiar plant, of the same Class with the Orobanche. Hill says it begins flowering in May. This was ladies traces.

Sep: 7. Fine ripening weather. Grass, & garden-plants grow apace. Howed & thinned my two plots of turneps. Earwigs eat the Nect: by night, but not the peaches.

9. Beautiful Autumnal weather: most of the Corn housed. Gathered my only Nect: it was not ripe; but the earwigs had gnawed it so that it could not come to any thing. Gathered my first peach it's flesh was thick, tender, white, & juicy; & parted from the stone. It was a good fruit; but not so high-flavoured as some I have met with.

Gather'd some ~~of my~~ forward white grapes: they were very agreeable tho' not quite ripe: the black Grapes in general are backward.

On the steep chalky end of Whetham-hill I dis:covered a large plant of the deadly Nightshade [belladōna] full of ripe fruit: & on the bogs of Bean's pond in Wullmere forest the same day that peculiar plant the sun-dew [rorella] in plenty. There are it seems on the same bog plenty of cran-berry-plants: but I could not venture on the moss to look after them. Cranberries, [vitis Idaea]. I thought I discovered a small Parnassia but was not sure. Found also ~~the bastard toad-flax, [thesium]~~ & southern wood [abrotanum] in a lane; & dyer's weed [luteola] very vigorous, & full of seed in a farm yard at Faringdon.

Owls hiss round the Church in a fierce threat-ning manner: I suppose they are old ones that have young. There are young martens still in some nests. About five days ago Sr Sim: Stuart's game-keeper kill'd an wood-cock in the moors. Not true.

11. Gathered my second & last peach: it was from a different tree from ye first, but seems to be the same sort.

13. Bagg'd up between 40, & 50 bunches of black grapes in Crape. Ty'd up all the best endives for blanching: they are but small.
Procured several Cranberry-plants from bean's pond with berries on them.

15. Fine Autumn weather for many days.

~~10.~~

Septr: 16. Gathered some good white Grapes. Took in the Hand-glasses, & cut the two last melons; not ripe.

17: 18. Went down to Ringmer. The second day there was a moderate rain for eight Hours, during which I lay-by at Brighthelmstone.

In a lane towards the sea near a village call'd Whiting not far from ye above-named town, I disco:vered a shrub of the rose kind, that had heps of a jet-black Colour, & very beautiful small pinnated leaves. As the leaves resembled those of Burnet, quæ: if this was not the Burnet-rose, which I think is said to grow wild. As it was quite out of bloom I had not ye satisfaction of seeing the flower.

I saw a flower afterwards, & it was white & single.

On the poorer parts of ye Sussex-downs I saw the smaller Burnet in plenty; but it had shed it's seeds. I find the rich pasture-grounds at Ringmer very bare of Grass: they seem to have suffered by the drought this summer as much as in any parts of the Country.

Ladies-bedstraw frequently in flower on the downs; & a thistle with an echinated head, & ~~no~~ little down to ye seeds.

Sep^r: 20. Discovered plenty of the prickly rest-harrow (Ononis) & dier's broom, both in bloom & pod, in the pasture-fields at Ringmer.
Mrs Snooke's grapes are very good; especially the black. Her crop of apple's fail. Blue Scabiuss in plenty still. The rooks frequent ye nest-trees great part of ye day. I saw a few wheatears (birds) on the Sussex down as I came along. Vast quantities are caught by the shepherds in the season; (about ye beginning of Harvest) & yet no numbers are ever seen together, they not being gregarious. Showers, & some brisk winds. Hawkweeds all ye Country over from the highest downs to ye lowest pasture-field. Wasps seem at present to be very much check'd: they have gnaw'd the Grapes pretty much. This very dry summer has damaged Mrs Snooke's buildings by occasioning such vast chops in the clay-soil, that they loosen the walls, & make settlements. Since I came, there were cracks in the ground deeper than ye length of a walking-stick.
24. Made a visit to Mr John Woods at his new mill. On the downs near Bpstone I found the downs covered with Burnet: & in one place, where the Ground had been devonshired the beginning of

~~in~~ the summer, the ground was cloath'd over with Burnet & filipendula, whose crowns had been severed with the turf. Found French-mercury (mercu~~ry~~:rialis ~~crambe~~) the smallest sort of Cudweed; & saw abundance of sea-plants on ye shore which I had not time to examine.

Septr. 26: 27: 28. Returned from Ringmer. Fine dry soft weather; & the roads quite dusty. Very little rain has fallen yet: the deep pasture Grounds round Ringmer are bare of Grass, & in great want of water. Many ponds on ye road are quite dry.

Saw plenty of the whortle-berry plants on Rogate heath. I found my grapes in general very backward, notwithstanding the dry sunny weather. The wasps seem to have done very little damage; they seem to be quite gone.

30. Made 10 quarts of elder-juice ~~syrup~~; to which when I had put 10 pds. of sugar, & boiled them up together, there came 13 bottles of syrop.

Ivy in full flower. Scabius, some mulleins, throat-worts, bugloss, hawkweeds, wild basil, marjoram, eye-bright, mallows, knapweeds, &c: still in bloom.

Found the Woodroffe (asperula) in plenty in my beechen Hanger. The beeches begin to be tinged with yellow.

A great rain.

Septr: 30. The men are weeding the garden, which is very much over-run with groundsel.

Octr: 1. A very cold, blustering day. Began fires. Began gathering the white apples, & golden pippins. Earthed up the Celeri, some rows to top. Used ye first Endive: it is too small to blanch well. Planted a row of Burnet-plants brought from ye Sussex downs. The cater-pillars have been pick'd off the savoys several times: those that have not used that precaution have lost every plant. The Cucumbers, & kidney-beans are cut down with the Cold. The ashes, & maples in some places look yellow. The wood-lark sings, & the wood-pidgeon coes in ye Hanger. John took his bees.

3. Vast showers with frequent claps of thunder. Discovered the Enchanter's nightshade (Circæa) it grows in great plenty in the hollow lanes.

4. Gather'd in my baking-pears, about three bushels. The wood-ruffe, when a little dryed, has a most fragrant smell.

5. Examined the wild black Hellebore (Helleboraster niger flore albo) an uncommon plant in general, but very common in Selborne wood. ~~Discovered the nipple-wort (lampsana.)~~ Vast heavy showers, with a tempestuous wind.

~~14~~ Octr: 6. Vast showers: the Ground is well-drench'd.

8. Planted a row of cos-lettuce along against ye fruit-wall to stand the winter.

Gather'd some very good grapes, both black & white, from the fruit-wall: but there are an abundance on the House, that seem as if they never could be ripe.

10. Discovered the small creeping tormentil (tormentilla) the gromwel (lithospermum) & the small Centaury (centaurium minus.)

The wren sings. Martens are plenty flying about under the shelter of the Hanger.

8. A great light seen, & a vast explosion from ye S: about a quarter past nine in the evening: the Cause unknown. It shook peoples houses very much. It seems to be meteorous.

10. Discovered common fumitory. Ray classes it under his anomalous plants.

11. Discovered the Common-figwort (scrophularia) in bloom, & in pod; & the Common dog's mercury (cynocrambe)

12. Discovered in Mrs Etty's garden the silvery Alpine Crane's-bill (Geranium argenteum Alpinum), & the red Valerian (Valeriana floribus rubris caudatis)

Snakes are still abroad, & wood ants creeping about.

A great rain again last night.

Octob^r: 12. The black Hellebores are budded for bloom on the Hill. The small creeping tormentil pretty frequent on Selborne common.

15. Set-out for Oxon. Saw ye first field-fare, martens still flying about. Saw none of the swallow-kind afterwards.

Farmer Knight sowed Baker's hill with wheat.

16. Discovered on the banks of the Thames as I walked from Streatly to Wallingford --

The water hoar-hound (marrubium aquaticum) the yellow willow-herb, or loose-strife (lysimachia) the purple spiked D^o (lysimachia purpurea) & the Comfrey (symphytum magum) in bloom, being one of the Herbæ asperifoliæ: water figwort (scrop: aquat:)

I also saw in Oxford dry specimens of the less stitchwort (Caryophyllus holosteus arvensis glaber flore minore) & the Cross wort (cruciata)

I saw at the Physic garden Madder (rubia tinc:torum) the Cymbalaria (linaria) hederaceo folio glabro: the stinking Gladwin (Iris sylvestris) stinking hoar-hound (marrubium nigrum) white hoarhound (marru:bium album) a large sort of Burnet: moth mullein (blattaria) Bugle (bugula) Water-scorpion-Grass (myosotis scorpioides palustris) the hawkweed called Hierachium echioides capitulis cardui benedicti; al: lang (de beuf.

Octobr: 21. Weather uncommonly mild: grass
& garden-plants grow very fast.
26. Returned from Oxon to Selborn. A very white
frost in the morning. I have seen no Swallows since
the 15th: Planted in my Garden nine large plants
of small burnet, which I gathered in a Chalkey lane
on my Journey.

John planted in my absence a plot of cabbages
to stand ye winter. The garden-burnet still conti:
:nues very vigorous; & the Celeri is grown very gross.
28. A very smart frost that made the ground crisp,
& has stripp'd the mulberry-tree & some ashes.
The Hanger looks very much faded; & the leaves begin
to fall. In general the new-sown wheat comes up well.

Plants still in bloom are the wild-basil, white
behn, common mallow, several Hawkweeds, bugloss,
the hoarhounds, Hedge-nettles, dead-nettles, dandelion,
wild succory, Ivy, furze, blue-bottles, thistle, sow-thistle,
mullein, fumitory, yarrow, wild Marjoram, (origanum)
tufted Basil, (clinopodium) small Centaury, honey:
suckle, wild; Arbutus, Bramble, clover, charlock,
~~[illegible]~~, throat-worts, crane's-bill, Scabious,
Knapweed, - Mother of thyme, wild red Campion,
butter-cups, stinking Mayweed, the common daisey,
the great daisey, ragwort, broad-leaved All-heal, fluellins.

Octr. 29. Discovered in the lane leading to the North-field base-hoar-hound with a white blossom, but just going out of bloom (stachys) common Self-heal out of bloom (prunella) Nettle-leaved throat-wort or Canterbury-bells (Trachelium) Cluster-flower'd, or little throat-wort (Campanu:la pratensis flore conglomerato) Dwarf spurge (tithymalus pumilus angustifolius) creeping mouse ear (pilosella repens) Crow's foot Crane's bill (Geranium batrachoides)

30. Discovered in my Ewel-close, a wheat-stubble, Sharp-pointed fluellin just coming into bloom (Linaria, Elatine dicta, folio acuminato) & round-leaved female fluellin (Linaria, Do. dicta, folio subrotundo) in plenty: also Mouse-ear scor:pion-grass (Myosotis scorpioides hirsuta): & broad-leaved little All-heal (Sideritis humilis lato obtuso folio)

The skie, & wood-lark sing in fine weather: rooks frequent their nest-trees. The ground is now full wet for a wheat-season. The wren sings.

31. Discovered the Ivy-leaved Sowthistle, or wild lettuce (Lactuca sylvestris Murorum flore luteo)

18. in a most shady part of the hollow lane under the cove of the rock as you first enter the lane in great plenty, on the right hand before you come to the nine-acre-lane: there was also male fern, (filix mas) & hart's tongue, (Phyllitis) discovered also common nipplewort (Lampsana) it is distinguished from Hawkweeds by having no down to it's seeds.

Novr. 2. Gromel, figwort, & viper's bugloss, & mouse-ear-scorpion-Grass still in bloom. I suspected I saw the leaves of the parnassia, ~~[illegible]~~ on a bog. Examined the viper's bugloss, (echium vulgare) & the small wild bugloss (buglossum sylvestre minus) the wild tanzy (tanacetum) great water horsetail, (equisetum palustre majus) Sun spurge (tithymalus helioscopius) wood-spurge (Tithymalus characias Amygdaloides) common St. John-wort (Hypericum vulgare) dwarf-hawkweed with sinuated very narrow leaves (Hieracium parvum in arenosis nascens, seminum pappis densius radiatis) Knawell, ~~common ground pine (chamæpitys vulgaris~~) Clown's allheal (Sideritis fœtida) small procumbent St. John wort (Hypericum procumbens minus) Herb Gerard, Gout-weed, or ashweed (angelica sylvestris minor seu erratica)

Novr: 4. Racked-off my half Hodsh: of raisin-wine, which began to ferment again: there was a great deal of sediment at bottom.

5. A Considerable snow for many Hours: but it melted pretty much as it fell. Gathered-in a great quantity of Grapes, which are still very good. 6th: A hard frost, & ice. Gathered-in all the grapes, about a bushel, the weather threat-ning for more frost. Spread the best bunches on a sheet in the dining-room.

12. Replaced the rasp-plants that dyed in the summer. The leaves of ye Butcher's limes but just begin to fall. The leaves in general hold-on well this year, thro' the mildness of the season.

17. I planted the border by the wallnut-tree in ye best Garden with two rows of my fine white, & blue Hyacinths: the blue are altogether at the end next the House. The border was well-dunged; & planted in good dry order. I planted also a good large spot ~~with~~ with smaller roots, & offsets to make a nursery. The blue at the end next the House.

Dark still weather for many days, with some small rain sometimes, & a very high barometer. The water is much sunk away in the roads, & lakes.

20\. Nov^r: 18. Discovered the common polypody (polypodium vulgare) in the hollow lane; & the stinking flag-flower, called Gladdon or Gladwin, (Iris fœtida, Xyris dicta) in the hollow lane between Norton-yard, & French-meer just without the gate: it was thrown, in all probability, out of the garden which was formerly just on the other side of the Hedge. In general it is esteem-:ed a bad blower; but this parcel of plants has produced many flowers this summer; & have sever-:al pods, which open in three parts, & turn out y^ir scarlet berries much in the manner of the male piony. There is but one seed in each berry. Discovered the common Spurrey (alsine, spergula dicta major) in pod, & bloom in a ploughed field: most exactly described by Ray.

22\. A very fierce frost for two nights: it froze with-:in the second. Discovered little field-madder (rubeola arvensis repens cærulea) & the small-flowered pansy (viola bicolor arvensis) in a wheat-stubble in great abundance.

The potatoes turned out well beyond expectation after such a burning summer: those planted on peat-:dust were superior to those on old thatch.

Garden Calendar for 1766. & 1767.

Feb: 8: 1769. Brewed half an hogsh: of strong beer, with six bushels of Rich: Knight's malt, & three pds & an half of John Berriman's hops.
The water was about three parts rain-water.

Feb: 27. 1769. Mashed an hundred of Malaga raisins in order to make twenty gallons of wine. The raisins were good & cost 23s per hund:
Put 6 buckets & two thirds of a bucket of water.
March 21. Tunned the raisin-wine, & added to it ten bottles of elder syrop.

March 2. 1770. Brewed half an hogsh: of strong beer with six bush: of Rich: Knight's malt, & 3 pds & an half of Berriman's hops.
Mem: put one bush: of brown malt to the second mashing.

March 12: 1770. Mashed an hundred of Malaga raisins in order to make twenty gallons of wine. The raisins were good, & cost 23s pr hund:
Put 6 buckets & 3/4 of water to the raisins.
April 6. Tunned the wine & put to it eleven bottles of elder syrop. There was barely liquor enough to fill the barrel.

Feb: 16. 1768. Made then 20 gallons of raisin-wine in a new barrel with one hund: of Malaga-raisins. The raisins were good, & cost 25 S. pr hund: Put 6 buckets, & two thirds of water.

March 8. Tunned the raisin-wine, & put to it 10 bottles of elder syrop. It just held out.

March 9. Brewed half an Hogsh: of strong beer with six bushels of Rich: Knight's malt, & three pounds of Turner's hops. Well-water. The beer work'd well.

May 19. Rack'd off the elder-wine, which worked too much: took from it two quarts of grout, & put to it one pint of brandy. It is sweet, & well flavoured.

Sep: 12. Bottled-off the elder-wine made Feb: 16: it was fine, & well flavoured. The cask ran seven doz: of bottles: some bottles were very large.

Sepr: 22. Bottled-off the Hogsh: of port: it was very bright: my share ran 11 doz: & 10 Bottles.

Septemr: 23. Made 12 bottles of elder-syrop: put to it 10 pounds of coarse sugar.

Dung borrowed in 1768.

March 5.th

Of Kelsey dung pd car: pd 4 loads.

Of Parsons car pd. dung pd 2 loads.

7. Of Hale dungpaid car pd 2 loads.

25. Of Hale - - - - dungpaid car pd 4 loads.

- - - - Of Kelsey - - - - dung pd car pd 8 loads.

- - - Of Parsons - car pd. dung pd - - - 4 loads.

Ap: 19: Of Parsons - - car pd - dung pd 2 loads.

June 10. Of Parsons - car pd dung pd 1 load.

Dung borrowed in 1769.

March 6. Of Hale dung pd - car pd - - 4 loads.

Of Benham - car pd - dung pd - - 3 loads.

Apr: 13.th Of Hale dung pd - car pd - - - 4 loads.

Of Benham - car pd - dung pd - - - 4 loads.

May 12. Of Benham - car pd - dung pd - 1 load.

June 12. Of Benham - - car pd - - - - - - 2 loads.

Dung borrowed in 1770.

Feb: 22. Of Hale car pd: dung pd — 5 loads.
23. Of Benham car: pd. dung pd 3 loads.
Dung pd: Of Benham car: pd: 6 loads.
Of Hale car pd dung pd 5 loads.
June 8. Of Hale dung pd car: pd 4 loads

Garden Calendar

Aug: 2. Master Hale brought me in one load of Hay. pd

for the Year

1766.

& 1767.

June 1: 1770. Racked off the raisin-wine made in March, & put to it one pint of brandy. Took out a gallon of grout.

Dung borrowed in 1771.

March 8. Of ~~Bent~~ Hale Dung pd car pd. 5 loads.
11. Of Benham Car pd 3 loads.
April 1. Of Hale dung pd one load car pd 1 load.

Nov^r: 29. 1771. Brewed half an hogshead of strong beer with 6 bush: of Rich^d: Knight's malt, & 3 p^ds & an half of Berri=:man's hops of the year 1770. The water was all from y^e well, but it was drawn some days before, & stood in the open air.

March 24. 1772. Brewed half an hogshead of strong beer with 6 bush: of Rich: Knight's malt, & near 4 pounds of Berriman's hops of the year 1770. All rain water. Put one bush: of brown malt to the second mashing). The beer works well.

March 5. 1773. Brewed half an hogshead of strong beer with 6 bushels of Rich: Knight's malt, & three pounds & an half of Berriman's hops. All rain water. Put one bush: of brown malt to the second mashing. Beer works well.

Nov^r: 1: 1773. Brewed half an hogshead of strong beer with six bushels of Rich: Knight's malt, & three pounds & an half of Berriman's new hops. All rain water. Put one bushel of brown malt to the second mashing.

1766.

Jan: 1st. The last Year concluded, & this began with a very dry, still frost.
Wheeled into the melon-ground a parcel of my own dung that had never taken any wet; there having been no rain worth mentioning for many weeks.
4. Made the seedling cucumber-bed.
10. Sowed about 30 cucumr: seeds.
13. The bed heats well, & the plants begin to ap:pear. Severe, still frost yet. The ground has never thawed at all in the middle of the day, since this weather began; but is covered with dust. There have been several small flights of snow; but never enough quite to cover the ground: & yet several redbreasts, & some red-wings have been found frozen to death. It froze within very much to night.
17. The same still, dry weather continues, with a dark sky, & high barometer. The snow is quite gone; &

4. the ground all dust. To day the frost has lasted just three weeks. The cucum:rs come-up well: sowed more.

Jan: 18. Somewhat of a thaw.

19. A thaw still with an high barometer & a fog: the first Cucum:rs are potted, the second-sown are come-up well.

21. A dry thaw with a N: wind, & high barometer. There has been no rain now for seven or eight weeks. The ponds are very low, & the wells sink:ing. The wind has been remarkably still since it has been so dry.

25. A gentle thaw still, with vast fogs, but no rain. The ground that was so dusty, is now very dirty with:out any fall. The soil is strangely puffed-up, & lightened. Sowed a box of Mr: Gibson's polyanth-seed: & five rows of marrow-fat-pease in a very mellow, well-dunged quarter.

Some of the Cucum:r plants keep dying for want of sun, being rotted by the reek of the bed.

28. The same still, dark, dry weather with the glass higher than ever.

Jan: 29. A vast white dew; & fog in the day. The barometer is higher than ever.
The Cucum:rs hang their leaves, & want Sun.
30. Sowed half the border under the melon-skreen with lettuce, & radishes. All the stiff soil is taken-out of that border, & laid-up to the frost to make melon-earth; & mould that has been in the frames is laid in it's place. Very fierce frost, & partial fogs.
Feb: 1. A thaw: rain & wind with a sinking glass. The first rain for many weeks.
3. Severe frost returns.
8. Severe frost.
10: 11. Rain, soft weather, & a thoro' thaw.
13: 14: 15. Continued Rains from the East which occasioned vast floods in some places. This fall was in several parts of the Kingdom a very great snow; & in others a rain which froze as it fell, loading the trees with ice to such a degree, that many parks, & forests were miserably defaced, & mangled. A strong E: wind contributed much to this damage.

~~4.~~ Feb: 18. Made a fruiting-bed for Cucum:rs with 8 loads of dung.
19. Planted six rows of Winsor-beans.
25. Planted the Cucum:r bed with plants that have two joints, are stopp'd down, stocky, & well-coloured.

Mild, grey weather, with a tall barometer. Land is in excellent mellow, dry order: people are sowing pease in the fields.

March 1. Dry weather still with a sinking glass. Brewed half an Hogsh: of strong-beer with 6 Bushels of Rich: Knight's malt, & two pounds & three quarters of good Hops. The water was from the well.
Sent a large flitch of bacon to be dryed to Mr Etty's chimney: it lay seven weeks & three days in salt on account of the frost, during which it did not seem to take salt.

The sun broke-out after many shady days.
2. A white frost, & very wet afternoon.
3. Sun-shine morning, the first for a long time.

Put some fresh Cucum^rs plants into some of ye Hills: the first removed were coddled in their own steam for want of Sun.

Sowed the first Succades.

March 6. The succades appear: the bed is full hot this mild weather.

7. Potted the succades: sowed more.

Finished a low rod-hedge between ye garden, & the orchard.

Soft delicate weather.

Planted some wood-straw-berries along at ye back of ye new hedge.

8. Transplanted some burnet, self-sown last sum: :mer: sowed carrots, coss lettuce, radishes in ye border under the melon-skreen.

Brought in 10 loads of dung for the succade-bed; & one load to line the Cuc^r seed-bed.

Cucum^rs begin to shew runners.

10. Planted one Chaumontelle-espalier-pear at the S: W: side of the second middle quarter; & one Crasan-burgamot-pear opposite across the alley; & one D^o near the standard nonpareil tree. These trees are from Armstrong at N: Warnboro; & are

~~&~~. to supply the place of those that failed.
Planted two more fan-elms at the back of the necessary-house.

Hot, sunny weather. The cumcum:r bed is full warm.

March 12. Sowed five rows of pease in the orchard the first crop begins to appear.
No rain for ten days. Sunny, hot days, with an E: wind, & frosty nights.

Made half an hogsh of raisin-wine with one hund: of Malagas, & half an Hund: of Smyrnas. Put to the raisins ten buck:ets & an half of water. The raisins were new, & fine: the former cost 24s: the latter 17.

13. Racked-off my last-made wine the third time. It is very good; but will not be quite fine, as it moves a little still. Took away about two quarts of very thick Grout.

Planted some stinking gladwins in the garden, a sweet bryar, and a black hellebore from ye wood.
Raked-down my asparagus-beds: the mould every where falls in a dust.

March 14. Turned the melon-dung, which is very hot.
15. Earth'd, & moss'd the seed-cucumber bed, which has the forwardest plants.
Hot sun-shine, & cold E: wind.
17. Pegg'd down the Cucum:rs which were grown up to the Glasses.
The succades are very fine, & have two rough leaves.
Hot sunshine with frosts. There has been now no rains for fifteen days.
18. Turn'd the melon-dung a second time. It is very hot. Black, windy weather, with some small flights of snow.
20. Thick Ice.
Made a Celeri-bed for an hand-glass.
Sheltered the wall-trees (which are too much blown) with boards, & doors.
22. Sowed Celeri.
Some rain after 19 very dry days.
Sowed rows of parsley.
23. Snow with thick ice, & a severe North-wind.
24. More snow, & fierce frost.
Covered the fruit-trees against the wall with

~~8~~ boards, & mats during these frosty nights. Made the succade-bed with ten loads of dung that had been twice turn'd, & had heated much. It is a very stout bed, & seems in good order. The fruit-trees against the wall are much blown-out, & in danger from this severe weather.

25. Snow in the night, & Ice.

26. Rain in the morning from the S: till twelve; then the wind turned N: & there came a violent snow for six hours, which lies very deep on the ground; & is but a bad sight so late in the year. The wall-trees have been boarded, & matted all day; & the hot-beds have scarce been opened at all.

27. A very heavy snow all day; which by night lay a vast thickness on the Ground; in many places three feet. All the shrubbs were weighed flat to ye earth. The hot-bed was never un-covered all day; but the plants lived in dark-ness. The boards & mats were kept before ye wall-trees.

28. The snow melted in part with a strong sunshine: but it is still as deep as an horse's

belly in many places.
The Cucr. plants look very well to day.
March 29. Warm air, & a swift thaw: yet ye snow is very deep in some places: all along ye N: field it is deeper than an Horse's belly.
Stopped-down the Succades: they are fine plants.
30. Snow goes away with a gentle rain.
April 1: 2. Great rain.
Female bloom of a Cucumber blows-out.
3. Black moist weather: the Hot-beds want sun.
4. Put the hills on the succade-bed: the earth is rather too moist, not being housed before ye snow.
The dung has been brought-in ever since the eight of March: the bed seems now to be mild.
5. Turned-out the Succades into the Hills: the plants are stout, & well-rooted; but look rather pale for want of sunshine.
Sowed some Romagnia melon-seeds from Mr. Humphry; & ~~so~~ some Cantaleupe-seeds.
5. Tunn'd the raisin-wine after I had let it settle a day & a night: I kept back a great quantity of grout. There was a gallon or two over for filling-up. Coloured it with 15 bottles of

~~10.~~ elder-syrop.

April 7. Mowed the grass-plot for the first time

9. Planted five rows of large fine potatoes, with a layer of peat-dust in every trench.

Sowed a crop of Carrots, parsneps, coss-lettuce & onions; a plot of leeks; double-stocks, dwarf Sunflowers, & savoys.

Sowed twelve basons more of Selborne-saved larkspurs.

The ground in curious, mellow order.

10. The last-sown melons are coming-up.

Dry, March-like weather.

The succades push-out runners.

12. Potted the Cantaleupes, & Romagnias.

Cucum:rs throw out fruit very fast.

Beautiful weather.

19. Cut the first Cucumber.

Small showers.

22. Cut ye second cucumber.

Soft showers.

Cucumbers show a great succession of fruit.

April 26. The succades have runners with three joints, are stopped, & shew third wood. Cut three Cucumbers. Cucumbers grow very fast. Soft, showery, growing weather.

26. Finished moving my barn, which I set at the upper end of the orchard. It began to move on thursday the 17, & went with great ease by the assistance of about 8 men for that little way that it went in a straight line: but in general it moved in a curve, & was turned once quite round, & half way round again. When it came to the pitch of the Hill it required 20 hands; & particularly when it wanted to be shoved into it's place side ways, parallel with Collins's hedge. Near one day of the time was taken up in making new sills, one of which was broken in two by skrewing it round sideways. No accident happened to the workmen, or labourers; & no part of the frame-work was broken or dislocated, so as to do any material damage.

The Workmen were three days in pulling down ye shillings, & blocking & removing obstructions, previous to ye removal. The barn is 40 feet long.

April 28. Made some holes for the hand:
:glasses, fill'd them with the mowings of the walks,
& sowed some large white Cucumbers.
Summer-like growing weather.
Cut 4 large Cucumbers.
Put the sticks to the pease. Weeded & thinn'd
the lettuce.
29. Sowed a plot of lucern-seed to transplant.
Earth'd the succade-bed pretty near to ye full; &
moss'd it all over.
Most beautiful, shady, growing weather.

May 5. Made the second melon-bed with eight loads
of hot dung, & some grass-mowings. The dung is
full hot still. There will be dung this year only
for two frames.
The succade plants show fruit, & grow, & look well.
Black wet weather of late.
6. Sowed seven rows, one pint, of dwarf-white-
-kidney-beans: the Ground has been dug three times
this spring, & is very mellow.
8. Made an annual-bed with grass mowings, &
sowed it with African, & French Marigolds, pendu:
:lous amaranths, & China Asters.

8. Sowed some snap-dragon seeds, & some dwarf-sun-flowers.
Planted five short rows of globe-artichokes, sent me by Mr. Fort of Salisbury.
Black, showery, growing weather for many days.
12. Turned-out two pots of Romagnia-melons, & one of Cantaleupes into the new bed. Bored holes in ye bed, which is still full hot.
Succades shew male, & female bloom.
Thunder, & heavy cold showers.
The wheat, & barley turns somewhat yellow.
13. Vast heavy showers, with Hail, & frosts at night.
14. Covered the mould all over under the succades with whole wheaten straw: beat down the earth first.
Moss'd the hills of the new bed: the bed is very hot, & requires Care.
18. Began mowing grass for ye Horses.
Hot, summer-weather.
20. Black, wet weather with a fierce N: wind, that tears-off the leaves from the trees.
May 27. Thinn'd-out, & tack'd the peaches, & Nect: & laid some of the gross wood of last year bare

14. of their willow-like shoots, in order to make room for more moderate wood. The Nect: that was blistered last year, is blistered again: & the first Nect: from the house is curled, & lousy, & wants good shoots. Yet in the whole there will be fruit on each tree which grows well: the apricot abounds with fruit.

The succades abound in strong healthy haulm, & begin to shew promising bloom.
The last bed begins to be more moderate: the plants are just not burnt, & have not very weak runners, which are stopped-down.
28. Succades begin to set.
Planted 50 cabbages.
Prick'd-out a plot of Celeri.
Black, cold, showery weather.
31. Lined the succade-bed; but did not put any mould on the lining.
June 2. The succades keep blowing with good fruit. The frame is crouded with vigorous vines: but the plants want some sunny weather.
Earthed the second frame the second time. The mould is somewhat burnt under the Hills: but the plants look pretty well, & send-out second wood.

June 3. Prick'd-out more Celeri. Black wet weather.

4. Very wet night, & morning.
Thinn'd-out the succade-vines, which quite choak the frame; & begin to rot for want of air & sun.
Plenty of melons are sett, & setting.
Every thing is strangely wet; & grass & corn begin to lodge.

5. Mended-out the rows of french beans, which are come-up very poorly.

7. Succades as big as pidgeon's eggs.
Earth'd-out the second melon-bed, where there is pretty good Haulm.
Sowed a few Indian-turnep-seeds, given me by Sr. Simeon Stuart.
Pricked-out a large Quantity of Savoys.
Hot, summer weather.

10. Fine weather.
Plenty of Succades, which are as large as a goose-egg.

13. Sowed six rows, a second Crop of dwarf-white-french-beans. The first Crop is in a poor Condition.
Earth'd-out the lining of the Succade-melon-bed, & raised the frame. Thinn'd-out the haulm, which is full of fruit.

16. June 13. Set several Cantaleupe, & Romag-
-na melons. The succades are half grown.
The frame now raised stands too high.
Very windy weather.
16. Sowed a crop of curled, & Batavia Endive,
& a crop of Coss lettuce; & planted out a bed
of Leeks.
21. A week of most uncommon weather; nothing but
wet, & cold winds. Planted out annuals.
23. Summer-like weather. The Succade bed
has plenty of fruit well grown: the Cantaleupes
& Romagnas have fruit set; but the Haulm, &
stems of the fruit are too much drawn.
The shoots of the peaches, & Nect: are very
curled, & lousy.
24: 25. Cut my Hay, a good Crop.
26. A vast rain all night.
27. Showers.
28. Showers.
Lined the Romagna bed with hot dung. Some of
the Romagnas are large fruit: the Cantaleupes
are only just setting.
The hay in a poor Condition.

June 18. Received an Hogsh: of port from Southtōn between Mr. Galden, & myself.
29. A very wet day.
July 1. The hay toss'd about a little.
2. Vast rains from the N:
5. Ricked my hay on the 12th day from cutting: it was as well as could be expected, but has but little smell. The Crop was great.
6. A storm of thunder, & lightening.
Cut a brace of melons. They come very quick from the time of setting; but are not curious this wet shady summer.
8. Cutt a brace of melons.
11. More melons.
Vast showers.
15. Melons come in heaps.
19. Planted-out a plot of curled endive, & a plot of savoys: put sticks to the large frechbeans.
Finished cutting the hedges.
Sultry weather, & showers.
22. Planted-out more curled endive, & some Batavian Endive; & planted-out some rows of German turneps.

~~18.~~ July 26. Planted more rows of German turneps.
Shady, showery weather still. All the succades come; but none good.
Aug: 4. Bottled-off the hogsh: of port between Mr. Galden, & myself.
5. Hot, summer weather, with an high glass.
6. Trimm'd, & tack'd the fruit-trees.
Romagna melons are come; but not good.
8. Sowed three ounces of prickly-seeded spinage; & some Cos-lettuce: planted-out more savoys.
Severe heat, & fine ripening weather.
15. Trenched three rows more of Celeri in Turner's Garden.
Septemr: 13. Found the rows of Celeri backward, & not thriving.
The Crop of spinage fails.
Peaches & Nect: begin to ripen well: they are both large, & fair.
Grapes do but just begin to turn.
13. Tyed-up endives both curled, & Batavian, they are curled well, & well-grown.
One crop of Savoys was well nigh destroyed by ye

dry weather.

All the Nect: trees this year produce fine fair fruit; but the first tree is distempered, & shrivelled.

The Apricot-tree produced a decent crop of fine fair fruit.

There are filberts, & nuts without end.

Potatoes are large, & good.

Peaches, & nectarines were fine in Septemr: being brought-on by the delicate autumnal weather.

Octobr: 4. Black grapes are very good.

The first great rain with much distant thunder, & ~~litening~~ lightening.

5. Planted-out two long rows of polyanths from the seed-box: the seed came from Mr: Gibson's. Planted-out some stock-july-flowers.

The endives by the heat of the weather run much to seed.

25. Planted 100 of Cabbages to stand the winter.

Planted Coss-lettuces to stand the winter against the fruit wall.

~~20~~. Octobr: 25. Grapes, black-cluster, are very delicate. Autumnal rains come on.
Novr: 10: & 11. Trimmed the vines against the House. Those at the end of the dining-room are weakly towards the top.
13. Dug-up all the potatoes, a good crop, & large bulbs.
The Celeri arrives at no Growth, & is cropp'd by the Hogs.
Novr: 17: 1766. Planted a new Nectarine-tree against the fruit-wall, which the nursery-man, Armstrong, calls a Violet.
Planted a standard golden-pippin in the orchard

Garden-Calendar for the Year 1767.

Jan: 1. Hard frost begins to set in.
10. Intense frost.
11. Very deep snow.
14. Very hard rain on the snow for many hours.
17, & 18. Most severe frost, & the Country covered with ice.
19. Made an hot-bed.
21. 22. Regular thaw.
Feb: 6. Cucum^{rs} plants shew a rough leaf.
14. A very wet season.
House-pidgeons begin to lay.
Cast dung in the farm yards.
25. Made half an Hogsh: of raisin wine with one hund: of Malagas, & half an hund: of Smyrnas. The former cost 25^{s} p^{r} hund: & the latter the same. Put to the raisins ten buckets, & an half of water.
Vast rains still, with wind & lightening.
March 4. Great rains.

(2)

March 5. Sowed some Succade seeds.
Stopped down the Cucumr: plants that have got several joints.
A fine spring day.
10. Sowed a crop of pease, the first. Sowed a small crop of Carrots, lettuce, & radishes.
Began planting the bank by the stable.
12. Made the Cucumber-bed with 8 loads of dung. Some plants in the seed-bed show male-bloom. Beautiful sunny weather.
17. Turned-out the Cucumber-plants into the Hills of the bearing-bed; they are fine plants, but full tall. The bed is hot & requires care. The plants for fruiting in the seedling-bed have good side shoots, & shew the rudiments of fruit.
Made a Celeri-bed with an Hand-glass.
18. Sowed Cantaleupe-seeds.
23. Tunned the raisen-wine which filled the half-hogsh: there was about one gallon over. The wine, after drawn from the raisins, stood two days in a tub to settle, by which means a large quantity of grout was kept back. Put to the wine ten bottles & one pint of elder syrop.

Mem: the syrop by being made with only one pound of sugar to a bottle of juice, fer-mented, & broke one bottle, & blowed-out some corks. Put one p^d^ of sugar to the wine to make amends for the bottle of syrop which ~~wa~~ was lost. The wine ~~was~~ is very sweet now.

March 25. Brewed an half Hogsh: of strong-beer with six bushels of Rich: Knight's malt, & three pounds of hops: well water.

28. Cucumber-fruit blows out.

Planted some strong cuttings of my sweet-water grape against the fruit-wall, & against the wall of the House near the fig-tree, & brew-house door.

30. Many Cucumber-fruit blown. Lined-out the seedling-bed for the last time.

31. Swallow appears.

April 2. Put three Gallons of wine, half of which was of the strongest sort, into ye vinegar-barrel.

3. Rain, gentle & warm constantly for four whole days to this time. Grass grows wonderfully. Earth'd-out ye seedling-cucum^r^: bed: fruit swells.

April 4. Motacilla trochilus Lin: Regulus non cristatus Raii; & Parus ater Lin: & Raii, Angl: colemouse, sing.

6. Saw more than twenty swallows & bank-martins at Mrs Cole's at Liss over the Canals.

10. The nightingale, motacilla luscinia, sings.

The black-cap, motacilla atricapilla, sings.

The red-start, motacilla Phœnicurus appears.

Raised, & earth'd-out the large Cucum: bed to the full; & mossed it.

11. Cut a very large Cucumber.

12. Cut five large ones, & sent them to London.

13. Miller's thumb, Cottus gobio, spawns.

14. Planted three rows of potatoes in a mellow quarter near the fruit-wall.

15. Made the melon-bed, ~~[illegible]~~ for two frames only, with 16 loads of hot dung, which had been cast, & turned over twice. The bed is stout, & consists of short, solid dung. Put a good layer of cold dung at the top to keep down the steam.

Cold dry weather; & the fruit-trees are matted every night.

April 15. Sowed carrots, parsneps, radishes, onions, leeks, lettuces, savoys, German turneps.

16. Sowed Baker's hill (which is about an acre & an half of ground, walks, & melon-ground excluded) with seven bushels of Saint-foin along with a crop of barley of dame Knight's. The field was winter-fallowed, & has had two plowings besides: but by reason of the wet spring is sown in a very rough Condition. It has been hand-pick'd of the weeds by women, & is got clean; & is to be rolled, & harrowed again.

Made an hand-glass bed for large white Dutch-Cucumbers.

Cold winds, & sleet.

The brambling, fringilla montifringilla, appears. The cock is a fine gay bird.

17. Some snow, with Ice & a fierce cutting wind.

18. Went to London.

June 12. Returned to Selborne.

Cold black weather; & the fruit of all kinds cut-off in general.

~~6.~~ June 16. Lined the melon-bed with four loads of dung: the succades are full of haulm, & the fruit beginning to blow: the Cantaleupes look poor, & distempered.

18. Succades begin to set.

Sowed a plot of endive.

9. Planted-out annuals on a showery day.

29: 30. Cut my hay, a good Crop.

July 2. Ricked five jobbs in excellent order: one jobb in large cock catched in the rain.

3. Pricked out savoys, & German turneps.

Some Succades are large: Cantaleupes begin to blow.

Alauda minima locustae voce, the titlark that sings like a Grass-hopper seems to have finished his song.

The stoparola builds in the vine.

Spipola prima Aldrov: the white-throat, sings.

~~Emberiza alba, the bunting~~ the titlark, sings.

Great showers about.

Planted-out Cucumbers for pickling.

July 5. Rain & a tempestuous wind that da:
:maged the garden much, & blowed down a
green-gage plum-tree.
7. Housed the last load of Hay.
8: 9. Strong winds, & heavy showers unfa:
:vourable to the wheat.
11. Vast showers still. Slip'd & planted
out pinks, & wall-flowers.
The ~~bunting~~ titlark sings still.
Young swallows appear.
The Stoparola brings out it's young.
18. Vines begin to blow.
20. Ananas are in cutting at Hartley.
Trenched-out some Celeri.
Planted-out some endive.
Hot, summer-like weather.
The ~~bunting~~ titlark sings still.
The Nect: trees put-out some young shoots,
& look better; the peach-trees shrivel up,
& get worse, & worse.
29: 30. Vast rains, & wind.

~~8.~~ Aug: 1. The first crop of Succades were all cut: they are not good for want of sun, & dry weather.
Parus ater, the cole-mouse, sings.
10. Hot, dry weather for some time.
Sep:r 11. Much wheat abroad, & some standing.
Second crop of Succades good. Cantaleupes good, but small.
Regulus non cristatus chirps.
Peaches begin to ripen.
Peach, & Nect: trees a little recovered from y:r distempered condition.
17. Discovered the yellow centory, Cent~~a~~urium luteum perfoliatum of Ray, in plenty up the sides of the steep cart-way in the Kings field beyond Pull's.
This is a very vague plant for ascertaining according to the sexual system. Linn: makes it a gentian, & places it among the pentandrias: but it has commonly seven stamina. Hodson makes a new Genus of it (Blackstonia) unknown to Linn: placing it as an 8andria digynia. It is best known by it's boat-like, very perfoliated leaves.
Moist black weather, which much retards harvest.
19. Sultry weather, with a very high barometer.

Peaches are good, & Nectarines delicate, & large. Black grapes begin to turn colour. Wheat in general is housed, & housing. The black-cap, red start, & white-throat still appear.

Cantaleupes small with me, but good.

Succades good.

24. Tyed-up many large endives.

Sweet Autumnal weather.

Ear-wigs, when small, fly about with ease: but, when full-grown do not attempt to rise; as if their wings were not then adequate to their weight. This is a mistake; there are two species.

Melons over.

18. Musca meridiana of Linn: & Scopoli appears.

Octob.r 5. Great hail-storms, & cold weather.

Martins appear still.

Very few wasps.

Missle-thrushes come to the Yew-trees.

Endives are very fine.

8. Celeri is blanched.

Gathered my apple, & pear-crop, which consist-ed literally of one Golden-pippin, & one Cadillac.

Dung borrowed in 1766.

Feb: 7. Of Kelsey -- dung pd car: pd: 4 loads.
--- Car: of my own 1 load .. car pd

Feb: 7. Of Parsons - Dung pd Cr pd 4 loads.
March 8. Of Parsons Dung pd Cr pd - 5 loads.
- - - Of Kelsey - - dung pd car pd - 4 loads.
Car: of my own 2 loads.
April 17. Of Parsons Dung pd - Cr pd - - 4 loads.
18. Of Kelsey - dung pd car pd - - 1 load.
26. Of J: Hale - Dung pd car: pd - - - 3 loads.

Dung borrowed in 1767.

March 6. Of Parsons - dung pd Cr pd - - - 3 loads.
- - - - - - - - Of J: Hale little cart car: pd: dung pd - - - 3 loads.
- - - - - - - - Of Kelsey - car: pd: dung pd - 2 loads.
April 2. Of Parsons - dung pd Cr: pd - 4 loads.
2. Of Kelsey - car: pd dung pd - - 4 loads.
3. Of Berriman car: pd: at three times 4 loads.
3. Of J: Hale a little cart car: pd: dung pd - 4 loads.
June 15. Of J: Hale Do car dung pd - 2 loads.
of F: Parsons dung pd Cr: pd 2 loads

Octob^r: 20. Being on a visit at the house of my good friend M^r: John Mulso Rector of Witney, I rode out on purpose to look after the base horehound, the Stachys Fuchsii of Ray, which, that Gent: says, grows near Wit: ney park: I found but one plant under the wall: but farther on near the turnpike that leads to Burford, in an hedge opposite to Minster Lovel, it grows most plentifully. It was still blowing, & abounded with seed; a good parcel of which I brought away with me to sow ~~it~~ in the dry banks round the village of Selborne. It is not known to grow in any County save that of Oxon, & Lincoln.

29. Saw four or five swallows flying round & settling on the County-hospital at Oxon.

Nov^r: 4. Bees & flies still continue to gather food from ye blossoms of Ivy.

5. Gathered the first grapes; they are very sweet, & delicate; tho' the buches, & berries are smaller than usual. There is not one fifth part of the usual crop.

12. Continual wet, & high winds. People are

11. much hindred in their wheat-season.
Nov^r: 12. Bro^r. Benjⁿ: saw a Marten flying in Fleetstreet.
16. Vast rains.
18. The first considerable frost.
23. Put the Hyacinths in rows in part of a Quarter near the fruit wall. Many of the roots were decayed; & the rest would have been better, had not the rains prevented their being put-out for several weeks.

Earthed-up all the Celeri. Some of it begins to pipe.

Grey still weather with an high Glass.
Dec^r: 1. Dug-up the potatoes, a good Crop.
4. A very hard frost with a little snow.
Car: away the melon-bed.
Sent two field-mice, a species very common in these parts (tho' unknown to the zoologists) to Thomas Pennant Esq of Downing in Flintshire. They resemble much in colour ye Mus domesticus medius of Ray; but are smaller

than the Mus domesticus vulg: seu minor of the same great Naturalist. They never enter houses; are carryed into ricks, & barns with ye sheaves; abound in harvest; & build their nests, composed of the blades of corn, up from the ground among the standing wheat; & some:times in thistles. They breed as many as eight young at one time.

Decemr: 6. Planted one golden-rennet, & six curious sorts of Goose-berries from Armstrong.

10. The nuthatch, sitta, sive picus cinereus, chirps. It runs about on trees, & hangs with it's back downward like the titmouse. It builds in hollow trees, stopping-up great part of the hole with clay, so as to leave barely room to go in & out. There have been several nests in an hole in the yew-tree in Selborne church-yard. Some of the clay remains still at the top of the Crevice.

15. Planted one Roman Nectarine, & one melting peach from Armstrong.

13. Decem^r: 16. Mild, pleasant weather. Daiseys, Herb Robert, ragwort, hepaticas, primroses, in bloom. Crocuss, & snow-drops spring.

22. Strong frost after a long dry fit with:out any.

24. Strong, bearing Ice, & a severe N: E: wind. Covered the Celeri, & put straw to the roots of the new planted trees.

26. & 28. Frequent flights of snow, & severe frost within doors.

30. Severe frost, & still sunny fine days. It freezes even in the Kitchen.

31. It froze under people's beds. Great rimes, & beautiful sunny days.

March 6. 1771. Brewed half an hogshead of strong beer with 6 bushels of Rich: Knight's malt, & 3 pds & half of Berreman's hops. Kept it in the tun-tub, & laded in the yeast til the 8:th Severe frost at the [illegible] All rain-water save one bucket.

NOTES

1751

January

7 *Spanish-beans*: longpod beans.

23 *Loaf-cabbage*: early sugar-loaf cabbage.

24 *Little garden*: the original garden behind the house.

February

23 *Dutch-currants*: red or white currants.

March

7 *U. White*: Charles White, Gilbert's uncle.

9 *Persian-jessamin*: white jasmine, *Jasminum officinale*, a native of Persia, India and China.

22 *Mays-seed*: Miller's *Gardener's Dictionary*, 3rd edn, says maize 'is seldom propagated in England but is a curiosity in some fine gardens'.

Holy-oaks: hollyhocks, *Althaea rosea*.

Grange: the granary of the former Selborne Priory.

Chardoons: cardoons, *Cynara cardunculus*.

April

6 *Skirret*: a variety of water-parsnip, *Sium sisadium*.

Scorzonera: *Scorzonera hispanica*.

Sea-cale: a plant not in general cultivation until after 1799, when William Curtis, the originator of the *Botanical Magazine*, published his pamphlet *Directions for Cultivating the Crambe Maritima, or Seakale, for the Use of the Table*, and began to sell the seed from his nursery at Lambeth Marshes.

Sliped: slipped; i.e. filled gaps with cuttings or young plants.

27 *Lassams*: a cottage at the southern end of the street; Gilbert White later bought the upper part of the orchard belonging to the property.

May

14 *Common beans*: broad beans.

24 *Basons*: large holes dug into the clay soil and filled with good loam.

October

5 *Stock-gilliflowers*: probably yellow wallflowers, although stocks were sometimes called stock gillyflowers.

26 *North-warnboro'*: a village near Odiham, Hampshire, where White occasionally bought nursery stock from two nurserymen, Armstrong and Forster.

1752

As White was following academic duties in Oxford, entries in the *Kalendar* are understandably fewer this year and next. At times it will be noticed that they are made in another hand. White was back in Selborne from 22 July to 4 August, and from 18 September to 25 October when he set out for Oxford again and did not return until 18 December. It was during this Christmas vacation that he helped his brother John to construct the famous zig-zag path up Selborne Hanger.

March

5 *Quincunx*: trees planted in squares, one at each corner and one in the centre. Repeated, these form a regular grove or wood.

10 *Plashed*: plashing, or pleaching, is the interweaving of live twigs and branches to form a hedge.

Quick-set: hawthorn, may or quickthorn, *Crataegus oxycantha*.

April

8 *Ringmer*: near Lewes in Sussex, where Gilbert's aunt Mrs Rebecca Snooke lived.

13 *Cups*: 'basons'.

16 *Painted lady peas*: variety of sweet pea.

Miller: Phillip Miller, author of the *Gardener's Dictionary*. Directions under the entry 'Leucojum—Stock—July—flower' are 'for if they are too much exposed to the Sun in the Heat of the Day, they are very subject to be eaten by a sort of Fly, as they often are when young, upon a hot, dry soil: to remedy which, you should always sow a few Radishes amongst them, which will secure 'em from this Mischief; for the Flies will always prey upon the Radishes, wherby your July-flower Plants will be preserved'.

May

18 *Finochia*: Florence fennel, finnochio, *Fœniculum azoricum*, grown as a pot-herb.

1753

On completing his University duties in May, White travelled for some months until taking-up a curacy at Durley in September. It is clear that unlike most curacies that he held, this necessitated residence within the parish for some of the time at least.

In this most eventful of years it was only to be expected that the recording of garden activities was severely restricted.

January

1 *African beans*: broad beans.

October

25 *Laurustinus . . . Mulberry*: i.e. propagation by layering.

1754

Although still curate at Durley, Gilbert White must have made frequent visits to Selborne, as the *Kalendar* entries are numerous and continuous, and he even brought plants from his temporary home for 'Wakes' garden.

March

12 *Cockscombs*: probably here a species of *Amaranthus*.

April

10 *Ewel-gate . . . Ewel-close*: the Ewel is a field on the north-west boundary of the 'Wakes' property.

May

21 *Pendulous amaranths*: probably *Amaranthus caudatus.*

October

1 *Dorton*: the source, on the other side of Selborne's street, of the 'warm, forward crumbling mould, called the black malm, which seems highly saturated with vegetable and animal manure' (see p. xviii, and letter 1 of *The Natural History of Selborne*).

15 *Campan. pyram.*: chimney bellflower, *Campanula pyramidalis.*

22 *Opulus*: guelder rose, *Viburnum opulus* a shrub native to the chalk around Selborne.

Berriman: one of White's farmer neighbours.

24 *Dr. Bristow*: then Vicar of Selborne.

Spiraea frutex: flowering shrub of the genus *Spiraea.*

November

20 *Mazagon*: mazagan, a tall variety of broad bean.

1755

At the start of the year, ownership of 'Wakes' passed to Charles White, Gilbert's uncle. Later, during the summer, Gilbert took-up the curacy of Dene, within easy riding distance of Selborne.

March

15 *Cantaleupe-seed*: this entry closely follows Miller's instructions in the *Gardener's Dictionary.*

20 *Waverley*: near Farnham.

Ilex-acrons: acorns of *Quercus ilex.*

Pine and Chili strawberries: the introduction of the large-fruited Chile strawberry, *Fragaria chilœnsis*, in 1714 had been the most important event in strawberry culture. It was crossed with other species; the most celebrated of the hybrids was the pine-apple strawberry.

April

16 *Three-thorned acacia*: honey locust, *Gleditschia triacanthos*, introduced to Britain 1700.
Boorcole: borecole or kale.

29 *Storax-trees*: *Styrax* sp.
Will Yalden: the partner of Gilbert's brother Thomas in London.

1756

The curacy at Dene was relinquished early in 1756 and more time could be spent in the garden at 'Wakes'. Among the trees planted were two consignments from the Lambeth garden of Thomas White. A vista for an obelisk was opened up and the large urns erected.

For the second time Gilbert became curate at Selborne; it is clear from the Parish Registers that he did most of the work in the parish between 1755 and 1759.

February

14 *Farina*: pollen.

March

15 *Post-chaise*: as roads around Selborne were often impassable in winter it was notable that so large a vehicle could be brought to the door so early in the year.

22 *Althaea frutex*: *Hibiscus syriacus*.
Ribbon-grass: *Phalaris arundinacea*.

April

2 *China-arbor-vitae*: *Thuya orientalis*.
Arbor-judae: Judas tree, *Cercis siliquastrum*.

6 *Parson's dung*: Parsons was a farming tenant of White.

August

24 *Turn'd colour before it began to smell*: according to Miller maturity was indicated by a crack near the stalk, and the smell, not by the changing colour of over-ripeness.

1757

At the end of the year, White became the absentee incumbent of Moreton Pinkey in Northamptonshire. This brought him an additional £30 per annum, after paying his curate, and made little encroachment on his time.

March

4 *Bush'd*: covered by lightly brushing with hazel or other twigs.

14 *Melon paper-house*: see *Every Man his own Gardener*, by Thomas Mawe and others, 5th edn, 1771. The frame of the house was covered with paper: 'the best sort for that use, is the best printing paper, or thick writing paper, such as is sold for eight-pence or ten-pence a quire'. The paper, after pasting on to the frames and being allowed to dry, was oiled with linseed oil that had been boiled to 'render the paper more transparent, and make it proof against rain'.

April

25 *Mrs. Snooke*: Gilbert White's aunt Rebecca.

October

1 *Lord Keeper*: Sir Robert Henley, soon to be Lord Chancellor and to become successively Baron Henley and Lord Northington.

17 *Mr. Bridger*: a yeoman farmer from the parish of Selborne.

December

26 *Brother Barker*: brother-in-law.

1758

On the death of his father in September after a long illness, Gilbert officially became master of 'Wakes'. He was now responsible for paying the rent for the property to his Uncle Charles, who was still the landlord.

February

6 *Hitt*: Thomas Hitt, *A Treatise of Fruit Trees*, 1755. 'The characteristic of his plan is to check the rise of sap by making the stem take a tortuous course' (G. W. Johnson, 1829).

14 *Tan*: tanners' waste, tree-bark from which tannin has been extracted, used in hot-beds to provide long and steady heat.

23 *Dr. Hales*: Steven Hales, 1677–1761, Rector of Faringdon and close friend of the White family. A remarkable experimenter, he is chiefly known for work on the motion of sap embodied in his *Vegetable Statics* (1727).

March

28 *59 potatoes*: see letter XXXVII to Barrington in *The Natural History of Selborne.*

September

5 *Hermitage*: the original hermitage near the top of the zig-zag.

November

20 *Damascene-plum*: damsons originated in Damascus, where they had grown from pre-Christian times.

1759

The main activity in the garden this year was the beginning of the construction of the ha-ha. In June White went to see Philip Miller at Chelsea Physic Garden and discussed canteloupes with him.

February

3 *Hambleton*: Hambledon, Hampshire.

March

6 *Untriged*: unraised.

April

16 *Lythe*: the Lyth, i.e. the Short Lyth plantation, and the Long Lyth in the valley beyond Dortons.
Tree-primroses: *Oenothera biennis*.

May

4 *Cherrysucker*: spotted flycatcher, *Musicapa striata*.
31 *John*: Lassam; Bowdler Sharpe's foot-note reads 'his nephew', but Gilbert's nephew John had only just been born.

July

21 *Mr. Cane*: White's cousin.
Tull: Robin Tull, employed occasionally in the garden.

September

8 *Crape-bags*: to protect from wasps.

1760

At the end of 1759, White began a six-month holiday; his first task on returning was to cast a critical eye at his own garden, as the first entry on 17 May shows.

June

28 *John Wells*: the farmer whose land was between 'Wakes' garden and the Hanger and from whom over the years White bought fields to extend the garden.

August

4 *Mezereon-seed*: *Daphne mezereum* grew wild on the Hanger.

October

22 *Dr. Hill's mummy*: apparently some form of rooting compound.

1761

This was a year of great achievement in the garden. The ha-ha was finished, as was the long fruit wall. In February, the terrace adjoining the ha-ha was levelled and new walks prepared 'so far that they will want but very small amendments before they are turfed'. A wicker screen was erected to shelter the melons and early crops.

April

11 *Basoms*: balsams, probably.

May

15 *Forest-chair*: rustic wooden chair.

20 *Crickets*: an extended version of this entry became letter XLVI to Barrington in *The Natural History of Selborne.*

October

24 *Cornflags*: *Gladiolus.*

December

30 *Halimus*: a foliage plant, *Atriplex halimus.*
Groundsel-tree: *Baccaris halimifolia.*

1762

March

10 *Mr. Roman*: Rector of Faringdon.

1763

In March Gilbert White became the owner of 'Wakes' and other property in Selborne when his Uncle Charles died.

February

21 *Jobbs*: cart-loads.

July

28 *The Hermit*: Gilbert's brother Henry, dressed as a hermit.

1765

The purchase of Hudson's *Flora Anglica* this year stimulated him to take up botany seriously and systematically, as many of the entries in the *Kalendar* show. White continued to use the lengthy Latin descriptions of Ray, however, rather than the Linnaean names which the *Flora* was the first to use.

May

14 *Kiver*: shallow wooden vessel or tub.

July

16 *Fern-owls or goat-suckers*: nightjars, *Caprimulgus europaeus.*

August

4 *Ponds*: see letter XXIX to Barrington in *The Natural History of Selborne.*

14 *Tremella*: apparently not the fungus *Tremella* but the blue-green alga *Nostoc*, which colonises wet soil.

16 *Aster with yellow thrums*: *Aster amellus.*
Aster with a black thrum: perhaps black-eyed Susan, *Rudbeckia hirta*, introduced 1714 from N. America.

September

5 *Fungus kind*: flowers of tan, *Fuligo septica.*
Ray's methodus: White had acquired a copy of John Ray's *Methodus Plantarium* in 1753.
Dentaria aphyllos: toothwort, *Lathraea squamaria.*
Hill: John Hill (1716–1775), surgeon and botanist. Author of several botanical treatises including one on the *Vegetable System*, he later became gardener at Kensington Palace.

9 *Wullmere*: Wolmer Forest, where Selborne residents enjoyed turbary.

17 *Shrub of the rose kind*: burnet rose, *Rosa pimpinelli folia* (=*Rosa spinosissima*), locally common.

20 *Wheatears*: caught to satisfy the trade in 'ortolans' for fashionable dinner tables.

24 *Mr. John Woods*: the father of Gilbert's brother-in-law, Henry Woods.

October

5 *Black hellebore*: White is describing the green hellebore, *Helleborus viridis*, which elsewhere he calls bear's foot.

1767

This was the year in which Gilbert White started the correspondence with Thomas Pennant, that, with some alterations, became the first part of *The Natural History of Selborne*—the first and third of the letters that were actually sent to Pennant (X and XII) refer to the 'field mice' that are mentioned in the entry in the *Kalendar* this year under the date 4 December.

April

4 *Motacilla trochilus*: willow warbler, *Phylloscopus trochilus*.
Regulus non cristatus: chiff-chaff, *Phylloscopus collybita*.
Colemouse: coal tit, *Parus ater*.

July

3 *Alauda minima*: grasshopper warbler, *Locustella naevi*.
Stoparola: spotted flycatcher, *Muscicapa striata*.
Titlark: tree pipit, *Anthus trivialis*.

20 *Ananas*: pineapple, *Ananas comosus*.

September

18 *Musca meridiana*: *Mesembrina meridiana*, a large black fly with yellow wing bases.

October

20 *Stachys fuchsii*: downy woundwort, *Stachys germanica*.

December

4 *Field mice*: see letter XII to Pennant in *The Natural History of Selborne*.

PUBLISHER'S NOTE

Reproduction of this manuscript is from photographs taken by the British Library. Every effort has been made to reproduce the matter of the manuscript as faithfully as the interpolation of an intermediate photographic process will allow. Inconsistencies in the photographs have meant that the pages of the manuscript as reproduced may differ fractionally in size from the originals and some minor retouching has been necessary in order to remedy defects in the prints provided.